When I Get To
HEAVEN

Bobbie Eriksson

The Book Guild Ltd
Sussex, England

To 'Big Bother'
from 'Tag-Along'

This is a true story, although I hide behind an assumed name. The names of most of the characters have been changed, to protect the innocent and the not so innocent.

The Book Guild Ltd.
25 High Street,
Lewes, Sussex

First published 1992
© Bobbie Eriksson 1992
Set in Baskerville
Typesetting by APS,
Salisbury, Wiltshire
Printed in Great Britain by
Antony Rowe Ltd.
Chippenham, Wiltshire

A catalogue record for this book is
available from the British Library

ISBN 0 86332 766 4

CONTENTS

When I get to Heaven, I know that I will find
contentment, love and happiness, with quiet peace of
*   mind*
people who will care for me, no matter what I do
when I get to heaven, and my life is through.

1

All the Nice Girls Like a Sailor

It was December 1937, rumours of war with Germany were rife, an air of restlessness swept through all walks of life. 'Your Country Needs You' posters looked down from billboards in most towns. The armed services were on the alert, despite the fact that there was not enough money to equip them. There was money to be made if you happened to be in the wool trade, rag trade, or had a foundry. All those uniforms and equipment had to come from somewhere. Not everyone was happy when it all ended, many dark months later. What were black days for Britain, meant easy pickings for the unscrupulous.

Living was for today, the future was too uncertain to make any permanent plans, and service personnel felt it more than most. There were many hurried little weddings, some within hours of a posting. A sense of urgency hung in the air like a vast black cloud. There was also an air of 'we are in this together', and people who had mostly just kept to themselves became more community minded. It was this air of camaraderie, and sheer determination, that was to see the people of Britain through years of deprivation and war. The 'pen-pal' network was to come into its own; with so many people far from home, a letter could mean so much.

They had been pen-pals for some months, and had arranged, finally, to meet. He was in the Royal Navy, based at Chatham, but his ship would be in Rosyth for a few days. She saw him in his Petty Officer Uniform, very smart too, and she fell, hook, line and sinker. I cannot help thinking that had she met him in his 'civvies', she would not have looked twice at him. A whirlwind courtship followed, with neither seeming to give much thought to their future, and very little money between them.

He had been disowned by his family for deserting the family business to enter the Royal Navy when he was twenty-one, in 1932. He had suffered years of verbal and physical abuse, at the hands of a tyrannical, bullying father. He had arrived late in the marriage, and the couple had wanted a girl. They already had a son, he was almost grown up, and they wanted a daughter to spoil and indulge. Instead, they got a skinny, bawling boy, but they indulged their whim for a girl by dressing him up as one, letting his fine, fair hair grow into long ringlets.

This he endured until he was almost six, when it was time for some form of schooling.

In 1917, the family went to live in France, father was working as an engineer in Paris. At six, he adapted to the new life, and soon learned the language, but his mother found it too difficult, and for her it was to be quite an ordeal. There was trouble in Paris, and during a riot the family had to hide in a wine cellar, listening to all the noise from the street above. There was a metal grid in the ceiling, which could be opened on the street, to lower wine barrels into the cellar. The small boy, bored with his incarceration, ventured out of his hiding place between some barrels, and went for a peek on to the street above. By climbing on some crates he managed to reach the lower part of the grid, but all he could see were people's feet, and a horse's hooves. Amidst all the clamour, something metallic clattered on to the grid, rolling to a stop just above the boy's head. He pushed it with his hand, and saw that it was a trooper's helmet, with the head still inside it.

That was the last thing he remembered of that awful day, but what happened later was that the owner of the wine cellar had waited until dusk, then managed to bring his horse and cart into the yard at the rear of the premises. It was laden with empty casks and barrels on the outside edge, but a space had been left in the centre, just large enough to hide one large man, a small woman, and one very frightened boy.

In this ignominious fashion, they left Paris for the relative safety and peace of the Alsace region of France. The boy went to a boarding school in Nancy, and his parents eventually returned to Paris, when things calmed down.

He was happy there, and made good progress in the school. On parents' days, however, he was nowhere to be seen, he had found a place to hide away, and no one ever found it, or could make him reveal its whereabouts. Holiday times were not so good, there was no hiding place, and he had to endure verbal abuse and beatings from an oversized, sadistic bully. 'One day,' he promised himself, 'one day I will not always be so small.'

He had cause to remember one Christmas in particular. Father told him Santa Claus had left him a broom, it was one of those child-sized sweeping brooms. He showed it to him and told him it had been left for a boy who was only fit to sweep dirt, and the handle was to remind him of that. With that, he beat him soundly with the present from Santa.

When he was sixteen, the family returned to Manchester, and the boy was put into the factory to learn what he might. He had plenty of help, especially at dodging his father, for many of the employees knew what life had been like for him. Back in Manchester, he had relatives to offer him sanctuary, particularly an Aunty Irma, who he adored, but they could do little to save him from a constant barrage of abuse. The small boy was getting bigger and stronger, and could teach tricks to the most artful of dodgers. He was well-warned when his father was around, and would make himself scarce. He was secretly having boxing lessons and doing body-building exercises. Aunty Irma saw to it that he was well-fed, and the eight stone weakling started to fill out. Sarcastic comments from father only determined his resolve to get fit and strong. He tried to join the Manchester police force, where he had two uncles already serving, but he was not quite tall enough. Just before his twenty-first birthday he informed his parents that he was joining the Royal Navy. There followed the grandfather of all arguments or family rows, with his father shrieking abuse at him. He stood by stolidly, listening, until he stopped to draw breath. With a terrifying calm he took hold of the father, who for years had ill-treated and derided him, picked him clean up off the floor, and hurled him into an armchair. Years of hatred went into that act of defiance, he had waited so long to be able to hit back. What may have been said, I can never know, but it was to be some years before they saw each other again. The ill-treatment and verbal abuse he had suffered as a boy was to haunt him for the rest of his life.

He never forgot his love for the Alsace region of France, he looked on it as home. I feel it was a strange irony that he later married a girl called Nancy.

She was a coal-miner's daughter, last of a family of four, brought up on the east coast of Scotland. She was born in South Queensferry, which nestles under the Forth Bridge, but the family home town was Kelty, in the Kingdom of Fife. Her father was in the army during the First World War, many of his comrades did not return home, but he was one of the lucky few who returned more or less uninjured. He returned to what was to be a land fit for heroes, but there was no work, and by 1925 he had decided to emigrate to Canada. Spanish influenza had robbed him of one child, another was in the army, so he left Britain, taking his wife, one son and one daughter. To emigrate they needed a guarantor in Britain, in case anything went wrong in Canada, and the son who was in the army was chosen, which meant that there was no room for him in the family's plan for a new start.

Life in Canada was hard, working on remote farms with only miles of prairie to see. After the mountains of Scotland it was a very lonely sight. The Canadian government used to move the families on after two years' stay on a farm, probably in an attempt to ease the feeling of isolation.

Her life consisted of getting up at daybreak to help feed the livestock, then cooking breakfast for the farm-hands. That was followed by household chores which had to be done before it got too hot during the summer months. Her day ended when it got dark.

Having only been in Canada a few months, her mother fell ill and had to be removed to a hospital in Alberta. To visit her meant a lengthy train journey, and the girl joined in the impromptu concerts the passengers held to pass the time. Her schooling had ceased when she left Scotland, and now she had all the chores to do. When her mother died of cancer, aged forty-three years, the family decided to move into the city, and they made their home in Toronto, Ontario.

The winters took terrible toll of the girl's health, and her doctor advised her to return to Scotland. The brother who had gone to Canada with her was killed in a road accident, and her father eventually remarried. It was 1932 when she arrived back in Scotland, and she managed to find a job in a hospital in Oban.

The hospital work depressed her, she had never got over her mother's illness and untimely death, or the loneliness of life in Canada. Most days at the farm had been spent working hard, and her only companion was a cat called Pie-face.

She left Oban for her home area of Fife, and found work in domestic service with the family of one of Scotland's well-known whisky manufacturers. She was happy there, but worked very long hours, and although they were kind to her, the growing family wanted her to be at their beck and call. She soon told them where to get off, years of poverty and loneliness in Canada's outback had not dulled her spirit. She was nobody's fool, until she met him.

1938, what would tomorrow bring? Who could wait? They did not. They went to her elder brother, the one who had been left in Scotland when the family emigrated, to borrow some money so they could wed.

He was based at Chatham, and on a cold day in February they were married. A shipmate stood for him, and they asked a man in the street to be the second witness. They knew very little about each other, had no money, and seemed to give little thought for their future prospects.

I wondered if she married him to either avoid war work, or just to spite someone else. Wherever that marriage was made, it was not in heaven, but John had his Nancy. All was right with their world, but it would not last.

2

England Expects

He was recalled to ship, went back to sea, and she found work and lodgings in Kent. He sent her postcards and letters, and all seemed well. The little boy arrived in November 1938, well-received, his parents did not mind one bit that the baby was a boy, and named him John Jnr.

The threat of war was imminent, and she moved with her son to be near whichever dockyard her husband might be at. It was difficult to find lodgings for herself and the baby, but she was often lucky enough to find a helpful landlady who would baby-mind, so she could work.

He was not supposed to inform her of his whereabouts, but they had devised a code so she would know roughly where he was. His letters would arrive with red crossings-out on them, all mail was censored.

September 3, 1939 was a gloriously sunny day in Kent, but the little boy was fractious. She was trying to listen to a crackly radio for news, but all she could make out was the voice of Neville Chamberlain declaring that Britain had declared war on Germany. The baby shrieked with rage, and she discovered he had cut his first tooth. She paced up and down the tiny kitchen, rocking the baby and wondering what it all meant. Her husband was on H.M.S. Rodney, part of the Atlantic convoy that was a tempting target for lurking German submarines. Where would it all end?

It ended for him, many dark months later, by being inva- lided out of the service, like so many before him and even more after. I will not go into his colourful naval career, but he had got himself into a deal of trouble and was reduced to the ranks. Seems he was staggering back on board ship after a night on the town, aided by two shipmates, all the worse for drink, when an officer he did not like witnessed his noisy arrival. The officer made some comments, and for a reply he got a hefty punch on the face from someone who knew how to punch. By the time John was taken to task for it he could not recall anything of the incident, just the four-day headache it left him with.

He learned, some months later whilst on another ship, that the hapless officer was having trouble with his eyesight. He resolved never to drink again, and he never did. Being stripped of his rank before the whole ship's company seemed light punishment by comparison. He was more fortunate, he had excellent eyesight and could spot an enemy aircraft while it was still just a dot on the horizon. He had the unhappy task of shooting enemy planes down, or so it seemed to him, and years later he was still shooting them down in his sleep.

Meanwhile, Nancy moved around the coast to be as near to his base as possible, this was done with the aid of their code. During a brief stay in Sheerness she would take a walk along the cliff path, pushing the baby in his pushchair, watching planes, sometimes witnessing a dog fight in the air. It was summer 1940, she could see far out to sea, and would watch the planes ducking and diving in the clear blue sky. One day an A.R.P.* warden moved her on, telling her to keep off the cliff path; she asked him if he knew that some of the guns along the cliff were dummies.

Back in town, she had been befriended by a woman who frequented the café where she worked. The baby was being looked after by the landlady, so she was able to work most days. This woman had been asking all sorts of questions. Was she married? Was her husband in the navy? When would she see him again? She had told her that she had only recently moved to Sheerness, but was unhappy about the questioning. There were posters up everywhere, warning 'careless talk costs lives'; these were dangerous times, you could trust no one. She was convinced she detected a hint of an accent, and it bothered her enough to report it to the area A.R.P. warden, who said it would be investigated.

Shortly after that incident she found out, via the coded cards, that the fleet was due to come in. It seemed several people knew, for the beach that day was crowded, and a

* Air Raid Patrol

whisper went round 'the liberty boats are due'. She had taken a towel to sit on, a flask of tea, a book, and toys for the baby, to make it look like a normal beach outing.

It was not liberty boats that came in, but enemy planes, flying in low, and strafing the crowded beach with bullets. Pandemonium broke loose, panic everywhere, but it was over in minutes, leaving many dead and injured. She had thrown herself over the baby, and they lay still while all hell erupted around them. There were dead all round her, and for one dreadful moment she feared the baby was too, he lay so still and silent; he remained silent for days. The warden later informed her that the woman had been arrested, she had been asking questions all over town about when the boats were due.

The said boats came in about eighteen hours later, with leave for the sailors. A few snatched hours was all anyone could hope for in those troubled days, but once again, inevitably, it was time to rejoin the ship. As he left and turned to wave at them, the little boy broke his silence and yelled 'Daddy.'

Her next move was to Weymouth, where again she found a helpful landlady, and got work in a cafeteria in the town. It was not a wise move, for the enemy had embarked on a series of morale breaking raids, intending to destroy anything that was at all interesting, old or historic. Weymouth had an interesting old clock on the promenade, which they kept worrying, but it is there today, as a monument to their poor aim. London was taking an awful battering, food rationing was causing great hardship, but the black market flourished. You could not get meat, eggs, butter, sugar and many other products, but for the right price you could get almost anything. Things were getting too hot for comfort, it was time to move again.

Whether the wanderlust was from necessity, or mere fancy, only she could know, but it was back to the East of Scotland for her and the baby, to Rosyth, a busy dockyard town.

She had not been back long when news arrived of Hitler's deputy Rudolf Hess. He had flown to Scotland, and crash-landed near Glasgow. 'Damn cheek,' she thought. Was he on a peace mission, or was he defecting? No one ever really knew.

For John, there had been a set-back at sea, a shell had hit a cable, sending it lashing across deck, killing three seamen, and injuring many. It meant a spell in hospital, and of course, sick-leave. It was obvious to her that his injuries were not all to the body; he was having terrible nightmares, and he had lost a lot of weight.

He was severely depressed; apart from the incident on his ship, he had lost friends from H.M.S. Hood when it had sunk. He lost ex-colleagues when the Royal Oak was sunk at anchor in the Scapa Flow, and the Bismarck, pride of the Germany Navy, was giving his shipmates the run-around.

Whatever happened in his life during the last few months of his time in the navy, only he knows, he never spoke of it. He was eventually invalided out of service, like some tired old battleship, but there was to be no refit for him. He was mentally and physically destroyed, a bad case of what was loosely termed 'shell-shock'. It covered a multitude of disorders, culminating in uncontrollable shaking. For some who never experienced, or indeed suffered it, it was sneeringly referred to as 'lack of moral fibre'. A poor and shameful epitaph to the deeds and events that had caused it.

It was off with the navy blue, and into grey demobilisation suit. What was it they said about a land fit for heroes? Most heroes are dead.

3

Mean Means Test

It was like having another baby in the house, at times he shook
so badly that he was unable to feed himself, or speak coher-
ently. The little boy had a bad stammer, perhaps from
mimicking Dad, or did he have his own traumatic memories?
The day on the beach at Sheerness, or any one of the lived-
through bombing raids, or could it be the spiteful pinches he
got from Dad, when Mum was not looking? He had been seen
doing just that, by the brother-in-law who loaned him the
money to get married. That brother-in-law had many a reason
for wishing he had not.

Because he had not been crippled or blinded, and could not
prove insanity, it was only shell-shock after all, there was no
pension from the navy. He was only one of many to be dealt
this blow, many widows were just as shabbily treated. The
expression 'there is a war on, you know' must, for many, have
had a very hollow ring to it. I have no doubt that the 'lack of
moral fibre' brigade, sitting comfortably in their offices, did
not have to suffer the ultimate insult, a means test.

Being reduced to ranks had found him on a rating's wages.
He had earned an extra one shilling per week for volunteering
for duty on a submarine, but being invalided out, and unfit for
work, he had to go on the dole. The amount of money he got
was assessed on how much he had earned previously, depen-
dants or not, so for him it was very little.

They left Rosyth and went to Kirkcaldy where he eventually
got a job, rent collecting for the council. Things looked a little
brighter, then there was another baby on the way. He always
managed to eke out a few pennies each week, to fill in and send
off a football coupon.

The baby arrived on the same day as the pools win notification, a seven pound girl and a five pound win. I know which gave pleasure, it was not the former! It was a lot of money in those days, and it was used as part payment on a leatherette put-u-up type settee. There seemed to be a lot of that awful leatherette material around then, and the only thing I can say in its favour is, it lasted.

October 1942. They had wanted another boy, well, they only had boys' clothes, and he was to be named after the grandfather in Canada, but here she was, large as life and twice as noisy. John Junior was not impressed – no teeth, no hair and so angry. I had arrived in what was once a stately home that had been converted into a maternity home, Forth Park nursing home, overlooking the beautiful Ravenscraig Park. Quite the thing, but I was soon home in the drab surroundings of Overton Road, no wonder I was angry. I screamed for weeks; did I know what I had come home to, where it would lead? It would have been very appropriate had my parents carried me home in a suitcase, or a carton. My cot was the bottom drawer of an old dresser, from where I screamed my rage at the world in general.

After one week at home, the little boy wailed at his mother, 'Do we *have* to keep her?' When told 'yes' he sobbed, 'Can we not send her back?'

I had come to stay and the whole street knew I had arrived. Mum was weak and ill after the birth, and the burden of looking after me fell on Dad. It could not have been easy, for he was not fully recovered from his illness. Mum got very little sleep; what with me serenading the neighbourhood, and Dad fighting the battle in the Atlantic, it is a wonder she did not murder both of us. His nightmares went on for years, starting with a yell 'enemy aircraft sighted', then would follow some garbled orders, ending with another yell, 'FIRE'. Mum could not sleep in the same room for fear of being torpedoed, or shot down in flames.

No one in her family seemed to be called by their Christened names. She was known as Nancy. Her brother, who had been in the army when she went to Canada, was Robert, known as Bob, and her other brother who had died in Canada was John, known as Jack. Being inventive, if not different, I was named Bobbie Jacqueline, after them both. Brother was John Junior and Martin after Dad's best man, but I was to go through life with a name suited to footballers and small dogs. A cablegram was sent to Canada with the news, very posh!

I had arrived, and life would never be quite the same. Britain was still 'digging for victory', food was rationed, as was petrol and many other things. The songs *White Christmas* and *We'll gather lilacs* were hits, along with the nostalgic *We'll meet again*. There was victory at El Alamein, and a lot of fuss over the Beveridge Report – I always thought that was a hot drink. And still I yelled my head off.

Babies are supposed to bring their own luck, and it seemed I brought a little. First the pools win, then early in 1943 Dad was offered a job at Rosyth dockyard, with what was then called the Admiralty, now Ministry of Defence. With the job went a house in Rosyth, so we were on the move, things were looking up.

The threat of invasion had subsided and life seemed more settled, people were hopeful of better things to come. Church bells could be rung on Sundays and special occasions. For so long they had been silenced, only to be rung on threat of invasion. 'Make do and mend' was the message on the posters, clothes rationing made a necessity of that little snippet of wisdom. 'Pay as you go tax' was another bright idea, all devised no doubt to make sure nobody got too hopeful.

Things were happening overseas that were horrific, making Britain's problems seem paltry by comparison, but it was to be some years before the full horror was revealed. Dad kept scrapbooks of newspaper clippings of news and events during the war years, they made fascinating reading. One he had underlined in red was about a court appeal to the House of Lords, where their Lordships had ruled that money saved on the housekeeping belonged to the husband. That must have made many a housewife's day, no wonder the Yanks were so popular. They came with their chewing gum, nylons, chocolate, music, and a whole lot more I need not mention! They must have been like a breath of fresh air in those dark days.

A tidal wave of sentimentality was sweeping the country, which must have been a relief after so much despondency. April 6 was the first day of pay as you earn income tax. While all this was going on, I sat up in my pram, viewing life with suspicion; the world was indeed a very strange place.

My first memory is of being in a pram, watching a baby boy

in a pushchair next to me. Our mothers were chatting, and I was looking at the boy, or at least at his glorious head of blond curls. It was all too much, and I reached over the edge of my pram and grabbed handfuls of hair, chortling with delight at his shrieks. Both mothers struggled to free his hair from my grip, but I cannot recall what the outcome was. That baby is now probably a middle-aged baldie, thanks to me; even at an early age I could not appreciate the injustice of nature, to endow a boy with blond curls.

I was very slow to walk, probably enjoyed being wheeled about, but talked very early; no secret was safe when I was within earshot. When I was still quite small, I had got over the usual 'Mama, Dada' stage, and Mum had schooled me to say 'Winnie the windbag' as my party piece. Whenever Winston Churchill's voice was heard over the radio, Mum would ask 'Who's that?' I would reply, 'Winnie the windbag.' I felt in later years that that was most unfair, whatever else he may have been, he was a great statesman. It happened once when the vicar called, and he was not amused, seems he was an ardent fan.

It was around this time, I think, that the parents decided to move again. There was a transfer to Wiltshire on offer, it was accepted, and they started packing. Uncle Bob had remarked that it was as well we did not keep chickens, for every time a large van went past they would lie on their backs to get their feet tied.

It was early 1945, and all I can remember of moving day is being told to keep out of the removal men's way. I was playing on the pavement outside the house in Rosyth, and could hear music coming from the direction of the dockyard. Mum said it was a party and the music was to dance to, so there I was, dancing on the pavement with the removal men trying to load up a van. I was told brother John would travel in the van, all the way to Wiltshire, and I was livid, but then I was going on the train, much more fun. The train to London was full of soldiers, and I ended up full of chocolate. Being small had its advantages. I also had the loan of a soldier's greatcoat, to keep me warm during the cold night's journey.

All I remember of our arrival in London was a busy station, full of people in different types of uniform, I was terrified. I had never seen so many people, it all seemed so frantic, hurrying here, there and all those kit-bags. Something of that scene touched a chord somewhere, and I felt very sad.

John of course was with us, he also got stuffed full of chocolate; his coming down in the van was all a big wind-up to get me going. It never failed, and I was off again, bawling 'I want to go home.'

The scene in the busy London station was not the only sad thing I saw that day. We had a lengthy wait for our connecting train to Corsham, so Dad said we would visit an old landlady of his. We had a drink and something to eat in a station café before going into the street to find a bus. I loved London, all the hustle-bustle, but there was a lot of mess, and falling down buildings almost everywhere you looked. I commented on it, and was told to be quiet, then it was our stop. As we alighted I saw more mess, heaps of rubble, bulldozers knocking things down, and a lorry full of rubble coming out of what looked like the remains of a street. It was odd, half-way up the street was what looked like two huge blackened holes. Dad had gone over to one of the workmen to ask something, when he returned he was crying. I was puzzled, what did it all mean? When I could contain my curiosity no longer, I asked, and wished I had not. It was the street Dad had been looking for, at least it had been until a few months previously, before it received more than one direct hit during a bombing raid.

We made our way to Paddington station, to get on the Bristol train, the last lap of our journey. It is not surprising to realise I cannot remember much of the last part of that journey, it had been a very long time since we left Rosyth, but there was one more surprise in store.

I awoke to find myself in a strange room, in an even stranger bed, I seemed so far off the floor. I would need a chair to get in and out of it. I was used to sleeping in John's old cot. The curtain's were closed but I imagined it was daytime. I could hear voices, ladies chatting, I think it was their loud chatter that woke me, but something was wrong. I did not know much, but I had heard a Welsh accent before, and we were supposed to be in England, it was very perplexing. I was beginning to worry about where I was, and where was everyone else, when Mum came into the room. I voiced my fears to her, and she laughed, telling me that there were many with Welsh accents in those parts. Those beautiful lilting accents were to become as familiar as the rolling Wiltshire ones. I was informed that we were in lodgings, and Mum told me the lady's name. We were to remain there until our things arrived from Scotland and a place was found for us to live. It was another beginning.

4

New Friends, New Faces

I do not remember how long it was before we were allocated a place to live. There was a shortage of accommodation, but priority was given to ex-forces personnel and government employees, so people who worked for the Admiralty had a house with their job, when available. We were given a place in part of an air training base that was being phased out of use. There were planes still flying from Rudloe Manor, which made it noisy at times, but I loved it. I would watch them flying over, with my fingers stuck in my ears. There were several civilian families there, so we had plenty of playmates. My mother would not let me out on my own as I was too young, so long-suffering brother John had to take me everywhere. That meant that I played with his friends; not for me dolls and skip-a-rope, it was tree climbing and kicking things around. Having a famous footballer as a namesake was just by the by, there was no doubt about it, little Miss was a tree-climbing boy-basher. No self-respecting girl, or her sister, would be seen dead with me. I cannot recall any particular toy I had, or favoured at that time, and there were no pets, but that was all to change.

We were moved out fairly rapidly, after only a few weeks; there had been a few scares with the close proximity of the aeroplanes, and it was considered unwise for civilian personnel to be so endangered. Wiltshire Council had had some prefabricated dwellings erected in Corsham, but we did not get one straight away, we were given one end of a converted Nissen hut. There were two to a unit, end on, with the doors at either end opening outwards. They were similar to prefabs, without some of the modern conveniences. They had a family room that housed a stove type fireplace, a small kitchenette, small bathroom and toilet, and two bedrooms. The floor was covered

24

with thick brown linoleum, called battleship linoleum. With a bit of floor wax and a lot of work, you could get up a nice shine on it. We had some French knitting rugs that Dad had made whilst he was on submarines in the navy, they lasted for years. Many submariners took up knitting as a pastime, as there is not much room to move about, and it made a change from reading. The more ambitious did Fair Isle, Dad said it was incredible what some of the sailors turned out, really beautiful things. It was difficult to get wool, but Mum used to buy old woollies from jumble sales, unravel them, then wash the wool for re-use. A lot of people were doing that, so it was not easy to find unwanted hand-knitteds. Later on he used cut up rags to make rugs, and turned out some really nice ones.

We settled in, and life went on, Dad at the Naval store depot at Copenacre, John at school, and me being a help at home! We would walk down to collect John from school, then go for a stroll around Corsham, getting to know the place; everything seemed right with the world. Things had gone on, and were happening, that I was blissfully unaware of. Japan had suffered an atomic bomb blast, European cities had been liberated, the blackout was over and servicemen were being demobilised. We had had Victory Day, but it was by no means over, many must have wondered 'would it ever end?' I skipped happily up the lane, picking wild flowers, singing an irritating nonsense ditty that went something like:

'Chickery chick, chelagh chelagh, chickery romy
Willicka wollicka can't you see?
Chickery chick for me.'

The horrors of the German concentration camps were lurking round the corner, the people of France were dealing with collaborators, and Stalin wanted an atomic bomb for Christmas.

No wonder nobody smiled much. One of the hit songs was *We'll gather lilacs*, John went down with measles, and I was annoyed because I did not get them. It was during his illness that I discovered boys, it was quite a revelation. I mean, I was three, and knew it all. Oh, there was John, but then he was just John. I needed a playmate, my spotty minder was feeling sorry for himself, and would not let me look at his comic. I found

Dennis, a quiet unsuspecting boy from a few doors away. I am not sure who made the decision, or who suggested it, and if you are out there Dennis, I will deny everything, but it was decided and agreed upon that we would play doctors. I would add that Dennis had no sister, so he had least had an excuse.

We discovered we had similar chests, but could not determine what function the 'knobs' had. My 'nellie nutton' was much tidier than his. His was a mess, but my offer to tidy it up with scissors was not well received. When it got to the interesting bits I was amazed – all that, just to pee with! Well it did seem a bit excessive, but I saw the wisdom of it when a demonstration was arranged. He could nearly fill a jam-jar, from feet away, no way could I do that, there was just no contest. At that point his mother arrived, and walloped the pair of us for taking all our clothes off. He should have known better, a big boy of five.

I heard, years later, that he and his family had emigrated to Australia, so I think *my* reputation is safe. I had told my mother that I wanted to be able to pee like a boy, I am so glad she did not ask why! My mother called me in from play one afternoon, and I found her with one of our neighbours. She had two grown up sons, and had found a teddy bear that belonged to one, when she cleared out a cupboard. She had smartened it up with an old baby frock, and yes, it was for me. I called it Ted, and we became inseparable, despite John's sneers. I adored that bear, old and worn as he was, even a new doll could not take his place as number one. The doll was a birthday present, she was French, so I called her Jacqueline. She had a flat head that was piled with soft brown hair that fell in long ringlets, and she was dressed in a fancy party frock, but Ted had nothing to worry about.

John and I had plenty to worry about, we seemed never to be out of trouble, of much the same sort, i.e. silly pranks. At first we were suspicious of each other, one trying to land the other in trouble, it was too silly. In the kitchen, like many others, we had a pulley fixed to the ceiling, which could be lowered to dry or air clothes on. Things would go missing from it, odd socks, pants, sometimes larger items, and they would be found later, pushed down the back of a chair or settee, under pillows, in the bath, even once in the coal bunker. We both got walloped for that one. We could not blame Dad, he was at work when most of it happened. We insisted we did not do it, and everyone was tense.

My mother had her suspicions confirmed one evening, when we were all seated round the tea table. For no apparent reason the clock lifted off the mantel shelf, flew across the room, and smashed onto the floor. I laughed, the others paled, even I sensed something was amiss. Not one to keep secrets, Mum explained, as matter-of-factly as she could, that it was a poltergeist. 'A what?' A poltergeist, noisy ghost. Wow, this was really something, but what to do about it? You could not ignore a 'something' that hurled things about a room. Wait and see, it was decided.

A quick visit to the housing department was what was done, and mother was told, 'Yes, we have heard there is something odd about that place, no one ever stays.' A move was promised, but it was to be a few months before it happened.

I came in from playing in the garden one afternoon, as I thought it might be time for us to collect John from school, and found Mum in tears. I had never seen her cry, she looked dishevelled, hair all hanging down, with her hairpins all over the floor. I was sent to ask a neighbour to collect John with her children, and when I returned she seemed a lot calmer. She had picked up all the pins, but I could see she was trembling still. I had never seen her hair loose before, and did not realise how long it was, I was amazed. A lot of ladies then used to roll their hair into a long sausage curl, around a sort of headband. Mum did hers in roll curls, all over her head, each one being pinned in place individually. It was years before she told me what had happened. She had been sitting in an armchair, dozing, when she felt very cold. She was powerless to move, and terrified out of her wits, as, quite deliberately, the hairpins were removed, one by one, then dropped on to the floor. She was unable to even call out, until the last pin dropped to the floor.

The vicar was called, and prayers were said. He told Mum to leave a Bible on the table, open at a certain chapter, I cannot recall which, and that would deter 'it'. 'It' was not amused, but apart from knocking the book onto the floor, little else happened. It usually only happened if Mum or I were in the room.

Earl Attlee was telling MPs that the atomic bomb was

making the world an unsafe place, that must have been the understatement of the century. It was almost Christmas 1945, it was to be our last, things would never be quite the same, ever again. Adolf Hitler had killed himself, everyone was so bad to him.

5

Oh Come, All Ye Faithful

John had discovered a new song, that to his delight could really annoy me. he said that Ted should be renamed Fuzzy Wuzzy, to fit with his song which went,

Fuzzy Wuzzy was a bear,
Fuzzy Wuzzy had no hair,
Fuzzy Wuzzy wasn't Fuzzy Wuzzy.

Honestly, brothers! I told Ted to just ignore him. Dad had a vegetable patch, where there were rows of cabbages and Brussels sprouts. I loved to crawl about them, pretending I was in a jungle, and one morning I came face-to-face with a furry, greyish brown thing that was hanging upside down between some stalks. I lifted it off, noting that it was an ugly little thing, but it had beautiful soft fur, and long leathery wings. I took it indoors to show Mum, who shrieked in terror at it, but Dad said it was a bat. Well, I always thought a bat was something you hit a ball with, but no, that was what it was called. I asked if I could keep it, and got a very firm 'No' in reply. I took it back to where I had found it, leaving it on a cabbage plant.

I told Ted all about it, but he did not seem impressed, probably jealous, all that fur, and him with none.

That Christmas Eve I heard carollers going round the doors, and wished that I could go too. I still slept in a cot, the side being left down, so I could get out during the night to visit the lavatory. I heard them coming nearer and slipped out of the cot to go and look out of the window. They were standing by a street lamp singing *Oh come, all ye faithful*, and I thought it was just wonderful; oh, to know all those words and tunes!

I had wanted a pram, so I could take Ted out, but I had not

29

told anyone. I got a hand-made doll's bed, and an adorable little cottage. Both had been made by a neighbour. There was a small doll that Mum had made an entire wardrobe for, including a fur coat. Small gifts had been hidden around the room for John and I to seek out, finders keepers. I found a sporty red racing car, John found a skipping rope. I did not want to swap and there was almost a riot. 'Peace and goodwill to all men' does not include brothers, but I agreed to swap when he promised to let me play with it sometimes. The neighbour who had made me the doll's bed and cottage, made a lorry for John. It came to bits, with all the pieces painted in bright colours. Ted was allowed to have rides in it, and I soon forgot the racing car.

In the sitting room, which served as a family room, there were paper chains and lanterns, that John had made at school, and large, navy blue weather balloons. Balloons were rare then, and I was fascinated by them, forever asking to be lifted up so I could touch them as they hung from the ceiling. All went well until one went 'bang' and I was right off balloons.

The Christmas lights in Oxford Street, London, had gone back on in 1944, and there was no more black-out. There were pretty trees with fairy lights in some windows of the houses in the village, and we had been taken to Chippenham to see Father Christmas, but because of the crowds, got nowhere near him. It was a time of magic for me, we had gone to the children's party at the church hall, as we were Sunday School pupils, and I had my first encounter with a plate of jelly. I liked it so much that I helped the children on either side of me to eat theirs also. Little did I know, that it was to be my last childhood Christmas.

There was a coal shortage, so we would go out for walks in the woods, armed with an old jute coal bag, to collect firewood, then the snow came with a vengeance. We would return home, John and I soaked to the skin, red-faced, with chilblains on our fingers. Goodness only knows how Mum got our things dry with only the small stove.

We awoke one morning to a thick, white blanket of snow, which had drifted up against our gable end, making it impossible to open the door, which opened outwards. We were trapped, it was no use, somebody would have to get out and try to clear away some snow. As the windows were small and I was

30

the smallest, I was voted in for the task. Out the window I went, aided by Dad, coat, boots, gloves, bobble hat and don't forget – the shovel. The spade was in the shed, somewhere beneath the snow. Dad lowered me down the four feet or so from the window ledge, and I promptly disappeared into a drift, all that could be seen was the pom-pom of the hat. I was really annoyed, especially when they all laughed, but I managed to stand up in it, edging my way around the wall to the door. Dad called me to start digging by the door. I could not see the door! Luckily two men who were passing came along and started to shovel the snow from the base of the door. Dad kept pushing at the door trying to open it, and compacting the snow, making it worse, but eventually it was cleared. He need not have bothered, there was no transport due to conditions and he could not get into work.

There were many uses I found for that shovel, besides shifting coal and snow. It was a must for making snowmen, and I never went out in the snow without it. John and I were in the street, playing, when two older boys came along and started being a nuisance. They started a snowball fight, which we entered into with gusto, until one hit John's lip, causing it to bleed. He said it hurt, and I was puzzled. 'Cissy,' shouted one of the louts, and I noticed he was putting stones into his snowballs. In a rage, I went up to him and smacked him full in the face with the flat end of the shovel, making his lip bleed profusely. He went off howling for his mother, while the other one warned, 'I'll tell my Dad on you.' John said I should not have done that, but I felt quite justified, especially when I saw how swollen John's lip had become.

Sure enough, lout's father turned up at our door demanding to see the girl that whopped his darling with a shovel. I was brought to the door, the man looked a bit surprised, and I told him his son got what he deserved, and he should not put stones inside snowballs. He turned on his heel and stormed off, muttering that some kids should not be let out.

The Women's Voluntary Service were kept busy in those days, organising sales of work, jumble sales and clothing exchange marts. About once a month they held an exchange mart in the Corsham community centre, mostly for children's clothing and shoes. I had a winter coat I had outgrown, but needed some shoes, and Mum wanted some hand-knitteds for

31

the wool, so off we went. I took Ted, as I felt he could use a new frock. I got my shoes, and Mum found some things for John, then gave some money to a formidable lady in a navy blue suit, who positively scowled at me. I asked Mum if Ted could exchange his frock, but she smiled and replied, 'I don't think so.'

The battle cruiser in navy blue asked, 'Is the child backward?'

Mum glared murder at her, snapping, 'No, are you?' and stormed out.

John and I had discovered, with Mum's help, a toffee bar that we both liked, it was called Highland Toffee, costing threepence a bar, John always took charge of halving it, breaking the bar unevenly. He would then bite off a piece to make them equal in size, giving me the unbitten half. I let him get away with that for quite some time.

Another delight was a neighbour's garden that backed on to ours. She had a friendly nanny-goat that we liked to pet, and sometimes she would give us the goat's milk to drink, usually straight from the goat still warm in the glass. It was all right until the goat ate some nettles, and I was right off goat's milk.

There was to be a Sunday School picnic for the children, in the church hall. John and I were all spruced up, me all in white, hair in ringlets and ribbons, John all slicked and polished, hair plastered down, it really was expecting too much. Of course it did not last, I did not even make it to the party. We had to walk past the cricket field on our way to the church, and all along the wide grass verge that flanked the pavement, fine black silt had been spread. It had probably been dredged from a river, and used to fill up holes and hollows on the verges. I thought it was tarmac, and made straight for it. Before Mum could grab me, I was in it, ankle deep in wet sludge, and I fell over. Mum was angry, then she saw John laughing, and they both fell about laughing. Me, I was furious. John soon stopped laughing when he realised I would have to be taken home, meaning he too would miss the party – pesky sister!

We had visitors shortly after that disaster, once again I was prettied up and told not to wander off, or get dirty. John was indoors, I was wandering around the garden, which went around three sides as we were on a corner plot, when I saw two people coming through our gate. A small, frail looking lady and a huge man. The man looked a bit like Dad, facially that is, same bald head, but huge compared to Dad. As he drew near, I saw him staring at me, and I knew instinctively that this was my grandfather.

Mum and Dad came out to greet them, followed by John, scowling as usual. Dad seemed so pleased to see them, I felt sad for him, could this really be the bully we had heard so much about? He never spoke of his mother, who had died, this was his step-mother, and I was watching her closely. She seemed very sweet and gentle natured, and was soft spoken, unlike her other half. He hugged and kissed John and I, what an ordeal. I could sense that John hated it as much as I did. I did not like being touched, and certainly not by strangers. He was rumbustious, loud and full of energy, but I was surprised to realise that I did not actually dislike him, I was just wary. I needed time to get to know him, but they stayed only a short time, promising to come again, soon.

Loaves of bread were to be made smaller, and less beer would be brewed due to a grain shortage. School children were to get free milk and dinners, I could hardly wait, I had been longing to go to school for as long as I could remember. Boy, was I in for a let down!

6

A Death in the Family

We had moved to a prefab in Brunel Avenue, not far from the Nissen huts. An old pram, borrowed from a neighbour, moved most things, me and Ted included.

One afternoon, around Easter time, Dad came home with a big bag full of weird looking things that came in a bunch. They were yellow and curved, and you could snap each one off from the bunch. Dad announced, 'These are more fun than Easter eggs', but I had my doubts. Mum had boiled eggs in coloured food dye, then painted faces on them. I cried when I was told to eat mine.

John was sniggering, knowingly, like older brothers have a habit of doing, when Dad handed me one of those bent things, telling me I could eat it. After much coaxing, I tried. John roared with laughter, as did Mum and Dad, I could not see the joke, it tasted awful. Then smart alicky, worldly-wise, big bother informed me haughtily that monkeys ate them, but even they had the sense to peel them first!

A few weeks later I was given an orange, but you cannot catch me twice. It was incredible to know that thousands of children in Britain had never seen a banana, or an orange. There were few treats around then, but there was the Saturday film matinee at the community centre.

Poor John had to take tag-along, but he had managed to adopt an air of 'I've no idea who she is', especially when I got bored with Tex Ritter, or Roy Rogers and his bloomin' horse and insisted on singing – loudly. Mostly it went all right, until the six-guns started blasting, when I would stand up on my seat and yell, 'Stop that noise!' and to the kids 'Stop that shouting!' John would just sink low into his seat, and hope I would disappear. I found the projection equipment fascinating, and kept raising my hand into the beam of light above my head; it is a wonder I ever got out of there alive.

John engineered a very good system of getting out to play after school, without tag-along knowing, and I was left, more and more, to my own devices.

I had been given an old doll's pram, it had belonged to Gloria and Josephine, the daughters of a friend of Mum's, and when I tired of showing Ted the sights, John and I gave each other rides in it. Dad had brought home a tabby kitten, and he also got rides in it. One day it was all too much for the old pram and it fell apart, though why it had to do so whilst I was in it, I just do not know.

The kitten was named Monty, as I am sure half the pets in Britain then were called. Next door had a Jack Russell terrier also named Monty, and when you called one, they both came running.

I had been in the habit of parking Ted on the hedge by our gate, when I tired of carrying him around, and one sad day Monty the dog found him. He had a wonderful time mauling him to bits, and I was too afraid of the noise the dog was making to attempt a rescue. If you have ever seen a terrier 'worry' something, you will know exactly what I mean.

I ran for my mother, but by the time we got back to him he had decapitated my beloved Ted, and was working on an arm, sawdust stuffing everywhere.

I was heart-broken, and sobbed and sobbed. Mum eventually got up enough courage to retrieve the remains from Monty, who stood there, tail wagging, looking really pleased with himself.

I asked if he could be mended, and got the parents' reply to everything: 'We'll see.' What I saw was beloved Ted and bits, in the dustbin. I was livid, got him out and stormed indoors to Mum, demanding to know why he was dumped in the rubbish. She told me solemnly that the 'angel of death' had taken Ted, and that was just his remains. I was beginning to understand what 'dead' meant, and I insisted Ted had a decent burial.

Dad dug the grave in the garden, and the family attended. Give Dad his due, he kept a poker-straight face, Mum could hardly contain her giggles, and John was red in the face – grief, I think.

I said a prayer: 'Please God, if there are dogs in heaven, will you keep them away from Ted, Amen.' The grave was filled in, flowers were laid, and I went into mourning, I expect the whole street heard me.

Later, I caught that damned dog trying to dig Ted up. I threw a bucket of water over him, and was seen doing it by his owners. Monty the cat took to following me around, but I was bereft.

There was a new baby in a house across the road, and I used to go and watch him being bathed. He was all pink and new, soft and sweet, and I wanted one. I dropped enough hints at home, but they fell on deaf ears.

The baby's mother told me her grandmother had just died, and being wise in such matters, I informed her that the angel of death had taken her, and you must bury the remains, not put them in a rubbish bin. She gave me a really odd look.

Mum was in the habit of giving myself and John a spoonful of cod liver oil and malt, every day, and it was so funny to see Monty cat sitting on the kitchen floor at our feet, waiting for his share, even funnier when Monty dog also joined the queue.

We had only been at Brunel Avenue a few weeks when the grandfather visited again, alone this time. All seemed to be well, as we played with him in our small back garden, Dad taking snapshots with his box Brownie camera.

I was wearing a frock that one of Mum's friends had made for me, a button-through, cotton frock with cap sleeves and a small collar. The material had a floral pattern and each flower had a little face, how I loved that little frock.

Dad had been busy, de-budding some early blooming chrysanthemums, with me watching. He told me he did that so the flower would have one large bloom, instead of several small ones. I went round after him 'helping', but I popped off the wrong buds, leaving the plants budless, and Dad was not amused. Grandfather thought it was hilarious, and said I did not need garden flowers, I had them all over my dress.

Our prefab was semi-detached, and next door, the family that had Monty, the Jack Russell dog, had a daughter called Vivienne. She was a bit younger than I, but we often played together. We would knock on the partition wall separating the two halves, and call 'good night' to each other, when we remembered.

Vivienne and I had been at Dad's peas, and had wonderful

fun, shelling and eating them. When Dad caught us he just laughed and laughed. I found out why the next day, which was spent staying very close to the lavatory!

John wanted to go swimming with some friends, in a local disused gravel pit that had filled with water. He assured Mum it was only waist deep, and he would be with older boys who could not swim either. He had no swim trunks, so he could not go, but Mum told him she would use some red dye she had on an old pair of underpants of his, and he could go the following day.

She did just that, and he seemed content, but she was not happy about it until an older boy told her he would look after him. She shook her head doubtfully then, wagging a finger at John, told him, 'Don't you come home crying to me, if you get drowned.' He would not take a towel, he could drip dry like everyone else, but in less than an hour he was back.

He was in a foul temper, railing at Mum, 'Why can't I have proper trunks, like everyone else?' He had got into the water, and everything had been fine until one of his friends screamed. He thought John was bleeding, but it was the red dye oozing out of the trunks. Poor John had to walk home, dripping red water down his legs, with his pals laughing and poking fun at him.

That summer seemed very long, and all seemed well with our world, but unknown to us, it was all to change. The spectre of Dad's illness was threatening once more.

The billboards informed us that 'the war is over, but the kitchen is still on short rations', we were only too aware of that. Our 'uninvited' guest had not gone.

7

Door Knockers

I am not sure how, or when it all started, but Mum had been very fraught, and Dad was in a permanent ill-humour. The spiteful pinching had started again, for both John and me, and a favourite trick of Dad's was to trap our faces by the cheeks with his index and second finger, then twist hard. I do not know who taught him that piece of nastiness, but I can guess. It seemed to me that he went about just looking for a reason to slap or pinch either, or both of us.

My hair was below shoulder length, and Mum usually put it into rags at night, to make ringlets. How I detested those idiotic ringlets, I much preferred braids, but whether braided or in ringlets it was a target for all sorts of bullies. Dad used go grab me by my hair, rendering me helpless; I am not sure which was worse, the hair grabs or the hidings I got when Mum was not around. He was careful never to touch either of us when Mum was around, she once asked me irritably why I was always crying, she had not seen the pinch I got from Dad. I was told by her to stop playing with rough boys. 'You are covered in bruises.'

I wondered if grandfather's visit had annoyed him, for he seemed much worse after that.

On one occasion he declared that my face was grubby, so grabbing me by the hair, he dragged me into the bathroom. Holding my plaits in one hand, he turned on the cold water tap with the other. He then loaded up a wetted nail brush with soap then proceeded to scrub my face with it.

It was the last straw, my temper flared as I squirmed free of the hair-hold. I gave him a hefty kick on his shin before fleeing, yelling that I would tell Mum on him.

He came after me shouting, 'Don't tell your mother, she is ill and will worry.'

I shouted back something to the effect that he was a bully like his father, and he should know better. At that he offered me a half-crown for my silence, and I agreed.

I told my mother the raw looking patches on my face were where I fell over, and had to scrub the grit off, and kept my vow of silence.

Mum had answered a knock on the door one morning, to find two persons doing what I can only describe as peddling religion.

She was completely taken in, hook, line and sinker. She had had a bad fright over our poltergeist affair, and was an easy target for any Jesus freak. It was pathetically funny, but no laughing matter for us, we had to live with it. Everything went by the board, while she indulged in her new-found faith. She was out, all hours, all weathers, selling their magazines, attending their gatherings; she could think and talk of nothing else. It totally destroyed our family life, in as much as John and I, and no doubt Dad too, were completely ignored. Our childhood was to be written off as insignificant, and social contact with non-sect members, discouraged.

We were sat down and told, in her perfunctory manner, that there would be no more church or Sunday School. No more Christmas, that was all wrong, no birthdays, they were unimportant, and absolutely no presents of any sort, they were worldly, therefore wrong.

We gaped at her in disbelief, but she tossed her head and added, 'You are to read and study your Bibles, and be good.'

Fat chance, I thought, it was an invitation to war. She must have read the expression on my face, for she announced, 'I will tell you what parts to read, and you will be told what you can or cannot do.' She had thrown down the gauntlet, but she made no allowances for my nature, and I was a born rebel; it was a battle she could never hope to win.

There was no more of anything much, and certainly no signs of affection. Love it seemed was also wrong, along with kindness and words of encouragement.

I hoped it would not last, but of course, only good things come to an end.

We had to tolerate a house full of 'holier-than-thous', tut-tutting over the state of things in general, and listen to their predictions of gloom and doom. Mum's favourite starter was 'When this present system of things comes to an end, blah blah.' Had it not been so pathetic, it might have been funny, but nobody was laughing.

She alienated her neighbours with her door knocking. 'I am on the Lord's work,' she would say, but meanwhile there was very little work done at home.

John managed to dodge out of her visitations, but I got dragged round doors, being told incessantly to 'pay attention.' We got a lot of doors slammed in our faces, but sometimes people would give me things, a sweet or a biscuit. It made my day when one woman told my mother off, in no uncertain fashion, for 'dragging that poor child about, like a parcel.'

Dad had taught me some songs, and when I got bored to almost screaming, I would give a lusty rendering of *All the nice girls like a sailor* or *Lilli Marlene*. I would get a nudge and a snarled 'wheesht' from Mum, it never failed to amuse.

We were to visit the grandparents in Manchester, Monty would be looked after by a neighbour. Neither parent seemed keen to go, and Mum had wanted to leave us with a neighbour also, but it was decided we would all have to go.

I cannot recall anything of the journeys, there or back, but remember a couple of amusing incidents.

On the Saturday, we were taken round the city centre and shops, grandfather was telling John and I off, for walking under a ladder. He stepped off the pavement on to the road, to avoid said ladder, and was nearly knocked over by a double-decker bus. We all laughed, except grandfather, and I told him he should look before stepping into the road. He just glared at me.

On the Sunday, Mum and Dad were going out with grandmother, and I was not happy about the fact that John and I had to remain with grandfather. Dad said an odd thing to me, he told me quietly, not to worry, they would not be gone long. Perhaps he knew I was nervous.

They had not gone long, when Grandfather took John and I upstairs, in his big Victorian villa, and showed us into a lovely sitting-room. His home really was beautiful, a far cry from our little prefab in Corsham. The door was fitted with a latch, which was too high for me to reach, and as I gazed around that room I heard grandfather say to John, 'Leave her in here, we

40

will go downstairs.'

I did not like being shut in a strange room, or being separated from John. I liked the idea of John being alone with him even less, I did not trust him one bit and I wanted to know exactly what he was up to.

I dragged a large, high-backed dining type chair over to the door, and undid the latch, let myself out and crept quietly down the large curving staircase. I found them both, at the foot of the stairs, playing with a tray of marbles.

'How did you get out?' demanded grandfather.

'It was easy,' I told him.

As he glared at me, I realised how facially alike he and Dad were, they had similar expressions, although they differed in build.

I glared back at him, and shouted, 'You try to shut me in a room again and I'll kick your door!'

He gaped in amazement, and John smirked as grandfather said, pointing to the marble tray, 'Do you know what that is?'

'Solitaire,' I replied.

'Oh, you know,' he said, and I added, 'I don't know how to play it though.' All this time we glared at each other, then he asked, 'Do you want to know?'

I replied, somewhat rudely, 'Nope, I want my mother,' and sat down on the bottom stair.

When my parents returned, Dad asked, 'Everything all right?'

Not known for my diplomacy, I announced that I had watched John and grandfather, and never let them out of my sight.

Dad gave me a really odd look, and I swear the grandfather blanched.

'When can we go home?' asked John.

We never saw the grandparents again; if our visit had been an attempt at a reconciliation, it had failed dismally.

Both our birthdays passed, and were ignored, but Christmas was coming, the air was alive with the excitement of it. We were forbidden to talk about it, it was a taboo subject. I was puzzled, Mum imagined she was a Christian, holier than most, but did not Christmas start it all? I could accept the indifference to our birthdays, but to shun Christ's was beyond my comprehension. The festivities and pagan rituals could be

shunned, and did it really matter what time of year it suppo-
sedly occurred? But to treat it as a non-event could not be
right.

I asked a lot of questions, and got a lot of slaps for my
troubles, it was not for me to question her new-found beliefs.
'Ours was not to question why,' was the stock reply to
everything.

I was told about Satan, but as far as I could make out, he got
all the fun. We were given a book each, to read and study. I
used mine to play post offices with, tearing out pages for stamps
etc., and John used his to prop up a wonky leg on his chest of
drawers. I could read long before I went to school, but had
difficulty with a lot of words, and books without illustrations
were boring. I was choosy what I read, but I liked newspapers,
and Mum kept hiding them from me. Dad took the daily paper
to work with him, so they were ready for the fire when I got to
them.

The winter of 1946–7 was severe, we had a few days in
London, leaving Monty with a neighbour. It was a visit to do
with Dad's job, and I think he hoped it would lead to a move
there.

The Christmas lights were still up in Oxford Street, and
there was a huge tree with lights on it in Trafalgar Square. I
was mesmerised by it the night I saw it, I just had to nip back
for another look, and got lost. A friendly London 'Bobby' told
me to stay where I was and my 'folks' would come and find me.
I had my doubts, but they did just that.

It was the worst winter for years, and when we arrived at our
lodgings, about 9 p.m., the landlady looked at John and me,
then to the parents, said, 'No kids', and shut the door on us.

Dad had another address, which was for furnished rooms.
When we arrived there, tired and hungry, we found the
furnishings consisted of lino on the floor, curtains at the
window, and a standard lamp. The landlady demanded cash
in advance, and for a minimum of one week, which amounted
to almost a month's wages for Dad. We only wanted it for a
long weekend.

'Too bad,' she snarled, slamming the door shut.

By this time Mum was in tears, so we did what several other
families did, we spent the night on Paddington station.

Next day, Dad had to go to work at Whitehall, but before he

went he called at a colleague's home in Paddington, to beg lodgings for us.

I loved it, there was a house full of children, and we slept four to a double bed, two up, two down, but it was not for long. One of the younger children got scarlet fever, and we left in a panic, Dad and John to one address, Mum and I to another.

I was heart-broken at being separated from John, and just a bit vexed that I might be missing something.

We went to an address in Leytonstone, to an elderly lady who had a beautiful pet dog. He was called Sultan, which I thought was an odd name for a German shepherd dog. Mum told me she could hardly give him a German name, in view of recent happenings. We played in the snow in her garden, and had a wonderful time, but all was not well with the parents.

Perhaps the job did not shape up, or it may have been the shortage of accommodation, but we returned to Corsham and London was not mentioned. John returned to school, and life went on.

I was still sleeping in a cot which was in my parents' room, and one morning I found that I was sharing my blanket with a large, dozy spider. I had seen its like in the garden, and around the house, it was like a smaller version of a black widow spider. I picked it up, to put it onto the floor and it bit me. I shrieked, mother came running, she shrieked, father came running. He nearly fainted at the sight of it, he had a horror of spiders, but he went off to fetch a newspaper, and put an end to any worries it might have had. I discovered little red marks all down one leg, seems it had done its utmost to evict me from a warm place. I had realised that Dad had an aversion to arachnids, so from thence forth I spent hours searching for them, to leave in likely finding spots, all over the house, hoping he would happen upon them. I think Monty mostly dealt with them, but Mum was a nervous wreck, she could not understand what was attracting so many spiders into the house.

Mum had a job as a cleaner at John's school, and I tagged along with her in the afternoons. She did the infants' section, after they had gone home, then some parts of the junior section. I enjoyed wandering in and out of the empty classrooms, sometimes I would play with the caretaker's son, who was about my age. I would day-dream about who sat at which desk, longing to be part of school life, but I would have to wait

43

until I was five, which seemed eons away.

Dad had taught me to whistle, and I was getting on everyone's nerves. Mum declared, 'The songs were bad enough, without that din.' Honestly, some people just have no culture.

8

The Uninvited Guests

Easter 1947 had come and gone, and was ignored. John had come home one afternoon, with four one-day-old chicks that he had swapped some comics for. Dad converted an old tea chest into a run for them, and to keep them safe from Monty cat. There were rules or bye-laws about keeping chickens, how close to a house etc., and ours were too close. Our back garden was small, so much to John's annoyance, they had to be given back. That was the start of all sorts of 'critters' that came into our lives. John was always bringing something home, but not many were well received, least of all the nits that came home in his hair.

They were not uncommon in those days, and most households kept the odd tin of DDT powder, awful stuff, to get rid of unwelcome crawlies of one sort or another. I giggled at John's discomfort, when his head had to be scrubbed with smelly black gunge, but was not so amused when I got the treatment also, nits or no nits.

The nurse had sent him home from school with a note – oh, the shame of it! You would think he had the black plague.

It was all right for Dad, he had hardly any hair, and I think it was around that time that Mum had her lovely long hair cut short. Even the poor cat got the works, we did not see him for two days afterwards.

School was out, summer holidays stretched before us, John would have me tagging along after him for weeks, a fact he failed to appreciate. He would have to choose his school holidays to go down with chicken pox, and not to be outdone, I got them too. I was pleased, I had been cheated out of measles, despite being surrounded by them on numerous occasions. Rumour had it that I was a 'carrier', how else could I avoid them? It was around the time when my spots started to itch, that I decided I would not bother to catch anything else. I remember Mum telling me not to scratch, or my fingers would drop off, and she seemed to know about such things.

I sailed through it, but poor John was really ill, delirious with fever. He had his bed in a narrow bedroom, next to our parents' room, but whilst we were ill we were in their room, me in my cot, and John in the big bed. The parents slept on the put-u-up settee, in the sitting room. I would creep into John's bed to be near to him, I was worried about the 'angel of death', sneaking in at night to steal him away.

Mum found out, and angrily told me off. I told her I was frightened the 'angel of death' might come, but the old lady watched over him too.

She carefully asked me, 'What old lady?'

'The one that makes John laugh,' I replied.

I was annoyed that she did not know about the old lady. She would come when John and I played in his room. I never found it necessary to speak to her, we always seemed to know what the other was thinking. She was small, had her dark hair pinned back from her face in a low bun, and when she smiled, she had no teeth. She wore a white shirt-style blouse, with the sleeves rolled up, and a long, ankle length skirt. She looked like she was wearing black, laced up boots.

Her presence never worried me. I felt I knew her, or at least, that I should know her. I wondered if she was my grandmother who had died in Canada. John was unhappy about it, and mostly left me alone with her.

I told Mum, she could only come if you looked in the long mirror which was leaning against the wall in John's room. If you turned, however quickly, she would not be there, you could only see her in the mirror. We would play for ages, me trying to 'see' her. Her laughter seemed to come from far away, almost as if it was inside my head.

Mum seemed most put out about her, and I noticed she was shaking. I could not understand what was wrong, I was quite used to seeing the old lady, I liked her.

She told me to stay away from the mirror, and when Dad was told about it, they agreed to put it in the rubbish bin.

When we first moved into that prefab, I could not sleep at night for the noise. I would wake Mum up when I went for my late night visit to the lavatory and ask her why it was so noisy.

'What noise?' she'd say. 'I can hear nothing.'

It was like someone in big, heavy boots, tramp-tramping up and down the passage way, stopping at the bedroom door, then tramp-tramping away again.

I used to need to go to the bathroom most nights, and as I could not reach the light switch, I went in the dark. I had been told not to switch on any lights, or flush the toilet, in case I woke anyone.

I would wait for the 'boot' noises to stop, then off I would go, down the passageway, to the little toilet next to the bathroom.

Most visits were uneventful, but I had stopped closing the door, for on a couple of occasions I could not reopen it. The first time it happened, I struggled with the door handle for several seconds, to no avail, and I began to panic. I screamed for Mum, and she came and opened it, no trouble at all. She asked what was wrong, and I told her someone was holding the handle, so I could not turn it to open.

The second time it happened, I had started to panic, once again, then for some strange reason I felt really angry, and said to the empty space 'Open this door, or else', and to my amazement, it opened. As I reached the bedroom door, which was usually left open, I said, again to the empty space, 'Go away.'

I often had a feeling of 'something', a presence, but apart from the old lady in the mirror, saw nothing. I was sure this 'something' was not the old lady, for she never did anything to scare me.

On various late night visits, I would hear a tap on the bath being turned on. I thought it was John, sneaking out to play a prank whilst I was in the toilet, then it occurred to me that I had not heard his bedroom door open. I would go in and turn off the tap, saying, almost to myself, 'Leave things alone.'

I once heard someone laugh when I turned off the tap, and fled back to my cot, and the assurance of the two sleeping forms on the big bed. One night, Mum was waiting by the bathroom door, and when I came out of the toilet she told me off for playing with water, when I should be asleep.

It was such a relief to know that someone else had heard it, and I had not imagined it after all. I told her it happened a lot,

47

and it was not me doing it.

'Oh my God,' was her only response.

The banging stopped, as did the tap episodes, and the mirror from John's room had been thrown away. Things went quiet, but there was more to come.

I had woken about 2 a.m. for my nightly visit to the toilet, and found that I could not move, I was totally paralysed, I could not even call out. I was worried in case I had an accident, if I wet my bed there would be trouble. I was not dreaming I decided, and I had to get out of my cot.

I got really anxious, and then heard once again the tramp-tramp of boots on the lino in the passageway.

I was lying on my back, still unable to move, the sound coming nearer. Instead of stopping at the open door, the feet tramp-tramped into the room. I could not look away or shut my eyes. I just lay there, rigid.

Something seemed to fill the atmosphere, although I could see nothing, but I was surprised to see a faint hovering light move about the room in the darkness.

I had a peculiar sensation, like a prickling feeling all over my body, and for some unknown reason, I felt very angry. I had felt that odd anger before, and had the notion that anger was my weapon against whatever was trying (and succeeding) to terrorise me.

The light hovered over the end of my cot, and I could move. I shrank back, as far into the corner away from the light as I could get. I mouthed the scream, 'Mum, Mum', but no sound came out.

I watched in awe, as the hovering light got larger, forming a shape. It was a man's head, then came the face, I almost laughed out loud. It was a black, Negroid face, with a jolly smile. I got the impression that it was having to work really hard to show itself to me, and only managed to get to the shoulders.

So this was our prankster, our passage tramper and tap pest. It made no attempt to come near, it just grinned foolishly at me. All my fear went, it was just too silly. 'That would not scare the cat,' I thought. I sat up and shouted, 'What's your name?' and the sound must have reached Mum's sleeping form, for she stirred, then sat up.

The smiling visitor just faded away, as I said to Mum, 'Can

48

you see him?'

'See who?' she asked.

How could she have failed to see it?

'Goodness, it's cold in here,' she said, then, 'Go back to sleep.'

'I need the toilet,' I told her.

She sighed, then got out of bed to take me. I had never been so pleased to be led by the hand, the 'big girl' had had a fright! My grinning visitor was gone – but not for good.

We never went away on holidays, for so many children in Britain holidays were only in story books, but we made our own fun, happily playing in and exploring Corsham. There were still a lot of uniformed people around, but few cars, so it was fairly safe to play in the street.

We had the police calling on us, when some older boys had tied John to the railway lines. They had seen it done in a film and thought it was a good gag. Luckily for John, they did it near to the station, and were seen by a rail worker who soon freed him, none the worse. It was the busy Bristol to London line, so nobody thought it was funny.

There was a privet hedge growing along the front of our prefab, it probably was not that high, but I could not see over it. One day, I wanted to play with a ball, and there was more room on the road. I heard a noise I took to be a motor-bike, and assumed it was on the road, but as I walked through our gate I heard a shout, then something hit me, hard. I ended up in the hedge, with a motor-bike lying on the path near me, its wheels spinning, motor chugging. The rider had been hurled over the hedge, and was sprawled out in our front garden.

The shout I heard had come from a man walking his dog, he had yelled at the rider to get off the pavement. I had come through the gate, right into his path. The rider, who was extremely drunk, was only a few bruises worse off, but I had bruises all over me.

There was a car parked a few doors away, and a neighbour said it was a doctor's car. He came and looked me over, then told Mum I must have X-rays, to make sure there were no breakages. He took Mum and I to Chippenham hospital, where I was detained for a few days. I cannot remember much of the incident, I only remembered one doctor in particular. He was black, and trying to be friendly, but he was not 'my'

49

black friend, and I was worried in case he might disappear in front of me. Mum told me I was very wary of him, much to everyone's amusement, and when he tried to touch my face, I sunk my teeth into his finger.

Meanwhile, Mum had been back to the housing officer, at the council offices, to see if a move could be arranged. When she told him why he was quite sarcastic. 'What again?'

But a woman in the office chipped in to say she knew the place. She told him an old house had stood on the ground where some of the prefabs had been erected, and it had had a bad reputation. She added that she was not surprised that Mum was unhappy, no one stayed there for long. Mum was relieved that it was not just us, twice was too much of a coincidence, and 'they' would see what they could do about it.

'They' did nothing, we put up with the endless mischief.

The Eros statue had been replaced in Piccadilly circus, and we were taken up to London on the train, for a day out, to see it and other sights. We saw some sights all right, most of which were walking about on two legs. I had more fun watching people, I was enthralled by the colours, noise and general hustle-bustle of London. That visit was the beginning of what was to become a lifetime's hobby, giving endless hours of delight. I called it 'people watching', not for me trains or birds. I was fascinated by people.

I soon learned how to do it without being too obvious, after several 'What are you looking at?' remarks.

The parents were closely watched, and I felt that all was not well with them. Dad was not being quite so spiteful, but Mum was paranoid about her religion, and was becoming more and more remote. She was having trouble with her eyesight, and getting a lot of back pain. I caught her crying a couple of times, but when I asked her what was wrong, she would say, 'Nothing, dear, it's just my funny way of laughing.' I thought, 'Huh, what has she got to laugh about?'

I also noticed that Monty cat was spending more and more time outdoors, he was in fact very reluctant to come in at all. We even had to set his food and water down by the back doorstep, and he slept in Dad's small garden shed, Dad left the window open for him. Once I picked him up bodily, and carried him into the kitchen. He let out one awful yowl, leapt on to the draining board by the sink, and fled through the open window, his tail all bushy and fur standing on end.

I told Mum about it, and she said he was not to be made to come indoors if he did not want to.

One Saturday morning, Mum and I had gone into Corsham centre, to the shops, leaving John at home – 'in charge'. Dad worked Saturday mornings. John had been bouncing a rubber ball along the passageway, thudding it off the wall by the kitchen door, Mum told him to 'Stoppit.' As soon as we were out of earshot, he started to do it again, banging the ball against the wall. This he did several times, until he heard his name, spoken sharply, 'JOHN.' There was no one in the house, and he left his ball and fled outside. We found him, about two hours later, too scared to venture back indoors. He told Mum what had happened, and she said, 'Don't be silly, it's nothing but your imagination,' but she had a very peculiar look on her face.

It annoyed me that they seemed scared of whatever it was in that prefab, I was sure it was all being done to scare us, and to be scared was playing right into 'its' hands The idea of something unseen causing mischief, made me extremely angry, especially when it upset my 'big bother'. I got the feeling there would have to be a show-down, 'it' would have to go. I could not tolerate anything, or anyone, getting at John.

It was a beautiful sunny afternoon, John had gone out, but Mum wanted me to stay indoors, she was expecting a parcel, and did not want to miss the postman. She had to go out, only across the road to the lady with the baby, and she would not be long.

I soon got bored with my own company, and decided to climb up on to the draining board, to look out of the window. The kitchen window faced the front, and I could see the road. The table was by the wall opposite, just underneath a small service hatch that opened into the sitting room. I liked to open the hatch doors and climb through, having used a chair to first climb up on to the table. I did that quite often, much to John's amusement, and Mum's annoyance.

As I gazed out of the window, looking for the postman, I heard the hatch doors open. I turned around to look, and saw the black friendly face I had seen before, by my cot.

I was a bit taken aback, for only the head and shoulders were visible, but there it was, coming through the hatch way. I knew that I was small enough to get through that hatch, but this 'thing' was going to get stuck. I laughed out loud, and it hovered by the hatch entrance.

It did not like that laugh. I giggled again, and the facial expression began to change, into a look I can only describe as pure evil.

Most people know what 'evil' means, but only those who have been touched by it can fully comprehend its true meaning. It is perfectly true, that the hair on the back of your neck stands on end, your spine prickles as your body goes rigid. Time itself seems to stand still, you can practically taste and smell – evil.

This sensation of evil seemed to fill the whole room, and somehow, as that obscenity hovered towards me, I found the courage to yell, 'I don't like you, go away, now!' For some strange reason, and I will never understand what prompted me, I began to recite the Lord's prayer, as I had been taught at Sunday school.

I got as far as 'Thy will be done, on earth as it is in heaven,' I could not remember what came next, so I sobbed, 'Deliver us from evil, Amen.' I was gasping for air between sobs, I could not seem to breathe properly, it was as if even the air was fouled.

The shape, hovering close to me now, began to fade, as a strange fluorescent type light seemed to engulf it completely. I had a fleeting glimpse of the face, with a hauntingly sad expression on it, then nothing.

I was sick in the sink, then realised I had better clean it up before Mum came back. I was shaking all over, and sobbing uncontrollably.

Mum found me shortly afterwards, still sitting by the sink, sobbing. When she asked me what was wrong, I told her I thought she had gone away, and she told me not to be silly. Years later, I told her what really happened.

I never saw anything again, but I took great care never to be alone in that house, for I could not dispel the aura of something 'not quite right' about the place.

Monty cat had canker in his ears, and had to be put to sleep – it was that 'angel of death' again, and we had another burial in the garden.

The winter of that year had been the worst ever recorded,

and the spring had brought severe flooding, with many towns and country areas under water.

Another flood was sweeping the land, a flood of divorces. The number recorded was causing concern, probably a by-product of so many wartime 'quickie' weddings.

The government was trying to persuade women to return to work, and still food rationing was causing misery.

There were men who would go round the doors, selling so-called luxury goods, such as nylon stockings, perfume and chocolates. They were called spivs, the only thing that got rid of them was the sight of a navy blue police uniform.

The summer, with all its traumas and events, had seemed very long, but at last it was September, and I was to go to school.

9

New Faces and Places

For as long as I could remember, I had wanted to go to school, I was beside myself with excitement. John had gone up to the junior sector, and I was in infants. Mother handed me over to the teacher, who took me to where the coat pegs were, and I was shown where to sit. About six children started that day, but more came later in the week. I was in seventh heaven, but it goes without saying – it did not last.

From where we lived, in Brunel Avenue, there were two fairly busy roads to cross to reach school, not to mention a quiet back lane. At morning break we were told to put our coats on, to play outside. I thought that was it, and went home. Funny, no sign of John or Mum.

I arrived home to find Mum up to her elbows in suds, doing a wash in the sink. She stared at me then asked, 'What are you doing here?' I told her we were let out, so I came home. She had to dry her hands, take off her apron and the turban round her hair, and take me back again. The teacher was one of those dreadful old harridans, left over from some war or other, and let loose on Britain's schoolchildren to wreak revenge on society. It was a pity Hitler did not come across a few like her, the war would have been over in weeks. She was ancient, almost thirty.

When it came to reading lessons, she was most put out to find I could read, and I announced in disgust that the book she handed me was for babies. She slung a book at me that was not pictures and letters, i.e. C is for CAT, with a picture of a cat. It was *Jack and the Beanstalk*, no pictures. 'As you can read, Bobbie Eriksson,' she sneered, 'you can read aloud to us, show us how smart you are.' She leaned back in her chair, arms folded, and a smug 'we'll see' look on her face.

I got to page three, with no stumbles, and her look got blacker, then she roared out, 'That is enough, go and find something to play with.' I was thereafter sent off to play, while the rest of the class did their A is for APPLE etc.

I got from her, 'Of course, you do not know your alphabet.' It was a statement, rather than a question. I replied, 'I do, and backwards.' I started to rattle it off, when she snapped, 'Be quiet.'

I could not understand why she was so hostile. The more I was left to 'play' the more disruptive I got, mixing all the poster paints together, getting plasticine into places I would rather not mention, and putting bucketfuls of sand down the toilet. After about six weeks, and several head on clashes with the teacher, I was moved up a class, and was put with older children. I was to use scissors, pencils instead of slate and marker, proper ink. Oh, this was more like it, and 'this teacher,' I told Mum, 'does not have hairs on her chins.'

'Chins?' asked Mum.

'Yes, she's got three,' I told her. I did not think it was funny, but Mum giggled.

With hindsight, I think my expectations of school life were just too high, for I went straight into another confrontation, and it was not long before I was in trouble again.

I was left-handed, or at least, naturally used my left hand for most things. There was a boy in that class who was also left-handed, and we both went through hell with that teacher. She insisted we learned to use our 'proper' hand, and on one occasion even tied the boy's left hand behind his back. He used to cry, I used to throw things. If we were caught using the wrong hand, there would be a hard whack on the back of it, with a wooden ruler.

I made very little progress in that class, and as I had entered it early, I had to stay in it for over a year.

She would yell at us and say that the Devil was left-handed. When I told Mum, she laughed and replied, 'She should know.' She told me to try and use my right hand, to look on it as a challenge, it might even be fun, 'especially if you could use both.' To this day, I am ambidextrous, but looking back I feel it was a wicked and ignorant thing to do to a child.

There was to be a royal wedding, the Princess Elizabeth was to marry a Greek. I thought it sounded like something out of a fairy story. There was a street party, and the buntings were up in the village main street. Corsham is a town really, by Royal charter no less, but I have always thought of it as a village, much more friendly. We stood outside the entrance to the Methuen Arms, and waved our Union flags, but I was quite put out when told we would not see the royal couple, they were in London. The 'Greek' Prince Philip, had been given the title of H.R.H. Prince Philip, Duke of Edinburgh, by the King. I thought that was really something, straight out of Hans Christian Andersen. How I wished we could have been in London to see something of the pageantry, but small girls can dream – so can big ones, for that matter!

I wondered how she managed to get the clothing coupons for her wedding dress, but I presumed, being a princess, she did not need to think of such things.

One of the popular songs that year was *Maybe it's because I'm a Londoner.* Enough of dreaming for me, it was back to school.

The Christmas nativity play was a new delight for me, especially as the juniors required three small girls, who had long fair hair, to play the herald angels. I was chosen as one, much to John's embarrassment, I am sure it was at this juncture he decided to opt out – he was probably playing Herod.

One of the other girls chosen was in a class above me, and did not seem to think I should be there, she wanted her friend to have my place. She embarked on an aggravation campaign which included pulling my hair, pinching me, and trying to tread on my long white robe.

I could take just so much, and on the night of the performance, just as we were going on stage, me, the smallest in the lead, she tried to trip me up. When that did not work, she gave my hair, which was loose, a savage tug from behind, yanking my head back. That was as much as I would tolerate. I turned around and laid into her, knocking her sprawling across stage. Peace and goodwill did not abound.

The place was in an uproar, cheers and laughter from the parents in the audience, shocked disbelief on the faces of the staff.

Dad nearly fell off his chair laughing, as did John, but Mum had the 'I've no idea who she is' look on her face, and as the curtain was hastily lowered, the punch-up continued. The play eventually got under way, minus the herald angels, but it was a giggle from start to finish. It is hardly surprising to know, that that was the end of my stage career.

The Christmas holidays started, and everyone tried to forget. Christmas day was a disappointment, I had hoped we would at least have a traditional dinner, but it was just as dreary as any other day, the festive season was totally ignored.

I dreaded going back to school, and having to listen to all the excited chatter, and hoped that no one would ask me what I got.

A neighbour we met in the street asked Mum in disbelief, 'Did they get nothing at all, not even some sweets?'

Mum whined nasally, 'Oh, they get things at other times of the year, sweets and presents.'

I promptly told her that was a lie, we got nothing, ever. The woman's face was a picture, as was my mother's.

Sweets and sugar were still on ration, but sometimes Mum would make a tray of fudge. We had a neighbour who never used her ration of sugar and exchanged it for other things she could use. When it was our turn, Mum made fudge, absolute heaven.

One day she had made a tray of it, and left it on the window-sill to cool. She told John, who was hovering over it, not to touch, it was hot. We went outside to get some of Dad's Brussels sprouts from the garden, and were not long gone when we heard a yell.

Mum laughed, saying, 'I knew he could not leave it alone.'

When we went back indoors, there he was, hopping up and down, with the offending finger under the water from the cold tap, and a tell-tale dent in the tray of fudge.

The newspapers that Mum kept trying to hide from me were full of a story about a small Indian man, who had been shot. I thought it was very sad, there was a photograph of him, lying in his coffin, surrounded by flowers. I thought he looked like a doll in a box.

I asked Mum what a riot was, and she told me I should know, I had started enough of them.

We had a funny old bakelite-cased radio set, and although it was a bit crackly, and almost impossible to tune into, we could always find John huddled up to it, his ear almost part of it, listening to the latest adventure of Dick Barton, Special Agent.

Mum listened to Housewife's Choice, and I got in the way, as usual.

10

Bullies and Good Turns

Dad had kept scrapbooks, during and after the war, of newspaper cuttings, with dates and stories of current affairs. There were all sorts of wonderful snippets, clipped out and gummed into the folders.

I was not supposed to look at them, but I found them irresistible. There was an old shoebox full of Dad's cards and letters to Mum, sent whilst he was in the Navy. They were full of red crossings-out where they had been censored for 'careless talk', but Mum had usually managed to work out where he was.

She kept hiding them from me, but I usually managed to find them, there are not many 'hidey holes' in a prefab.

Mum still had her cleaner's job at our school. She would do the infant's classes after we finished, and two other ladies did the junior sector later on.

After class I would wait for Mum to finish, and John to come out of juniors, about half an hour after my class ended. Mum used to bring me a slice of bread, spread with margarine and a sprinkling of sugar. I was always ravenous.

I would sit down to eat it, near where she was working, watching her. Even to my child's eyes, she seemed so frail and thin, and it was such a pity she cut her long brown hair. I was never allowed to touch her, no hugs or kisses, and there was never any of the likes from her.

It felt sometimes like either she or I were simply 'not there', the loneliness of our non-relationship used to completely engulf me.

When I finished my snack, I would wander off around the empty classrooms, and sometimes into the playground. The infants and juniors had separate play areas, and were not allowed in each other's, so one afternoon, I was surprised to see three 'big girls' in the infant playground.

When one of them spotted me, she said to her companions, 'There she is, quick.'

Instinct told me to flee, and I did, back into the building, along the corridor where I had last seen Mum. There was no sign of her, and I guessed she would be in the toilets, sweeping the floor, so in I rushed, with the three girls in hot pursuit.

Mum was not there, so in panic I rushed into a cubicle and bolted the door after me, my heart thumping.

They had seen me run into the room, and soon found which cubicle I was in. As they banged on the door, I kept quiet, I was not going to make their day by yelling for my mother.

After what seemed like a long time, I heard them whispering amidst stifled giggles, so I listened. The plan, it seemed, was for them to pretend they were going, and when I tried to leave they would hold fast the door.

The cubicle doors went down to within two inches of floor level, but the partitions between were about twelve inches off the floor. I was in the fourth one down from the exit, so after a few minutes' silence, broken by the occasional smothered snigger, I crawled under the partitions until I reached the cubicle opposite the exit, and waited. The door, which opened inwards, was open, so they could not see my feet, and must have thought that I was still inside the bolted cubicle.

When my heart stopped thudding, I made a dash for the exit. They were after me like hounds after a fox, but as I raced into the corridor, there was Mum, talking to the janitor, good old Mum.

I was asked what on earth did I think I was doing, and I told them three big girls tried to lock me in a lavatory.

The three culprits emerged, trying to look the picture of innocence, and the janitor said, 'Not you three again.'

Seemed they amused themselves regularly, by bullying the babies, and had been in trouble over it before.

They insisted I was lying, saying they did not know I was in there.

When the janitor found the cubicle, locked and empty, it confirmed my story, and he told them the headmaster would be informed.

They glared murder at me, and I had the feeling I had not

60

seen the last of them.

About one week later, I was in the playground waiting for either John to come, or Mum to finish her jobs, when I saw the janitor working in the flower beds around the school building. I went over to watch him, and he handed me a daffodil that had been broken off at the stem. I was going off to show it to Mum, when there, in the infant playground again, were the three horrors. Despite being told off by the headmaster, they were back, bent on revenge.

The biggest and ugliest one, who seemed to be the ring leader, whooped with delight when she saw me holding a flower, and announced that she was going straight to the headmaster, to report me.

I could never understand how those three managed to get out of class so soon after the infants left, they must have been poised for flight the second the bell rang for end of lessons.

It seemed to take John ages to come for me. I was not worried, I knew where the flower had come from, but somehow, I no longer wanted it, so I let it drop on the playground.

Big Bertha turned up with a teacher on tow saying, 'There she is, and look,' pointing at the evidence, 'there is the flower.'

She stuck her pug face right in front of me, sneering, 'You are not supposed to pick the flowers.'

The teacher said to her, 'That is enough,' then to me, 'Did you pick it dear?'

I told her the janitor gave it to me.

'She's a liar,' shouted Big Bertha (that's what I called her).

'Be quiet!' scolded the teacher.

It was just beginning to get interesting, when the janitor came into view. He called over to me, 'Where's that flower I gave you Bobbie?'

I told him, pointing to the scowling girl, 'She said I stole it, so I threw it away.'

He stooped to pick it up, handed it to me, glaring at the girl, then turned and walked away.

John arrived then, and we went off to find Mum.

The teacher told the girl, 'You, come with me,' and as they walked away, I stuck out my tongue at the girl.

John said, 'You keep away from her, she's trouble.'

I told him I did not go looking for her.

When Dad heard about it, he told me to kick her in the shins if she bothered me again.

Some time later I was in the playground at morning break, with other children around, when she arrived with her cronies, once more bent on mischief. We were allowed to take a toy to school to play with at break, and my choice was a skipping rope.

I saw that oaf of a girl snatch a doll from a child half her size, and throw it on to the ground. She and her two pals laughed at the child's distress. Me – I saw red!

I stormed up to her, and demanded to know why she picked on someone smaller than herself. She grabbed my plaits, which were a target for bullies of all sorts, and started pushing me about. A crowd gathered to watch the fun, and one of her pals told her to leave me alone.

'Not until she cries,' said bully.

That did it, I lashed out at her in a rage, whacking her across the face with my skipping rope. She let go of my hair, gaping at me as the weals swelled up across her cheeks, then, letting out a howl, she turned and fled.

Strange, nothing came of that incident; I was dreading a summons to the headmaster, but it never came. I never saw her again either, she must have decided it was safer to remain in the juniors' playground.

When the three of us walked to and from school, we had to go down a lane that flanked some fields. Mostly there were cows in the field, but occasionally there would be a large farm horse, whose name was Dobbin. He was a gentle giant, all the children knew him, and he just adored being admired and fussed over.

One Saturday morning, I decided I would go and see Dobbin. He had been in the field on the Friday after school, so I supposed he would still be there. I cannot recall what happened, but Mum found me later, in the field, surrounded by some very inquisitive cows, no sign of Dobbin.

She managed to get me away from them, but they trailed after us up to the gate, and we had to climb over it for fear one might get out.

Shortly after that incident, John and I were on the lane, when we heard a cow bellowing. When we got to where the hedge ended, by the gate, we saw what all the commotion was about. A calf had a hind leg tangled up in some brambles, and the cow was standing nearby, obviously distressed. John declared we had to do something about it. Most of the cows seemed to be at the far end of the field, so we clambered over the gate. I was to distract the cow, while John freed the calf – I could run faster!

She was already upset, and I was just too much, she came at me and I ran and ran, with her after me. I nearly died of fright as I lunged headlong into the hedge that grew alongside the fence. She stood there bellowing at me, I was petrified.

A few minutes later, that seemed like hours, John was at the other side of the fence, the safe side, telling me 'Come out of there, the calf is freed now.'

I was all scratched from the dive into the hedge, and badly shaken. John was all smug and self-satisfied, having done his good deed. Brothers really are the pits!

It is hardly surprising that to this day, I am wary of cows.

When Mum went to shop in Corsham, and did not want 'tag-along' to go, I would visit the couple with the baby, who lived across the road. Any excuse I was there, it usually meant a biscuit or apple for me, and I could amuse the cute baby.

The baby's mother once remarked that I seemed to like apples, and I told her we never had them at home. She replied that surely my mother bought apples, but I told her Dad did not like apples, they were a waste of money. She gave me a queer look, and muttered something about Dad's cigarettes. She asked me a lot of questions, and like any average five-year-old, I told her all she wanted to know. Mum had gone on endlessly about being truthful, not that she practised what she preached.

I could not understand why that neighbour started avoiding my mother.

11

Trains and Surprises

John and I were informed that we were going to Wales; no, not for a holiday, for a religious convention. 'Oh no,' I wailed, 'not a Holy Joe Bible bash,' and got a slap from Mum. John said nothing, he did not need to, his face said it all.

It meant a couple of train journeys, one into Bristol, then on to Ebbw Vale. Bristol Templemeads station reminded me of our London visits, and I was having fun, so many people to watch, but the journey to Wales was magic.

We had to go through the Severn tunnel. I could hardly wait. I had been through the famous Box tunnel, built by Isambard Kingdom Brunel, and never tired of our journeys into Bath for Mum's 'meetings'. It was, for me, the only interesting thing about our visits into Bath Spa. We never got to see the shops, the Abbey, Pultney bridge, pump rooms, or any of the numerous attractions of that lovely Georgian city. I once had a glimpse of the famous Royal Crescent, and remarked on the pretty street. 'Hoomph,' was the only response from Mum.

John and I were playing in the corridor of the train to Wales, with some other children, when someone said we were approaching the tunnel. Mum grabbed me, just as I was lowering the window to lean out for a good look.

I was well and truly told off, and had to spend the remainder of the journey in the compartment, much to my chagrin. When I settled down, and had ceased fuming over the fact that John was still in the corridor, having fun, I took stock of my surroundings.

We had the compartment to ourselves, so there was room to move about. I noticed something glisten on the floor, and got down off the seat to investigate.

It turned out to be a pearl type bead, which I picked up to show to Mum and Dad, but they were both dozing. I spent a very happy half hour or so, grovelling about on the floor, reaching under the seat to collect as many beads as I could find or reach. Someone must have broken their necklace. I had about twenty beads, and I put them in my handkerchief, tied a knot in it,and then put it into the pocket of my overcoat which was on the seat beside me.

When Mum awoke, she went mad, I was absolutely filthy from crawling about on the floor. I told her what I had found, but she was not interested.

Dad laughed, and told her I should have been left in the corridor, the other children would have kept me out of mischief.

I kept those beads for a very long time, and I often wondered who they had belonged to, and why she had not collected them up. Probably did not want to get messed up, retrieving them from under the seats.

We arrived in Wales late Friday evening, had a bus journey, then reached our lodgings for the weekend. It was pouring with rain when we got to Ebbw Vale, and when we left on the Sunday evening, it was still pouring. As for the weekend, it was memorable for the sheer boredom of it.

I had been given a paper pad and pencil to keep me amused. John seemed in a permanent ill-humour, not that I blamed him, but it was clear I would have to find my own amusement. I did so by drawing faces on the pad, and passing them around to the people seated near us, who were pretending to listen to some oaf up on a platform. He was droning on about what an awful place the world was, full of sin and wickedness. I did not think that boring people stiff would make things any better.

My scribbles caused a lot of stifled giggles, and when Mum realised who was the cause of the mirth, my pad and pencil were confiscated, with a 'Sit up, and pay attention.'

I had seen all that was in front, it was time to have a good look at what was behind me. I turned round in my seat, getting on my knees, and took stock of the rows of faces. Much of the same it seemed, until I saw him.

He had a wonderful red beard and a moustache and a shock of the reddest hair I have ever seen. It was so different from

Dad, who had hardly any. He was pulling faces at me, which made his beard and moustache move. Not to be outdone, I made faces back. In what seemed no time at all, several people were pulling faces, they were obviously as bored as I was.

It did not last, I got a clip round my ear from Mum, and told for the umpteenth time to 'Pay attention.'

I was obviously a real pain in the neck, for on the Sunday I was left with our landlady.

Her house seemed very large and dark to me. On the upstairs landing there was a life-sized statue of a lady wearing a sari, carrying a basket on her head. Mum had walked into it when we arrived on the Friday, and had apologised, she thought it was real. John and I had giggled about that for ages. I asked the landlady what it was, and she told me that her husband, who was now dead, had brought it from India. Never one to be accused of tact, I told her he should have left it there. She proudly showed me around her home, showing me all sorts of things he had brought from India, including an umbrella stand made from an elephant's foot. I thought that was disgusting, but said nothing. At the end of her tour, I was wondering if there was anything left in India, he must have needed a ship to himself to bring so much junk.

I had lunch and tea with her, and she kept me amused all day. It was wet outdoors, so I could not play in her garden, but her house was fascinating.

The parents and John returned in the early evening, and as our things were already packed, we said our goodbyes and departed.

So much for Wales. It seemed that our parents were determined to see to it that we got no fun or enjoyment out of life; they certainly got none.

Shortly after the Welsh fiasco, Mum told us that she and Dad were going to a convention in Brighton. Thankfully, we were not! We were being sent away to stay with friends of theirs, to different addresses. I was to be apart from John again, and I let the whole street known about it. However, when I was deposited at their friends' home, I realised they had two daughters, so at least I would have playmates.

It was a visit that would be an eye-opener for me.

They belonged to the same religious sect as my parents, but it was clear they lived in a different world. The first thing I noticed was the affection shown for the girls, the next surprise was the bedroom they shared, where I was also to sleep. I had never seen so many toys, the dolls were unbelievable, I had to touch a doll to be sure it was really there. There seemed to be an awkward silence, as I gazed around that room at the pretty curtains and furnishings, and oh, those dolls.

The older girl asked if I liked the doll I had touched. I nodded dumbly at her, and she told me I could borrow it for the weekend.

I was dumbstruck as the younger girl blurted out that I could borrow all her dolls if I wished.

I managed to mutter a 'thank you' as her mother hurried out of the room, followed by their father.

I was alone with them and they pounced on me, neither could get over the length of my hair. They both had short, curly hair, and were desperate to play with mine. I sat passively on a wicker ottoman, whilst they brushed and fiddled with it, wanting to scream, but they had offered me the use of their wonderful dolls, so I just put up with it.

My eyes were smarting from the tugs with the hairbrush, but I was rescued when their father called, 'Tea's ready, wash hands.' That was a novelty for me, who only washed when dirty.

My mother had given me a small, brown paper bag to give to my hostess. In it was a block of jelly and a solid block of dates; that, it seemed, was her contribution to my weekend stay. When I went into their dining-room, I got another shock.

This time, I was convinced I must be dreaming. I had never seen anything like it, the table was absolutely laden with food. There was brown and white bread, home-made scones, still warm from the oven. The yellow stuff in a dish must be butter, my Mum used to mix a half-pound of butter with a half-pound of margarine to make it go further. There were three sorts of jam, all home-made, I wondered how they got the sugar for it. I noticed iced buns with coloured dots on them, hundreds and thousands they were called. The 'funny brown stuff', I was told, was peanut butter, and yes, that was jelly and custard, it is called a 'trifle', I was informed.

I sat down and stared at it all, and we had to say grace. 'For what we are about to receive, may the Lord make us truly thankful – AMEN.'

I did not need to be told twice to 'tuck in', but I quite unashamedly asked, 'How d'ye manage this lot wiv food an' sugar on ration?' The girls giggled, their parents exchanged glances. I was not told how, but that night I prayed that if I was dreaming, I might never wake up.

I had been given a bath the previous evening, so I was a bit annoyed that I was expected to wash when I got up on the Saturday morning. There was no school, so we could play all day. I had kept the borrowed doll on a chair by the bed I slept in, but I hardly dared touch it, let alone play with it, it seemed so fragile.

When we were allowed outside to play, I was offered a ride on a tricycle, but although I had seen one before, I had never ridden on one. It proved to be very easy, and I was soon careering about on it. Being a novice, and over-confident besides, the inevitable happened, I took a tumble.

The result was two grazed knees, and a fright, and the tricycle was put back in the garden shed. The older girl had a two-wheeler, but I did not dare try that.

I sat on the kerb, picking bits of gravel out of my burning knees, when the girls' mother took me indoors to clean up the wounds. It was such an indignity to have to sit up on the sink worktop, and be fussed over with wads of cotton-wool and disinfectant, and it stung like anything. I had to put up with it until all the gravel was cleaned out, but being given an apple to cheer me up made it all worthwhile. I wondered what I could go out and injure next.

That evening, I was appalled when told it was bath-time. I reminded them that I had had a bath the previous evening, and a wash in the morning. They all laughed, and the mother said she needed to be sure all the grit was out of my grazed knees. I huffily thought that John would not be suffering so much washing, and wished that I was with him. Sunday was much the same, more water, and so much food.

My parents arrived in the evening to take me home, they had collected John, who looked thoroughly fed up with his lot. I gleefully hoped that he too had been washed ragged. My mood was one of pure spite, and when it was time to say the thank yous, I announced that I did not want to go home.

Mum shot me one of her looks, Dad smirked, but John was still sullen, probably because he realised they were obliged to

68

take me home. It was some time before the parents went to another convention, I cannot imagine why!

Dad went to Scotland for a few weeks, with his job, and life for us went on. I missed going to Sunday school, and kept asking when I could return, I was always told 'NO'. John came home from school one afternoon, asking if he could join the cub scouts. What a fuss! Mother went on endlessly about 'worldly things' and it was forbidden to salute the flag. What utter nonsense, all he wanted was to be able to go somewhere with boys of his own age, and perish the thought, have some fun.

I was invited to a class-mates's sixth birthday party, but was not allowed to attend. The reason given was that I would be expected to invite her to mine, as birthdays were 'worldly' they were not allowed.

John and I were both sat down and told we were not to bring anyone home, or go visiting. We were to disassociate ourselves from outsiders. Well, I was not sure what dis-assoc whatsit meant, but it sounded really unfriendly.

I told my class-mate that I could not come to her party, and wanted to die when she asked 'Why not?' When I explained, as best I could, she gaped at me in disbelief, then told me my mother was horrid.

The day after the party, she brought a piece of birthday cake, wrapped in paper, and gave it to me, telling me that her mother said I was to eat it before I got home. I did, and took great delight in telling Mum all about it.

Dad returned from his visit to Scotland. I wondered why I had felt sad when he went away, for no one had missed him. Mum had seemed less fraught, and John and I were free of pinch bruises. He dropped a bomb shell when he calmly informed us that we were going abroad. He had a transfer to Ceylon, now Sri Lanka. He had put in for the move without Mum knowing, and she was furious.

We were all to be inoculated, that sounded nasty. When we called into the doctor's surgery, there were forms to fill in, and we all had to have a medical check-up prior to the inoculations. The doctor told Mum that my jabs would have to wait until my chest-cold cleared up, but the others were all right. I have no idea what vaccinations they were given, but they were all very ill from them. I was dreading my turn, but it was not to come. We were to move again, but not to foreign climes – well, not really!

12

A Foreign Land

John was annoyed that I missed the jabs, I did not mind at all.

The parents were to sell up; at least, they decided to, everything was to go, not that there was much. Most of it went to neighbours.

I was in my cot one evening when a lady from a few houses away came to look at it, and wanted it for her son.

She asked how old I was, and was told 'six'.

'Goodness, and still in a cot,' she remarked.

'Well, she is a bit small,' was the reply.

'Cheek,' I thought. I hated the way some adults would discuss you, as though you were either not there or stone-deaf.

Dad, who could never keep money, spent what they got for items sold, so there was nothing to show for the household sale. We were supposed to be going to a fully furnished and equipped bungalow in Kandy, Sri Lanka, so we ended up with a couple of tea-chests that contained unwanted and unsold items. The beds would go on our leaving day, there were no pets, so there were no problems there.

A neighbour, who was a carpenter, had made a toy lorry for John, which was painted in bright colours, and could be taken apart. For me, he had made an endearing little cottage about ten inches square, that had hinged walls and roof for opening. The front was painted with flowers around the door, it was just delightful, and my prized possession. He also made a doll's bed, which was painted blue, with a Red Riding Hood motif on the headboard. The cottage was treasured, but the doll bed was well-used; several kittens over the years were to find it irresistible.

After the sell-up, there were only a few things left, the aforementioned toys, which were the only reminders of a not quite forgotten Christmas, and an old bakelite radio set, which was temperamental. Seems no one wanted that, or the odds and ends of household bric-a-brac that were packed into the tea-chests, along with one of Dad's rag rugs.

Moving day, it seemed, was fast approaching, but I had still not been taken to the surgery for my jabs. Things had been a bit odd, with a lot of whispering going on, and my curiosity was at fever pitch. I overheard Mum say to Dad, 'I don't want to go there, either.'

'Go where?' I asked.

Mum blurted out that we were not going to Ceylon, an unmarried man had been given the job instead. She added with a sigh, 'We are going to Scotland.'

There we were, with two old battered suitcases of belongings, two tea-chests full of junk that nobody wanted, and probably not a penny to show for the items that had been sold.

We were to leave the tea-chests behind, John and I were told they would be sent on later, but it was to be almost two years before we saw them again.

I found out later, from Mum, that Dad had to borrow money to get us to Scotland, he had a travel warrant for himself, but not for the rest of us. The chests were left with a neighbour, who had loaned the money, and I suppose there was never any money to reclaim them. There was nothing in them that Dad wanted anyway.

I suspected that the move to Scotland was temporary, and Dad was trying to force the issue of a permanent stay, by dragging us along.

The Admiralty usually found accommodation for their staff, when possible, but we were to go to lodgings Dad had found in Bellshill, Lanarkshire.

I remember nothing of the journey back to Scotland, but vaguely recall our arrival at the lodgings. They were in an old house that had been split into four units by the elderly couple who lived there. They had the upstairs flat, which was reached by an outside wooden staircase that must have come out of the Ark. To say it was rickety is an understatement. We were given a room in their flat that was about fourteen feet square, with a large alcove near the door. There was one large window, a fireplace, and a curtain to cover the alcove. The furnishings consisted of an old leather three-piece suite, a table with four chairs, a small sideboard, and a double bed in the alcove. There was lino on the floor, and a rug which covered about two thirds of the main floor area. We shared bathroom facilities with the old couple, but could not use the kitchen. Mum managed to persuade the old lady to let her boil a kettle, but there was to be no cooking. We would have to eat sandwiches and cold food brought in pre-cooked.

There never seemed to be any money for food, and we usually had just bread and margarine, with jam or marmalade. John and I were given water to drink as we got free milk at school. Our new school was close to the lodgings, so we both came home to our lunch of sandwiches. The bread was different to what we had been used to, it was a tall white loaf, with very dark crusts top and bottom. When we had a 'pan loaf' with crusts either end, John and I used to fight over whose turn it was for the new crust. He usually managed to arrange to get it, by saying that I had had the last one, so it was his turn.

I knew that some children got free dinners at school, and I wondered how they managed that. When I asked a class-mate, I was told you got them if you were poor, and your father was out of work. I told her we were poor, but Dad was not out of work, he just never had any money. He never gave any money to Mum for housekeeping, she had to manage on the few shillings she got each week for child allowance, I could see no hope of ever getting school dinners.

My first day at the school in Bellshill had been unforgettable. I was left at the gate by Mum, and told to go across the playground, into the door marked 'GIRLS'. I had not been told to wait for John at lunchtime, but I supposed he would collect me to take me home. The boy and girl playgrounds were on opposite sides of the building, so I entered the door marked 'GIRLS', as instructed. Classes had already begun, and there was no one about, so I looked about to see where I should go. I stood for what seemed like ages, then a girl came out of a room and saw me and asked 'Ur ye new?'

I nodded, and she pointed to a door marked 'HEAD-MASTER'.

'Ye've tae gaun in therr,' she said, pushing me through the door, after knocking on it.

There was a man sitting at a desk, and he looked up as I was propelled through the doorway. He smiled, and pointed to a

73

chair by his desk, asking 'And who might you be?'

'My name is Bobbie Eriksson,' I informed him as I sat down.

'Oh yes,' he nodded, then added, 'You are in Miss Wilson's class.'

I replied, 'I have only just got here, I am not in anyone's class yet.'

He laughed, saying, 'Miss Wilson is to be your teacher.' He was filling in a card as he spoke, and I noticed he did not have the strange accent I had heard since my arrival in Scotland. He asked where I lived, and I told him I had not been told our address. He then asked my age, and I told him I would be seven in October.

'When in October?' he asked.

'I don't know, we are not allowed birthdays.'

He muttered something which I could not hear, then told me he would take me to my new class-room. He asked if I was worried about meeting new class-mates, and I told him, 'No, I quite like people.' He seemed to think that was funny, and took my hand as we walked into a room.

There were neat rows of double desks, and the seating arrangements seemed to be mixed, with a boy and a girl together where possible. I was to sit next to a girl. 'Thank goodness,' I thought.

I was introduced to Miss Wilson, and went up to shake hands with her – hoping mine were clean!

She looked me over, then in a sing-song voice remarked, 'So, ye've come frae England? Well, well.'

You would have thought I had just homed in from the planet Mars. There were thirty-eight pairs of eyes trained on me, as I was shown where to sit.

I was introduced to my desk companion, who said 'Hello.' That I understood!

I replied, 'How do you do?' and shook hands with her.

I thought Maggie's chin would fall off her face as she gaped at me, but she composed herself enough to exclaim, 'Jings, git you wi' yer pan loaf.'

I had no idea what she was on about, until she added,

'My, but ye're awfie posh.'

Miss Wilson settled her class down, and I could breathe normally again. I was dreading morning break, but Maggie was given charge of me and told to look after me in the playground.

Once out there I was fair game, and my class-mates wanted to know my entire life history.

My Dad was English. 'Well, she cannie help tha-at,' consoled one boy.

'Is yer mither posh, like you?' asked a girl with red plaits and a face full of freckles. I thought she looked like a baked rice pudding, and ignored her.

They were all around me, firing questions, I was beginning to get annoyed.

One boy remarked, 'Dinnie ye talk queer, kin ye no' speak English?'

I was itching to thump him, but managed to control the urge.

One girl asked if my name really was Bobbie. 'That's a laddie's name,' she sneered.

She nearly got thumped, but instead, I asked her what her name was.

'Fiona McFadzean,' I was told.

'Huh,' I replied indignantly, 'if I had a handle like that, I would not poke fun at anyone else's name.'

She looked shamefaced as she replied, 'Aye, it's awfie, wid ye like tae play tag?' and we became friends.

Miss Wilson decided she did not like my name, there was a boy in class whose name was similar, and it was causing confusion, much to our amusement, and her annoyance. She announced to the whole class that I was to be known by my middle name, Jacqueline. I hated the idea of that, it was bad enough being Bobbie, and I was not going to have any of it. My class-mates were well warned of the consequences of calling me anything other than Bobbie, as for the teacher, she could lump it, I would ignore her.

At lunch-time on that first day, I waited by the main gate for John, and waited and waited. When most of the children had gone, I decided I would try to find my own way home, I knew it was not far. I crossed over the road I knew we had crossed on the way to school, and walked down a street that seemed familiar. When I became unsure of where to go next, I hung about at a road junction, hoping John would find me. I was beginning to get really worried when I spotted Mum and John, hurrying down the pavement opposite where I was loitering, was I glad to see them!

Mum saw me as they crossed the street, she came hurrying up and demanded, 'Where *have* you been?'

'I didn't know where we live,' I wailed.

To that she replied, 'Well, John was supposed to wait for you, but he forgot.'

She then railed at him, 'You mind you wait for her this afternoon.'

As he glowered at me, I realised how galling it must be for him, to have to run around after me. 'Tag-along' was an embarrassment, no self-respecting, almost eleven-year-old boy would be seen dead with his kid sister.

A few days later, Miss Wilson informed me that the 'office' had got my date of birth wrong, and I was to go down a class, seems they thought I was a year older.

So, I had to run the gauntlet of another thirty-plus inquisitions. Maggie was still to 'mind' me, so it was not too bad. I was fast tuning into, and mimicking, the local 'lingo'. I spent hours learning to roll my Rs. Mum once remarked, when we were seated around the table, 'Would you just listen to that girl, she sounds like a savage,' then she turned on Dad with, 'It's all your fault, bringing us to this place.'

I was not sorry to leave Miss Wilson, I kept forgetting I was 'Jacqueline' and just ignored her, when the name was called. I would realise too late, as she stormed down the aisle between the desks to cuff me on the ear, or whack the back of my hand with a wooden ruler. She took to throwing the blackboard duster at me, and just before I changed classes, she scored a direct hit to the side of my head with it. It was about eight inches long, felt on one side, with a wooden back for a handle, and it hurt. I was so mad, I picked it up off the floor and hurled it back at her screaming, 'My name is Bobbie – Bobbie – Bobbie!'

She ducked, as it whizzed past her head, clattering off the wall behind her desk. I spent the rest of the morning standing in the corner, with my back to the class.

In the playground I was a hero, the class-room buzzed with it for days. John got to hear about it, and said, 'Trust you to cause trouble.' Mum was furious about it, and threatened to go and 'sort that woman out'.

The Princess Elizabeth gave birth to a son, just before John's

76

birthday. My favourite song was *Slow boat to China*. I often wished that I was on one.

13

Thank God, and Mrs Mac

Our sleeping arrangements at Bellshill were as follows: the parents in the double bed in the alcove, John on the settee, and me on the two armchairs, which were pushed together. John's problem was that he was a bit longer than the three-seater settee, and had to sleep curled up. This meant that either his knees stuck out, or his back got uncovered. The cushions he used for pillows kept falling off during the night, and he seemed to have a perpetual crick in his neck.

My two armchairs were snug enough, but also a bit short, so if I stretched out, they parted company as they were on castors, and I fell through the gap. I must have moved about a lot in my sleep, for most mornings I awoke on the floor, chairs apart, covers all over the place!

It never occurred to anyone to tie the castors together for the night!

Another problem was the light. Once asleep, it would take Armageddon to wake me, but sometimes getting off to sleep was a trial. John and I were always sent off to bed early, me first, so I always took my time in the bathroom.

When I complained that the light kept me awake, Dad had the bright idea of putting an old blanket over the tops of the chairs. When I further complained that it was stuffy under there, I was told to 'Shut up, and get to sleep.'

It was always 'Shut up, and get to sleep'.

No 'What is the matter?' or 'Goodnight'.

When he wanted me to get ready for bed, it was 'Get to your bed, you.'

I had decided that he did not like my name, for he never called me by it. To other people I was 'that girl', and to me it was 'you'.

The spiteful pinching had ceased, it left marks, they were replaced by straight finger-prods in the small of the back, where bruises could not be seen so readily.

John was very quiet, always sullen, and out of the lodgings as much as possible.

I spent my time with Mum, but I seemed to be a constant source of irritation to her, I never felt that I belonged with, or really knew her. I felt that if she said a kind word to me, it would choke her. Somehow she always made me feel so angry.

She was like a rag doll, no spirit or fight in her. I wanted to shake her out of her lethargy, it never occurred to me at the time that she was half-starved, and shamefully neglected, as indeed John and I were. We were always hungry, but we got milk at school, it was all Mum could do to get a cup of tea.

When John had ceased escorting me home from school, I would occasionally steal an apple from a display stall outside the greengrocer's shop. It is amazing how I never got caught doing it.

One night I awoke because of the light, the chairs had parted company once more, and the blanket covering had slipped. I could hear my parents whispering, they were always whispering, I suppose so as not to wake John or I. There was a strange smell, and it was several minutes before I realised what it was, chips – they were eating chips! I could hardly believe it. I turned over as gently as I could, to peek out at them, and I was seen by Dad.

'You get to sleep,' he snarled.

'Leave her be,' said Mum.

Dad had tried to cover the chips with the newspaper they had been wrapped in. I asked if they had chips, and Dad 'shushed' me.

'You'll wake John,' niggled Mum, then added, 'You can have some if you are quiet.'

'Have you got some for John?' I asked.

Dad shushed' me again, and whispered, 'There's not enough for 'im as well, besides 'e's asleep.'

I offered to wake him and was told to 'Shut up, or else'.

I replied, loud enough to wake the dead, 'If therr's nane fer John, then ahm no' wanting ony.' I always slipped into 'Glesga lingo' when I needed to annoy the parents, especially Mum.

John remained still during all of that, but I had a sneaking suspicion that he was not asleep. I sat and watched those two eat the chips, and was sure that neither of them enjoyed their supper.

One Saturday morning, Mum and I were going to the local butcher to get some cooked meat and potted haugh. I think it is also known as brawn, pork meat in aspic jelly. I hated the stuff, but it made a change from jam on our bread. Mum would buy two pound (in weight) tins of jam, usually blackcurrant, and when Dad was around at tea-time, every time John or I reached for the tin, he would admonish, 'Only a little, we must economise.' If he felt we had too much, he would make us scrape some off and return it to the tin, I thought that was a disgusting habit.

We had reached the shop, and joined a queue, and after a few minutes were inside the shop. It was bitterly cold outside, and it was a relief to be indoors. I disliked that shop, with all those carcasses and the sawdust on the floor it made me feel quite ill.

I was 'people watching' as usual, when I heard Mum call my name. I wondered what I had done, and turned round in time to see her slump to the floor in a dead faint.

Two women got to her before I did, and I recognised one of them as our neighbour from downstairs. One of the shop assistants fetched a glass of water, as Mum started to come round, and the woman I had recognised said she would see us safely home.

Mum was protesting and please-don't-bother-ing, but the neighbour would have none of it. She was staying until a doctor was fetched, regardless of Mum's protestations.

Somehow a doctor did arrive, with a 'What have we here?' The neighbour and I were told to wait outside on the landing, whilst he examined her.

John was out, and Dad worked on Saturday mornings, so that left me. When the doctor beckoned us into the room, he asked the neighbour who she was, then who I was. He then told us that my mother was very ill, she had pneumonia and would have to remain in bed and be nursed.

'He asked, 'Is there a husband?'

The neighbour replied, 'Aye, but he's nae bloody yiss tae man nor beast!'

She said it with some vehemence, and I was quite shocked.

She went quite red in the face, and added, 'Well, it huss tae be said.'

Mum was whimpering, 'I don't want any fuss.'

The neighbour replied with the same vehemence, 'You haud yer wheest, ye'll dae as yer telt.'

That neighbour was to be my salvation, I called her 'Mrs Mac', everyone should have a Mrs Mac in their life.

A Mrs Mac is one of those guardian angel women who, by some uncanny sixth sense, just know when someone is in dire need. They do not have to be told, or asked for help. I have been luckier than most, for there have been three such Mrs Macs in my life, every one a Godsend. It must be a great privilege, to be a Mrs Mac, but most of us are too busy looking after our own affairs to see the need in others. People of that calibre are a rare breed, God's gift to the rest of us.

When Dad returned from work, he seemed annoyed at having to get the sandwiches, and asked Mum how long was she going to be ill. When she told him she did not know, he told her, irritably, that she could not 'just lie there'. He looked at the list of instructions and prescription the doctor had left, and put both back on the table, muttering, 'More expense.'

The doctor had said there must be a fire in the grate, Mum was to be kept warm, and have hot soup.

I said to Dad, 'We'll need some coal,' and when he did not reply, I added, 'Will you get her medicine?'

'Shut your face,' was the only reply I got.

John and I crept round like shadows, and were only too relieved when, in the evening, Dad announced huffily that he was off to the pictures. He went to the cinema a lot, but he never offered to take Mum, and certainly did not take John or I.

The old lady who owned the house came in to see if all was well. She told us the doctor had said Mum was to have hot soup and drinks, and she would see to it. I thanked her, and she said as she left, 'Ah'm next door if yeez need me, ah suppose "it" has gone oot?'

She always referred to Dad as 'it'.

We kept watch over Mum, listening to her laboured breathing. She looked so thin, lying there, her face like a mask. I was terrified, I could not get rid of the image of a dark, floating, menacing cloud, bringing the 'angel of death'. How I detested that sneaky spirit, I vowed to keep watch, I was sure it would not dare risk being seen.

Mum had not made any contact with her religious sect, so we had no other visitors besides Mrs Mac, the landlady and the doctor.

I must have drifted off to sleep on the floor beside the bed, and John had fallen asleep in the chair, but I awoke with a start when I heard a noise. It was Dad returning, I wondered if he would bring some chips, but I should have known better.

We both got yelled at. 'Get to your beds, don't you know your mother is ill?'

John told him, 'Yes, we knew, but we did not go off and leave her.'

He got a back-handed swipe across his face that sent him reeling. I saw red and told him to leave John alone. I was told 'Get to your bed, you.'

I was bristling with rage, and mentally vowed to get him, one day. I had a mental flash of him, telling John and I about his promising himself vengeance on his father.

I heard Mum ask if she could have some water, he told her, 'Yes, if you get up and fetch it.'

She managed to struggle out of bed, and as she stood there, trembling with fever, he told her she had best sleep on the outside, so as not to disturb him in the night.

I got out of my armchairs, and told her to get into bed, I would fetch her water from the bathroom.

Dad railed at me, 'You, get back to yer bed or I'll fetch you a fourpenny one.'

I yelled at him, 'Make it a shilling, ahm fetching her water!'

When I was in the bathroom, running the cold tap until the brown stuff cleared, I promised myself that if he hit me, I would tell the doctor what he said to Mum.

Sunday morning I folded my bedding as best I could, put it in the corner, then replaced the chairs. They were easily moved on their castors. I then made some marmalade sandwiches for Mum. Dad had not stirred, and was still fast asleep, when I prodded Mum to try and get her to eat.

Dad stirred, grumbling, 'What are ye doin' up?'

'Someone has to see to Mum,' I niggled.

Mum refused the bread and marmalade, so Dad had it, then

he got dressed and went to boil a kettle for tea.

About an hour later, Dad announced that he was going for a walk in the fresh air, declaring, 'Ah'm not staying 'ere with all this illness.'

Whilst he was out, the doctor arrived. He was angry that Mum's prescription had not been filled, and there was no sign of it, or his list of instructions. I said that Dad must have it on him. He wrote out another list, handing it to me, asking, 'Will you see to it?'

I said to him, 'I can't read your writing,' so he told me I must wash everything Mum used, in disinfectant, and give her a receptacle to be kept near her for phlegm. I asked what that was, and he explained – I wished I had not asked!

He then sent John and I from the room, to examine Mum. I was annoyed, for I was sure Mum would spin him a yarn. Oh yes, she was all right, had everything she needed etc. There was not so much as an aspirin in the room.

When the doctor left, I looked in the sideboard cupboard for a 'receptacle'. All I could find was an almost empty jam tin, so I spooned out what was left on to a saucer. We had very little crockery or cutlery, only what the landlady had loaned us. I took the tin to the bathroom, to wash it out, and got told off by the landlady for playing with water.

When Dad returned, I told him the doctor had been, and was angry that Mum did not have her medicine. He ignored me, so I asked, 'Will you get her medicine?'

'Yes, yes,' he snapped, adding, 'Shut up about it, do.'

I realised it would be Monday night before she would get it, if at all. I also realised that Mum could not be left unattended, and asked him if he would stay home on Monday.

'You stay 'ome if ye must, an' stay 'ere, you're not to go out, d'ye 'ear?'

'What about her soup an' drinks?' I asked.

He thought for a minute, then told me, 'Let no one in, if anyone asses (he could not say 'asks'), tell 'em she's fine, just fine.'

So much for that, I had no intention of doing anything of the sort. Mum was to have her drinks and soup, or my name was not Bobbie.

She did not touch the cup of Bovril the landlady brought when Dad left on the Monday, or the chicken soup she brought at mid-morning. She had hardly stirred at all. When I tried to rouse her, to have her hot drink, she mumbled feebly, 'You have it.'

I was aching to have it, but could not, somehow it did not seem right.

I sat on the floor by her bedside after I was dressed, and had some bread and marmalade. She seemed very hot, beads of perspiration trickled down her face, and she made a funny noise as she breathed. I got very worried, she had not coughed up any of the nasty stuff the doctor had told me about. I could feel the panic rising in me, I had to do something, but what?

I thought, 'What *can* I do, oh please God, help her.'

I could feel the thumping of my heart, I wanted to scream. I got to my feet and paced round the room, kicking furniture as I went.

A feeble voice came from the alcove, 'Bobbie, stoppit.'

I thought, 'That's it! By Jove, that's it.' I had to make her move, somehow, she must move.

I went to her and asked if she could sit up. 'Please try to sit up,' No response.

I kicked at the chair leg, then banged it against the table.

'Bobbie,' wheezed the feeble voice, 'stoppit, for pity's sake.'

I do not know what got into me, but I yelled 'NO' and banged the chair again. I knew I was being hateful, but it did not stop me. Bang, went the chair once more. 'I must make her respond, she must move,' I told myself.

She managed, somehow, to heave herself up onto her elbows, then leaned back, gasping, 'You wretched child, stoppit!'

I rushed across to her bed, to prop her up on her pillow, and grabbed the cushions from the settee, to steady her. 'My God, she's skinny,' I thought.

She started to keel over, and as I pushed to steady her, I pleaded, 'Sit up, sit up, please.'

She gave a odd little cough, and motioned for the jam tin on the floor. I watched in shocked amazement as she coughed into that tin. She paused for breath, then another fit of coughing. It occurred to me that she must have been drowning in that filthy stuff.

When it was over, she asked me to fetch her a drink. It seemed to take an age for the brown stuff to clear from the water, and as the tap was running I emptied the contents of the tin down the lavatory. I thought I was going to be sick, but I was too rushed to get back to Mum to dwell upon it. I was rinsing the tin when I heard her call, back I dashed, reaching her just in time for her to use the tin once more. This time, I could not watch, but left for the privacy of the bathroom where she could not see me cry.

As I washed my face, I wondered if there was really a God. I decided there must be, I believed he had heard my plea, so I said a mental 'thank you' and returned to Mum.

I cleaned out her tin once more, and brought her a flannel and towel to wipe her face. She was sipping her water when there was a knock on the door. It was Mrs Mac from downstairs, she had brought a tray of food and two flasks.

She noticed the untouched drink and soup that the landlady had brought earlier, and told Mum off.

'Ah'll bide, until ye've eaten summit,' she announced, bustling around Mum, tidying her bed.

She turned to me, asking, 'How is thur no' a fire in that grate?'

I did not know what to say, so she added, 'Oh aye,' whatever that meant.

She watched Mum sip at some soup she had poured into a bowl, then told me to have what was left in the flask. When I had finished, she motioned me to follow her out on to the landing, then she closed the door.

She asked me what I was doing at home, and I told her, 'Minding Mum.'

'Whaur's yer bloody faither?' she snarled.

'At work,' I told her.

'Geeziz Mary,' she exclaimed, then told me, 'The morn, yer tae gaun back tae the skale, ah'll see tae yer pair mither.' She placed her hands on her hips and whistled through a gap in her teeth, adding, 'Suffrin' saints, imagine, leavin' a bairn tae mind a sick wifie.'

Mrs Mac took charge, but it was some days before Mum took any interest in anything. When she did, I got what for. She sat me down to lecture. 'You are not to tell people our business, we don't need anyone's help, we can manage.'

I wailed, 'But Mum, I could not manage, I did not know where to turn.'

'No matter,' she bristled, 'I won't have it, I have my pride.'

85

'Damn your pride!' I shrieked at her. I was furious, and railed at her, 'That would look great on your tombstone – she had her pride.' Before she could say anything else, I added, 'Not that anyone would bother to read it.'

She looked vexed, and I felt really rotten. I had been torn with guilt over my awful behaviour when she was really ill, and broached the subject of it. I told her I was sorry I had been so hateful.

She looked at me for a few seconds, before she shrugged, and said she believed it was all meant to happen, for it had actually helped her. I had a notion she was right, it had all been very weird.

She did get her medicine, but I would like to believe she was helped by a child's faith, and a neighbour's kind heart.

14

Goodnight Mr Day

After Mum's illness, the old couple seemed to take more interest in what was going on, and we saw a lot more of them, they would pop in for visits. The lady was nice, but I was not sure about the man, I felt he needed to be watched. He had been in the merchant navy until he retired, and was full of stories of his travels around the world. He had a concertina he could play, and tried to teach John and I to play it, without much success. I did not mind him when John was around, but felt ill at ease if left alone with him.

Mum had contacted members of her sect, and was back to 'door knocking', so when school was out, we were left with the old couple.

The only physical contact I was used to was when Dad slapped or pinched me, and when Mum plaited and fiddled with my hair. She would tug at it with the brush until my eyes smarted from it. It was even worse when she put it into rags at night, to make ringlets, how I loathed those silly corkscrews. I could not bear anyone to touch me at all, and the old man had found out about it. He delighted in tormenting me, by trying to grab whatever he could, and he grabbed things he had no business to touch.

I told Mum about it, and she told me to stay away from him, he was just being silly.

John showed me how to hold fast the door to our room, by wedging a dining chair back under the door handle. I would only move it to let him or Mum in. That way, I kept him out of our room, and away from me.

I had to sneak out if I needed the bathroom and one day he was waiting outside for me. He was annoyed that I seemed afraid of him, and told me not to be silly, he would not harm

87

me. As I made towards the door of our room, he said there was no need to jam a chair against the door. I felt that I should, at least once, give him the benefit of the doubt, but nevertheless, I was poised for flight. I entered our room, closing the door, as he went into the bathroom. He called to me to come and see what he had found, and warily I crept out on to the landing. He had left the bathroom door open wide enough to see into the room, and there he was, playing with his penis.

I remembered something Mum had once said, and I yelled it at him. 'The Devil finds mischief for idle hands.' Then, as I fled for the outer door, I flung back at him, 'You dirty old pig.'

The sound of his laughter followed me out on to the rickety staircase, and I found myself wishing it would collapse whilst he was on it.

Another time he locked himself in the bathroom with a book to read, and when I knocked on the door, saying I needed to 'go', he just laughed. I could not wait until Mum or John returned home, and I had an accident. I knocked on the door once more, to inform him that I had just had an accident all over his landing carpet. The response was a stream of obsceni-ties and expletives, quite a few of which I did not understand. I was worried about what would happen when Mum got back, but she seemed not to notice. I had to own up and I told her what happened. She laughed, and said, 'Serves him right, he'll get what for from his missus.'

She then told me he had been in a foul mood ever since the council had informed him that his house was condemned. I asked her what that meant, and she told me it was to be pulled down. I thought that was daft, the place was falling down by itself. We were given notice to find new lodgings.

A few weeks before we left, we met a new lodger. He had a smaller room on the same landing and also shared the bath-room facilities. One evening Mum brought him into our room to meet us, and I got the shock of my life. Mum said, 'This is Mr Day,' and I blurted out, 'But he is as black as the night.'

'Bobbie,' said Mum sharply, but Mr Day just threw back his head and laughed uproariously. I liked him, but he worried me, I mean, was he real? Would he fade away into a wisp of light? Mum informed us that he was a doctor at the local hospital, and I fervently hoped he was not the one I had sunk my teeth into, at Chippenham hospital some years before.

He spent a lot of time in our room, and I began to feel at ease with him. I would even sit on his knee, while he told us stories of his home in Africa. He seemed real enough, and I hoped with all my heart that he would not disappear into an evil, sneering grin. I simply had to be sure, the other black man had seemed real enough, then I had an idea.

If he was real, he would bleed, did all living things not have blood? If he was a spirit, I would soon know.

It was a master-stroke, but I could not bring myself to sink my teeth into him, one does not bite one's friends.

I asked, tentatively, if he had blood in his veins like us.

He replied, 'Of course – why?'

Dad laughed, John smirked, and Mum as usual said, 'Bobbie, stoppit.'

To me it was crucial that I knew for certain, I accepted that a phantom could seem as solid as a real person. He splayed out the palms of his hands, saying, 'Look – real.'

I saw my chance, and drew a finger-nail sharply across his palm. He winced, and I saw a tiny trickle of blood.

Oh the relief! I gasped and said, 'You *are* real, oh thank goodness.'

I was so happy, but Mr Day looked hurt. I expect I was being downright offensive, but to me it seemed the only way.

I began to explain, 'I once knew a black man who . . .'

Mum cut me off, mid-sentence, with a look that could kill, and a 'Bobbie, that's enough!'

We remained friends, however, and it seemed my apparent rudeness was forgiven.

He worked shifts, and when he was home nights we would play a game. He would wait on the landing outside the bathroom, with the light off, waiting for me to emerge. I could not see him in the dark, and he would pounce on me amidst squeals and laughter. I got wise to his tricks, and started to put out the bathroom light, before opening the door. That gave me a sporting chance of getting across the landing, without being caught. We would edge round the walls in the dark, I even crawled on all fours to evade him, and for several nights I made it to the safety of 'home', the door to our room. He asked how I managed it, and I told him it was easy, in the darkness I could see his white teeth when he smiled. When I reached the safety of 'home' I always said, 'Good night, Mr Day.'

He would reply, 'Good night, little girl.'

I am not sure who moved out first, but I never saw him again during our last few days at Bellshill.

There was always a lot of activity in the area where we lived, it was a busy road, with shops and a public house nearby. Saturday nights were always noisy, Mum worried when Dad went out, usually to the cinema, and would fret until he returned safe.

There were nearly always fights outside the pub around closing time, usually over football or religion. If things were too quiet, some wag would set things moving by yelling from a safe upstairs window, or the upper deck of a moving bus, 'FUCK CELTIC' (or 'RANGERS' depending on his allegiance) or 'PAPES' or 'PRODDIES OOT' depending on his religious persuasion. It never failed to start a punch-up. The protagonists would be back at work on the Monday, commiserating over the poor eyesight of some unfortunate linesman, or the sheer idiocy of an unsuspecting referee.

There was a piece of wasteland near our lodgings, and one week, a fairground was set up. We were duly warned not to go anywhere near it, it was not for the likes of us.

Just before we moved out, the old man came to Mum and asked if he and 'the missus' could take John and me to the fair, as a farewell gift. Mum would have none of it. He got the full lecture about dissassocia-whatsit, and mixing with 'those sorts' of people. You would have thought he was planning to take us to a slave market.

I was desperate to go, and could tell that John was too. Although I did not trust the old man, it would be all right with John and the old lady there also.

He persisted and got 'I don't want them going on any of those things, there will be gambling and goodness knows what else.' She shook her head saying, 'No, no.'

'Lands sakes, missus!' he exclaimed, 'Ah'm no wantin tae lead them intae sin and debauchery (I wondered what that was), only oot fer the nicht.'

My heart sank, but he would not give in, and finally she relented, with all sorts of prophesies of gloom and doom. He promised her we would only be looking, and off we went. We had to pass the chip shop on our way, and passing that shop, as we often did, was sheer purgatory for me, who was always hungry. I once told Mum that if I ever got to heaven, I would open a chip shop.

She replied that if I ever got to heaven, they would tie me to a tree, it was the only way they would know where I was.

We arrived at the fairground, it was all noisy music and flickering coloured lights, people milling about, around an assortment of rides. I was disappointed I could not go on anything, for we had no money, but it was fascinating watching the people.

John looked fed up, and I asked him what was wrong. He shrugged and replied, 'It's aye the same fer us, we're on the ootside, just lookin' in.'

I felt so sad for him, I wanted to hug him and say 'never mind', but I did not dare, 'big bother' did not need 'tagalong' fussing over him.

On our return journey, the old lady shepherded us into the chip shop, and bought us each a three-penny poke of chips. The old man grumbled at her, and was told, 'You haud yer wheesht, ye auld bugger.'

After we told Mum all about it, I asked her what an 'auld bugger' was, and got a thick ear for my troubles.

I had not seen a newspaper for months, Dad took them to work in the day, then Mum used them for the fire, before I could get to them. Dad and I kept whistling the 'Harry Lime' theme tune, I did not know who he was, but it was a catchy tune – Mum hated it. We had had our birthdays, and nobody noticed, and similarly, Christmas had been totally ignored. Dad had gone on at length about 'looking forward to a new decade for us all'. I had no idea what he was on about, we did not usually get anything 'new'.

It did not take long to pack, and we were on the move once more.

The wartime slogan posters had been replaced by advertising billboards, and there were two that really puzzled me. One was for Beechams Powders, it depicted a family of parents and two children, walking in the rain. The mother was sneezing. I thought it was talcum powder, and wondered why on earth would anyone want to use something that made them sneeze.

The other was seen all over the place, Barr's Irn-Bru. It was ages before I discovered that it was a fizzy drink.

Dad was still working at the Naval Store Depot in Carfin,

and he had found us lodgings in Newarthill, with a couple who had three boys. I was pleased, it meant playmates again, but I was worried about another change of school. Mum consoled me by saying it would be all right when I met the Maxill boys. I thought they sounded like a gang of cattle rustlers, out of one of John's cowboy comics.

15

Chookie Hens and Cheeky Kids

I met Robert and his two brothers, but decided not to shake
hands or ask 'How do you do?' I remembered Maggie's
reaction to that. The middle brother, whom I from then on
referred to as 'Middle Maxill', looked me over, and asked,
'Hoo auld ur ye?'

'Eight,' I lied, I would not be eight until October, months
away.

'Yer awfie wee,' he commented.

'So ur you,' I snapped, trying to dissolve him with a look. It
was loggerheads from the start

When school was out, I saw a lot of those boys. Robert was
about John's age, but they did not seem to want each other's
company, they were both loners. Middle Maxill was older than
me, then there was Billy, the younger one. We were more of an
age, but it was Robert I liked.

On meeting Billy, he proudly announced that he 'hud a hole
in his heid'. I was shocked, but apart from the one he was
talking through, I could see no evidence of it. His mother
chuckled, and informed me that his skull had not knitted
together at birth. 'Heavens,' I thought,' I have got a lot to
learn.'

For a while, Middle Maxill was openly hostile to me, but he
could not contain his curiosity. He wanted to know what John
and I had for Christmas, and when I told him 'nothing', that
seemed all right, for he and his brothers also had nothing. I
told him a lot of children got nothing, and he was not to let it
bother him. He asked where our toys were, and I told him we
had none. The few we had were in Corsham, waiting to be sent
for. He wanted to know when they would arrive, and I told
him probably never.

93

There had been a lot of news in the papers about the death of the author George Orwell, who had written a scary book about life in Britain in the future. Whenever anyone got up to no good, or thought they were doing something they ought not to, instead of a 'nod and a wink', it was 'Big Brother is watching you'. 'Big Brother' being the government, or controlling party. I felt that my big brother wanted watching, I never seemed to see him, he was getting too good at avoiding 'old tag-along'.

Our lodgings with the Maxills were, once again, one room, smaller this time, sharing the bathroom, and no use of the kitchen. There was a double bed in one corner, and a table with four chairs. There was no fireplace, one window which overlooked the rear of the four-in-a-block flats, and a large cupboard at one end of the room. The cupboard of course, had no window, but there was room on the floor for a single-sized mattress.

That was where John and I slept, end on, so we had each other's feet at our heads. It was worse for me, as John was much taller, his feet were in my face. When I tired of him tossing and turning I used to bite a big toe.

We had to be careful how we sat up in bed, as there were shelves in the cupboard, where Mrs Maxill kept her towels and linen. John was forever banging his head on them. When it was cold, or John had snatched the blanket, I would borrow some towels to wrap up in. I had to be sure to return them to the position I had taken them from, so no one would know they had been moved.

The summer was hot, and it got very stuffy in that confined space. Dad would shut the door and we had to wait until the parents would be asleep, before we dared open it again. I hated that cupboard, and used to have nightmares. I would wake up screaming, waking the whole household, then end up getting a hiding from Dad. He sometimes grabbed my hair so hard it made the scalp bleed. I had seen him unravel tufts of long hair from his fingers, dropping them to the floor with a look of distaste on his face. With him tugging, and Mum tugging on the hair brush, it is a wonder I was not bald.

I would go into Mrs Maxill's kitchen and watch her prepare food, or natter to her whilst she did her ironing or washing. She would lift me up to sit on the side of the sink, and this way we spent many companionable hours together. How I wished that my mother was like her, there was always a hug from her, and I did not mind at all, although I usually hated anyone touching me.

Mr Maxill worked shifts, I think on the railway, and when he was around he remarked, whenever he saw me, 'Oh, it's fair braw, tae hae a wee lassie in the hoose.' I am sure his sons, and John, did not think so!

I once watched Mrs Maxill trying to cram a cut up cabbage into a pan that was too small to hold it all. We both ended up in fits of laughter, and I asked her why she did not use a larger pan. Between gales of laughter she told me she did not have one. She would sometimes let me peel the potatoes with a peeler, or scrape the carrots. I was amazed to see her eat a piece of raw carrot, and she gave me a piece to try, saying it was nicer raw; she was right, it was.

Robert used to sit at the top of the outside staircase, by the door to the flat, watching the nearby railway track, waiting for trains to pass. He was fascinated by the trains, and once told me he longed to travel on one. He was quite put out when I informed him that I had been on them too often, up, down, back and forth, and I thought they were dirty, smelly things. He did not care, one day he was going to ride on one. I wished then that I had the money to buy him a ticket, to go wherever he wanted. He was a lot like John and I, it was always 'one day'.

Instead, I practised doing handstands against the wall by the door. I had seen a girl next door do one, and resolved to master the art. After several attempts, and a banged head for my efforts, Robert said irritably, 'Will ye no' stop that, I kin see yer knickers.'

I could not have cared less about that, then I remembered they were held up with a large safety pin, and realised he must have seen.

He went on, 'Huv ye no' nae elastic?'

Feeling my face colour up, I replied, 'Nope, John nicked it fer his catapult.'

'Hoomph,' was his only reply. I mean, I was only joking!

One hot afternoon, I was perched on the draining board watching Mrs Maxill work at the sink, and I gazed out of the open window on to the gardens below. The people in the downstairs flat kept chickens in an enclosure, which seemed to be very close to the building, if I leaned out of the window I was almost right over them. I wondered how it was they could keep hens so close to the house. I remembered John had to get rid of his chicks for that very reason.

Things were far too peaceful, there was a pot of scouring powder on the window sill, so when Mrs Maxill left the room briefly, I leaned out of the window, and sprinkled scouring powder all over the hens. There was the most awful commotion, the hens were careering all over the run, probably thinking it was food. It had never come from aloft before, I ducked back in, replaced the powder pot, and sat there, all angelic.

When Mrs Maxill rushed back into the kitchen saying 'Whit's up, whit's aw that racket?'

I told her, 'Ah think there's a cat among them hens.'

She dashed off to get the neighbour who owned the hens, but he was already out, peering into the pen, and scratching his head.

They exchanged opinions as to what could be the reason for the hens' distress, and I was tempted to go 'mee-ow', but thought better of it.

Mr Maxill had arrived, as his wife returned to the kitchen, and he yelled at her, 'Git that bairn aff that sink, afore she fa's oot that windy.'

As she lifted me down, she chuckled, saying 'It wiz you, ye wee monkey, whit did ye dae tae thae chookie hens?'

When I told her, she laughed until the tears rolled down her face. Everybody laughed, but Mum told me to leave the hens alone, as they would not lay any eggs if they were upset.

Dad had been off work ill for a few days, and Mum told us he had a gum disease that was making them bleed, and loosening all his teeth. I thought it served him right, they never saw a toothbrush, and he refused to waste money on toothpaste. He had a disgusting habit of sucking bits of food out of the gaps between his teeth. It was a shame, for he had nice teeth, very white, and they looked strong, but Mum said the problem was with the gums, not the teeth.

The lower ones had to go, but the dentist would try and save the upper ones. None of us ever saw a dentist, although John and I were seen by a visiting school dentist. The only doctor we saw was the school one except on a few occasions for inoculations, then there was the 'nit nurse', as she was scathingly called. John had been taken to see an orthopaedic surgeon and had been in hospital. One leg was a bit shorter than the other, and he had hammer toes. I always believed his toe problem was due to his feet being crammed into ill-fitting shoes when he was a baby.

Amazingly, we were fairly robust, but John had to endure taunts from other children: 'toe-dancer' and 'hop-along'. I had blacked a few eyes over those taunts, but hoped it would all be put right when he had his operation, when older. He was a very quiet boy, a loner, who had a nervous stammer, and I was inclined to be a bit over-protective, much to his annoyance.

When Dad came home, whining about his teeth, it was the last straw. All that John endured, without complaint, and that oaf was crying like a baby. I remembered how indifferent he had been to Mum's illness, the times when I had come home with grazed knees, to be told, 'Shut up, or ah'll give ye summat to witter about.' I was livid, and told him imperiously that he was a grown man, and should behave like one.

Mum pushed me out of the room, telling me to go to Mrs Maxill.

John was angry with me also, seemed I could not appreciate Dad's discomfort and upset.

One Sunday afternoon we had three surprise visitors, a man called Jack, and a lady and gentleman whose surname was Carter. Seems they were cousins of Mum's, and she looked really pleased to see them.

I had thought we must have some relatives somewhere, we had met grandparents in Corsham, and had visited them, briefly, in Manchester. Relatives were never discussed, if we asked about them, we got the 'dissassocia-whatsit' speech.

I thought they were just wonderful, I was desperate for relatives. Jack could do amazing conjuring tricks, and things with playing cards. Mum told me he also wrote poetry, and I wondered how she could keep quiet about a relative like him.

John was quite envious, and spent hours trying to perfect some of the card tricks Jack had taught him.

The Carters were lovely, and I hoped to see them all again, but I never did.

There was a war in Korea, I did not know where that was,

but it seemed to me that there was always a war going on somewhere. Did people never weary of killing each other?

16

Boys Will Be Boys

One of our neighbours had given me an old rubber football, it was soft and not very bouncy, but it was the only toy I had played with in months. Middle Maxill was quite annoyed about it and announced, 'A lassie shouldna' hae a baw, an' onyways, ah'v lived here aboots longer. Ah should hae it.'

After that, I was determined he would not have it, ever. He tried every trick and means he could devise to separate me from that ball, it became a vendetta. Had he simply asked to play with it, he could have had it any time he liked, it was his attitude that irked me. He resorted to open threats.

'Ah'll just tak' it frae ye,' he smirked.

'Just try, and Ah'll knock yer heid aff, ye kin yase that fer a baw,' I snarled.

He yelled back, 'It's no' yours, ah should hae it.'

'Awa' an' bile yer heid.'

It all got a bit out of hand, I even took it to bed with me, and hid it when I had to go to school.

Mum said I should just give him it, and have done with our feud. 'Besides,' she argued, 'you do not really want it.' But it had gone too far for that. I could be as stubborn as the next one, I would not back down.

He knew that John and I were sent to bed early, we had to go early, so that the parents could have their supper. I used to spy on them through the gap between the door and its frame.

One evening, he knocked on our room door and asked Mum, 'Kin ah play wi ma baw?'

Mum chuckled and replied, 'You mean Bobbie's ball.'

He blustered, 'It's mines, an' ah want it back.'

'It's nothing of the sort, yours,' argued Mum, 'it was not given to you.'

There was a pause, before he wheedled, 'Well, kin ah jist play wi' it fer a wee while?'

'Of course you can dear, if you can find it.'

'Oh, right then, whaur is it?'

I've no idea,' Mum replied, snootily, then closed the door.

'Good old Mum,' I whispered from the cupboard.

She knew I had it in the cupboard with me, and I think she was as wicked as me. The ball had been soft when I was given it, and it just got worse.

'Punctured,' said John, who knew it all.

Mum said I should leave it somewhere, not too obvious, for M.M. (as we called him) to 'happen upon', and try to look peeved when he found it.

I tucked it under the hedge, near the gate, trying to make it look like it had fallen out of a hiding place.

He whooped with glee when he found it, and came to meet me as I arrived back from school, flourishing it like a trophy. I tried not to smile and said, 'Oh jings, ah never thocht ye'd find it.'

He looked at me, puzzled, so I added, trying to sound vexed, 'Well, it's yours noo, ye found it, ye blasted nuisance.'

He looked triumphantly at the wizened ball, then scowled, 'It's no nae yiss as a baw, that's whit happens when ye gie' a baw tae a bloomin' lassie.'

Under normal circumstances, I would have probably rearranged his facial features, but I was trying hard not to laugh.

Mum and I had a good laugh over it, and she told me I should let him believe he had put one over me. I did, and from then on we were much more tolerant of each other. Isn't life funny?

I had found another playmate, her name was Anne, and she was in my class at school. She lived only a few doors away, their house was the last one in the row, and flanked the railway line.

She lived with her grandparents, at least, I assumed they were grandparents, for she told me she did not have a Dad. I told her she could have mine, but got a polite 'no, thank you'.

I thought how lucky she was, she never got pinched or punched, or had her hair yanked out.

She invited me to her birthday party, and I wanted to go, but was sure it would not be allowed.

To my utter amazement, Mum said, 'All right.'

I hurried off to tell Anne I could come after all, and she said, 'Good, now you will have to invite me to yours.'

My heart sank, as I informed her that we were not allowed birthdays, never mind parties.

She stormed off in a huff, declaring that I need not bother coming to hers then.

Next day she was at our door, asking me to please come, she did not mind if she could not come to mine, as I did not have such things.

The party was to be on the following Sunday afternoon, my mother put my hair into those hated ringlets, and I had a clean frock on.

When I arrived at Anne's house, I gave her the bar of chocolate that Mum had bought, and wished her a happy birthday.

She said, 'Thank you, whaur's the card?'

I noticed there were boys at her party, and wondered who on earth would invite boys? One of them came up to me, and asked who I was. Before I could reply he asked,

'Whaur's yer party frock?' I told him I did not have one.

'Then whit ur ye daein' at a party?' he asked rudely. I resisted the urge to kick him, and just walked away, saying, 'Didn't your mother teach you any manners?'

We were to play party games in the garden, we played 'the farmer wants a wife' and 'bee baw babbity' which is similar, i.e. you form a circle, with one person in the centre of the ring. When the music stopped, the person in the centre had to choose a person until everyone had left the ring. The last one chosen started all over again. I noticed no one chose me, so I left the games and wandered off round the garden. I had not been in a garden since we had left Corsham, and I delighted in all the flowers and plants. I found a jam jar and amused myself trying to catch a butterfly. I was so engrossed in that pastime, I did not notice the boy who had spoken to me earlier creep up from behind. I was standing on a crazy paving path, admiring my 'catch' when I was pushed hard from behind. I went sprawling on to the path, the jam jar smashed, and I fell on the pieces of broken glass. My left hand was bleeding, and as I scrambled to my feet I saw the culprit sneak off into the house. Anne's grandmother took me indoors, I stopped crying when she had cleaned up my hand, and it was not as bad a cut as it could have been. She bandaged up the cut, rather excessively I felt, but it got me a lot of attention. I got to choose where I wanted to sit at the table, and announced that I wanted that boy (pointing at the culprit) to sit next to me.

My attacker had the good grace to look shamefaced, as he seated himself down. The table was laden with all sorts of wonderful things, and when everyone was seated, we sang 'Happy Birthday' to Anne.

The boy asked me quietly, 'Are you all right, your hand is OK?'

I replied nonchalantly, 'Oh aye, it's fine, but I have to mind that finger, it's hanging off.'

I went on, 'It wiz oozing blood and gunge, but –'

Before I could elaborate further, he went white and hurriedly excused himself from the table, exclaiming, 'Ah dinnie want ony tea!'

I felt smugly satisfied, mission accomplished, and started to tuck in.

I heard a stifled snigger, and looked up to see Anne's grandfather watching me. I only just managed to keep a straight face as he winked at me.

Oh how I wished I could do that! Did one have to be grown up to be able to wink? Whenever I tried, both eyelids closed. 'Perhaps I should practice,' I thought.

Middle Maxill and I had fallen out once more, and I did not see much of Billy or John. I liked to sit on the step with Robert, and talk trains. We could watch the nearby railway track from the top step, and it was quite a busy line. I think it must have been the Motherwell/Glasgow line. I told him what I knew about Isambard Kingdom Brunel's famous Great Western Railway, and how the local enthusiasts referred to it as 'God's Wonderful Railway'. I enthused about the Box tunnel, and how I loved to go through it on our visits to Bath Spa. I told him of the times John and I had leaned over the parapet of the road bridge over the track, to watch the Bristol/London express thunder by, smoke belching out of its stack. How Mum and I picked primroses in the spring, from the railway embankment, waving to people on the passing trains. I described the tiny 'toytown' type railway station in Corsham, and the huge sprawling Temple Meads in Bristol.

He was green with envy when I told him I had been on the

Flying Scotsman and I had been over the great Forth bridge on a train. I told him about the Severn tunnel, en route to Wales, but my memories of Scotland were all jumbled up. I described the London station we had arrived at from Scotland, I could not remember its name, only hundreds of people in uniforms, milling about, all those kit-bags piled up on the platforms. There was something about that scene that had haunted me ever since.

Robert told me about a wonderful train that was really a luxury hotel on rails. It was called the 'Orient Express' and it was famous. It sounded wonderful, and we both agreed it would be magical to travel aboard it. He said that when we grew up, he would take me on it – Robert, I am still waiting!

Mum had made contacts with members of her religious sect, and once again we were going to her meetings. It meant many opportunities for me to 'people watch', and I made the most of it.

The meetings were held in a hall in Motherwell, which meant a bus ride. Buses are wonderful places to 'people watch' from, as are all forms of public transport. There were quite a variety of accents around, the most prominent being Glaswegian.

The Glasgow people are unique, in a class by themselves, and I could always pick them out from a crowd. They mostly seem to have a warm, friendly nature, droll sense of humour, and are as kind-hearted as you could ever wish to find. A lot of them would like you to believe that they are hard, even vicious, but that is only a thin veneer. Their local 'lingo' is also unique, and picturesque, to say the least. I had great admiration for those rough and ready people, and my love for them and their beautiful city will remain with me always.

I will never forget my first bus ride to Glasgow. I kept asking Mum, 'Is this Glasgow?' at almost every stop, getting, 'No, not yet.' People were getting off and on at every stop, and I was fascinated. Dad and John were sitting behind us, and they were both sniggering at my ill-concealed excitement. I had a new pair of shoes on my feet, they had been bought for me, along with a pair of new, shiny black Wellington boots. I could not believe it, we usually got second-hand things, and I longed for a pair of those shiny boots.

The boots were tied together with a piece of string, looped

through an eyelet hole near the tops. I could not wait to try them on, and John fell about laughing, saying I needed a longer piece of string.

I had put on the shoes for our day out, but had come a cropper on the stairs in the flat. The steps were stone, and with the shiny new soles on the shoes, I went my full length down them.

After that upset was over, I kept turning up my feet to look at the soles of the shoes, to see if they were still shiny.

Those two dinkle-berries thought that was just hilarious.

We had stopped at what looked like a bus station, and a lot of people were waiting to board. We were on a double-decker bus, and John and I had wanted to go upstairs, but Dad said 'NO.' One trip down the stairs was enough for one day.

Whilst the bus was waiting for people to board, and before the driver exchanged with another, I noticed a very unkempt man in shabby clothes make his way along the queue of people. As I watched him, I had the idea that he was not as old as his general appearance suggested, and nudged Mum, pointing.

She told me that he was a tramp, and explained that he lived rough. I could not believe anyone would choose to live like that, and was near to tears. As I watched, a woman went up to him, and out of her shopping basket, handed him a huge red shiny apple, then hurried away. He just stood there, staring at the apple as if he could not believe it.

It was all too much for me, I got a prod from Dad, and 'What ur you sniffling about?'

Mum soothed, 'Never mind dear,' and I wondered if she saw it too.

We arrived, at last, in the city and alighted on Sauchiehall Street, then crossed a few roads until we entered a street called George Street. There were small hand-carts all along each side of the kerb, in what looked like a square. They were piled high with all sorts of things that people were selling. A lot of fruit and vegetables, and all manner of curious objects. Dad said they were known as barrows, and you could buy anything from a safety pin to a battleship. I looked, but could see no battleships. It was a huge open market, with numerous barrow boys calling out their wares, it sounded like a foreign language to me.

If someone turned out in a new outfit, you could be sure

some wag would ask, 'Whaur d'ye git tha-at, the barras?' The market was known for its cheap goods, and if you did buy something 'frae the barras' you kept quiet about it.

We were to get on another bus, I asked if we were going home so soon, and Mum said there was a surprise for us, we were going to a circus.

I had read about them, but had never seen one and was beside myself with anticipation.

The big top was set up inside Kelvin Hall, and we filed into our seats. I did not like that part, walking on planks to reach our seats. I could see through the gaps to the floor a long way below, and discovered that I did not have a head for heights. All went well until the interval, I was too scared to leave my seat, but Mum and John went off to find the toilets.

A clown came around the audience, selling pink fluffy stuff on sticks, which looked like cotton-wool. Dad said it was candy-floss, but I knew better than to ask for some, and I did not like the looks of that clown.

I did not want him anywhere near me, but he would not leave me alone, tickling my chin, and trying to make me laugh. I got more and more agitated, and Dad told him to 'clear off', he was upsetting me. He persisted in trying to make me laugh, I did not like not being able to see his real face, and ended up sobbing hysterically, and Dad yelling at him, 'Get away from her!'

Everyone was staring, and Mum returned, wanting to know what had happened. I had to face the problem of getting out of that big tent, and I must have been upset, for I cannot recall our homeward journey at all.

I told M.M. all about it the next day, and he sneered,

'Huh, lassies, ah wouldna hae been feart o' a clown.'

I retorted angrily that I wished he had come, then we could have thrown him to the tigers.

'Thurr wurnie nae tigers, you're a fibber,' he shrieked. At that I smacked his ear, and stomped off.

Boys! They really are a pain in the neck. There was a new royal baby, Princess Anne. I wondered if she would find her brother was a pain in the neck at times.

17

Kind Hearts and Grubby Faces

Mrs Maxill was ill, and had taken to her bed. I missed pestering her in her kitchen, but Mum told me she was not sure what was ailing her. I visited her a couple of times in her bedroom, and thought she looked ill.

However, we were to move anyway, a house had been found for us on an estate the other side of Newarthill, and we were off again.

We still had the two battered suitcases, and Dad bought some second-hand beds and bedding. The flat was one of four in a block, similar to what we had just left, only all of it was for us; instead of being just in one room we had three bedrooms.

We had an upstairs flat, and once again there was a flight of steps, leading up to the main door, then another one inside. The bedrooms and bathroom-cum-toilet led off from a long narrow passage. A door at the end led into a sitting-room, and the kitchen led off from that. The sitting-room had a large window, and a tiled fireplace with metal discs that could be pushed over the fire, to cook or heat a kettle on.

The kitchen was small, with a hired gas cooker and an assortment of cupboards, which seemed to be made from very thin ply. The shelves were solid wood, but the doors were very flimsy. There was a window above a sink unit that had cupboards below. There was a gas tap fitting for a clothes boiler, and a double electric power socket. On the far wall was the gas and electric meter, the former being one that took pennies. There was an airing cupboard in the passageway, outside the bathroom, and on the opposite side, a coal cupboard. I thought it was a really weird place to put a coal cupboard, all that dust. We had an outside storage cupboard, under the staircase, but never had much in it.

The previous tenant had left linoleum on most of the floors, but in the room that I was to have, some of it was missing, and seemed to have been ripped off.

Dad had managed to get some curtains, and these were held up with string, tied on to a nail, hammered into the wooden batten on either side. The parents bought some furniture on hire purchase, I presumed that meant you need not pay for it all at once. They got a dining suite of a table, four chairs and a sideboard. The latter had a huge knob between the two doors, and coloured wood on the doors giving the effect of the sun. I thought it was hideous, but said nothing. They also bought another of those awful put-u-up settees, second-hand, and two small easy-chairs with wooden arms.

The tea-chests from Corsham were sent for, and so, slowly, bit by bit, the place began to look like home. Once a few pictures were nailed up, and Dad's rag-rug was by the hearth, it looked quite homely. Dad got a fender set for the fireside, with a small storage stool fixed at either end of the fender. I used to like to sit on one of them, and flame-gaze into the fire. Mum would be perched on the opposite one, and we would tell each other what we saw.

Slowly but surely bits and pieces were added, cutlery, crockery, a metal teapot. What a luxury that was! No more chipped spouts.

Dad came home with a black, plastic-framed electric clock. John could not rest until he had it in bits, to find out how it worked. He found to his horror that he could not put it back together, but Dad managed to get it working again. He had laughed about it, and we thought there would be a riot when he found out.

My bed was put over the part of the room near the wall, where the lino had been torn. When I made up my bed, I discovered two loose sections in the floor boards. I decided to keep my discovery a secret, it could prove a good hiding place for things I did not want nosey 'big bother' to find out about.

We had a home, at last. The address made me laugh, it was Larkhall Drive, but the locals called it Gowkhall, a gowk was a fool, so I supposed there must be a bit of street enmity on that estate. I soon found out why! Some were Catholic, others were Protestant, and never the twain would meet.

There were two girls in the family that lived downstairs. The elder was Nancy, who was a bit younger than John, and Gracie, who was a bit younger than I. There were grown up brothers, but they had their own homes.

I would have a playmate, and there seemed to be plenty of children around, for both John and me.

We did not need to change schools, as we were now nearer to it. John was in his last year at junior school and I realised that soon I would be left alone.

One afternoon, Mum came home with a tiny black and white kitten, we called him Fluffy, he and I were to become very close friends.

Dad seemed to be very unhappy, and was always snapping at us. The spiteful prodding and back punching had been replaced by blows to the legs, behind the knee joint. He would use the edge of his hand in a karate type blow. Several of those blows left the legs all shaky and numb, making walking very painful. The sensation of 'pins and needles' in the legs lasted several hours. He was always careful not to pick on us when Mum was about, but we hardly ever saw her. She was out all hours, all weathers, on her 'door knockings'. There were magazines and tracts all over the flat, in drawers, cupboards and left lying where she hoped we would 'read and study'. Her not-so-new faith was all she could talk about, family life and our needs were not her concern.

'You will have to get on with it,' was a stock reply, and to minor ailments, 'You'll have to keep it until it's better.' John and I would sit on the outside steps after school, awaiting her return, but when the weather turned cold, she gave John a key. I had to wait about half an hour for his return.

Mum never seemed to sell many of her magazines, I think she just put people's backs up with her attitude. She seemed determined to convert as many people as she could, regardless of the effect it had on her home and family.

John managed to dodge out of her door knockings but I got dragged about at weekends and school holidays. Those visits were not without their comical moments. As an avid 'people watcher', I had a lot of laughs.

One of our visitations took us to a house that we had reached by a way of a long path up to the front door. A middle-aged woman had answered our knock, she looked us up and down, then announced, whining nasally, 'you should be at the beck door.'

Mum launched into her 'I am on the Lord's work' speech, to be stopped short with, 'Wha-at do you want, monee? Are you beggars?'

I could tell Mum was getting annoyed, she tried again. 'Our purpose is to call upon . . . .' but she was cut short once more. The woman 'shoo-ed' us off her doorstep with, 'We don't want beggars or gipsies here, be off with you.'

I had an overwhelming desire to poke my tongue out at her, but Mum said, 'Come along Bobbie.'

I replied, over-loudly, in best 'pan loaf', 'What an awful woman, why was she so rude.'

As we reached her gate, she called nasally, 'Close the gate.'

I yelled back, 'Close it yersel, ye iggerant auld battleaxe,' and left it wide open.

I was surprised to see that Mum was laughing. We met all sorts, I soon learned to know when people were really hostile, but Mum seemed to be oblivious. I also learned a lot about human nature. It seemed to me that the nicest people were not necessarily the ones who lived in big, smart houses. With their polished accents and well-groomed appearances, they could still be rude and intolerant.

The Motherwell tenements revealed a very different sort of people. It seemed to my child's eyes that the grubbier the face, the kinder the heart; there were very few of those doors slammed in our faces. We were offered enough tea to float in and offers of, 'Lave that bairn, missus, ah'll mind her 'till ye've din.'

One woman sent Mum packing, but I was sure Mum did not fully comprehend what the woman said to her. Me – I laughed about it for weeks.

Mum had just gone into her conversion speech, as I called it, when the woman realised what Mum was at the door for. When it dawned, she let rip, 'Hoo durst ye come here, sellin' yer bloody books, an' me a guid cathlick!'

Mum was not to be put off, she tried to explain, but it was fuel to the fire – hell fire!

'Yous-yous, ye come here, foo o'shite, thurr's enough shite frae yous, tae fill a coal bag!'

'Well, really,' started Mum.

'Git aff ma doorstep, an' doon they sterrs, afore ah fetch the polis!' She waved her first.

That was Mum's cue to make herself scarce.

'Come along Bobbie,' and we were off, me giggling fit to burst. 'It's not funny,' whined Mum, and I giggled even more.

When we bussed out to some surrounding towns and villages, we would find a cafeteria to have a bun and a cup of tea; that was the highlight of the visit for me, and worth putting up with all the boredom. Sometimes, Mum could be successful, and someone would invite us into their home.

We went into one home, in the village of Ferniegair, where there were several small children, all looking pale and undernourished. There was little we could offer them, and their plight was pitiful. Only the older children seemed to have shoes. We were used to seeing poverty in our travels around Lanarkshire, so much so that we seemed well-off by comparison.

Another home we were invited into was occupied by a lady who was in her mid-thirties. She had two sons, both older than I, and had her sick father living with her. I use the term 'living' loosely, for life for that poor man was a burden of suffering. He spent his days seated in an armchair by the fire, with a pile of newspapers at his side. He rested between fits of consumptive coughing, ready to grab another newspaper to cough blood into, before throwing it on the fire.

My heart ached for him, I could not help thinking about Monty the cat, when he got his painful ear disease and we had him put to sleep, peacefully ending his misery. Here was a human being, left to cough up the remnants of his life. Where was that wretched 'angel of death', when it was needed?

The more I saw of life, the less I could understand, but it seemed to me that although I did not like or agree with what Mum was doing, we were a welcome diversion for a lot of unhappy and lonely people – surely, that could not be wrong.

The newspapers were full of the story and pictures of the wedding of the Shah of Persia. His bride wore a dress encrusted with diamonds. I supposed that nobody in his country ever went hungry!

18

Rule Britannia

There was to be a Festival of Britain, with a competition for school children, to draw or paint something appropriate. I wanted to a do a crayon and ink drawing, so I copied a Britannia, off a penny coin, placing it in the centre of a foolscap sized piece of paper. The piece of paper was coloured in as a Union flag, Britannia was copied in black ink. It did not win a prize, but got a 'highly commended'.

I was so pleased, and rushed home to tell Mum. I got a 'hoomph' from her, followed by, 'Pity you can't find something useful to do with your time.'

She seemed to be permanently cranky, and Dad was agitated, John and I kept well out of his way as much as possible. His moods were unpredictable, but when his face took on a certain look, I just knew there would be trouble. It was as if another person moved into his mind, or he slipped out of focus. He would rant and rave, all sorts of nonsense, and was beyond reason. I could never determine any specific reason for his outbursts, I just knew they meant trouble. When he had that look, he got very spiteful, it seemed to me that he went about looking for reasons to pick on us.

One Saturday afternoon, Mum had gone out on her door knocking, leaving John and I with Dad. He would not allow either of us to go outside, and told us to be quiet 'or else.' We were to sit in the chairs by the hearth, only leaving to go to the lavatory, and we were not to talk to each other. I had a fit of the giggles, especially when I saw the expression on John's face, it was total, absolute boredom.

Dad did not seem to notice, he just paced up and down the sitting-room floor, cracking his knuckles. I hated it when he did that, it turned my stomach. He left the room, as we had done in

111

turn earlier, to go to the lavatory. After a few minutes we heard him shout, 'Come 'ere, both of you,' then louder, 'NOW!' I thought, 'Oh, here we go, trouble.' John and I exchanged glances, then went into the bathroom.

He grabbed at both of us and demanded, 'Who did that?' pointing to the toilet roll, which had unrolled almost to the floor.

'No one,' I niggled, 'who would want to do that?' I had a sneaking suspicion that he had done it.

He roared, 'Someone did it, I want the truth, I will thrash the culprit.'

I replied, 'Really, well you were the last one in here.' He said, 'Oh', and I continued, really angry, 'Yes, go on, roll up that paper.;

He stared at me, and I yelled, 'Roll it back.'

'Why?' he asked.

'Just do it,' I snapped.

I had noticed once before, that he could not cope with anyone who stood up to him, and I was really angry.

He re-rolled the paper, and said, 'Well?'

'Now touch it.' He gaped at me again. 'Go on, touch it,' I yelled.

He did, and it unrolled itself once more, almost to floor level. He seemed very put out, and grabbing at us once more, he marched us back into the sitting-room, shoving John into an armchair, rather too roughly I felt. I was at boiling point by then, and when he barked at us to 'sit there, an' don't move', I told him to leave us alone.

That was his flash-point, he came at me with fists clenched, and instinct told me to move – fast. I dodged past him, making for the door, but my long plaits were, once again, my downfall. He grabbed hold of me and raised his fist, aiming a punch at my head, as he spun me round. I ducked, and the full force of his punch hit the partition wall between the sitting-room and kitchen. The wall was plasterboard in each room, supported by wooden framework, and his direct hit punched a dent in the plasterboard on the sitting-room side. It stopped him in his tracks, and he stood staring at it, like a small boy caught thieving.

I said quietly to him, 'I hope that hurt, and serves you right,' then added, 'whit ur ye goanie tell Mum?'

'Ah'll think o' somethin'' he muttered, then went into the kitchen.

John sat in his chair, staring at his feet, and I sat in mine, wishing I had never been born.

When Mum returned shortly afterwards, she breezed in, asking, 'Oh my, why all the sombre faces?'

Dad came out of the kitchen, and announced that he had just put the kettle on, for a 'cuppa'.

She saw the damaged wall, but before she could say anything, Dad ventured, 'Oh that, I'll see to that, just a bit o' horseplay,' he continued, thumbing in our direction, 'these were foolin' about, just an accident.'

Mum made no comment, but just went into the kitchen to prepare some food.

Later, when we were clearing up, Dad sidled up to me and whispered, 'Ta fer not snitchin' on me.'

I ignored him, but when Mum left the room, I told him 'You are a liar, as well as a bully.'

Some days later, Mum asked me what really happened, and I told her he put his fist through it.

'I thought as much,' she said quietly.

There was never very much to eat at home, I do not know how John managed, but Mum was out a lot, so I think she got her meals where she could. We had school dinners, which cost fourpence each day, and had free milk at school, but goodness only knows how the parents managed. They would have supper when we went to bed, as we had school dinners, Mum said we did not need anything else. Breakfast was usually bread, margarine and marmalade, when there was any, and on rare occasions we had cornflakes with milk.

The only money Mum ever had was the five shillings per week family allowance, and the few pennies she got for selling her magazines. She bought them for tuppence, and sold them for fourpence.

Sugar rationing was over, we had been given a shilling each by Mum when sweets came off ration, to go to the sweet shop and see who could get the most for their shilling. I won hands down, with twelve halfpenny chews in assorted flavours, three one-penny 'tooth breaker' lollipops, and three one-penny gob-stoppers.

We rarely had sweets, so I was annoyed when the school

dentist sent me home with a note for treatment. I was to have a number of teeth extracted, the milk teeth had not fallen out, and the new ones were pushing through. Mum explained that they had to come out to let the new ones grow in, and a few would be done at a time.

Being given gas was a horrific experience, and I fought like a demon. The rubber mask was pushed on to my face, as the dentist's voice droned on, getting fainter and fainter, telling the story of Peter Pan, until, nothing.

I came round, after a weird dream about being squeezed, time after time, between two large revolving pillars. I had heard a radio playing, somewhere in the building, when we arrived, and a voice had been singing, 'I'm a lonely little petunia, in an onion patch, oh won't you come and play with me.' For years after, I hated that silly song. I was feeling terrible, and felt worse when the nurse gaily informed me that they had done the lot, to save me having to come back. They probably realised wild horses would not get me back there.

'Oh dear, she's a bleeder,' she informed the dentist as she clamped a clean handkerchief of Dad's over my mouth, then wrapped a scarf around my head and mouth. It was mid-summer, so I did not take kindly to a scarf wrapped about my head.

When I got home, John poked fun at 'gummy' face, and laughed at me when I cried. He sneered that I had laughed at Dad when he got all his teeth taken out, so now I knew how it felt. I could not stop the bleeding, so Mum gave me a large towel, it was quite off-putting, and I was feeling really ill. I had been starved because of the gas, and now I could not even contemplate food. I lived on soup and milk sops for days, and went about gummy, apart from four upper and four lower teeth at the front, for months. The new teeth took a very long time to come through, but somehow, I managed to eat most things I was given.

During that summer, when I got really hungry, as there were no school dinners, I discovered a source of 'goodies'. On a road, near where we lived, were some allotments, surrounded by a privet hedge. I could hide in that hedge, and when nobody was about, would steal tomatoes, carrots, French beans and radishes. Only a few at a time, then I could hide, and eat whatever I had managed to snatch. I had to munch on them

114

like a rabbit, and I thought that was very funny, when I was hiding in a hedge.

Once, I nearly got caught, a boy from my class at school had spotted me in the hedge, and came over to see what I was doing. I had not managed to get anything, as there was a man working near some tomato plants. The man turned out to be the boy's father, and told me to 'come awa' oot o' therr' then, 'Whit ur ye daein'?' he asked. I told him I was trying to hide from my brother, and the boy and I watched him lift off some small tomatoes from the plants. I asked him what he was going to do with them, and he replied, 'Chuck them awa', why? Dae ye want them?'

I nodded, and he put them into a paper bag that he fetched from his shed. I thanked him, and hurried home to show Mum. She told me I was not to go pestering folk, but we would have them grilled, on toast, for tea. She put a penny in the gas meter and put on a kettle for a cup of tea, there was just enough gas to grill the bread and the tomatoes, after the kettle boiled. They were the best tomatoes I have ever eaten, but I felt a twinge of guilt over the stuff I had pinched from those allotments.

I had seen Fluffy cat, foraging around neighbours' dustbins, he did not get much either, and I wondered if I might try that. I decided I would only dare at night, for fear of being seen, and then I would not be able to see what I was doing, I would have to think of something else.

Fluffy had come home with Mum, not long after we moved to Gowkhall, she had swopped two of her magazines for him. It was usually John who swopped things, and I wished I had something to swop.

He was a funny, affectionate little cat, and liked to have a human to play with, usually me; I would sing the cartoon song 'I tawt I taw a puddy tat, a kweeping up on me'. Fluffy would creep up on me, whilst I pretended not to notice him, he would pounce, then scamper off, to do it all over again. I often thought we were a right pair of vagabonds, foraging for what we could, and being mostly left to get by as best we could.

Dad had been going from bad to worse, we just never knew what he would do next. Mum's eyesight had been causing her a lot of worry, and she had to see a specialist at New Stevenston hospital.

I had gone into the kitchen, one afternoon after school, to

find her pouring boiling water all over the draining board, she had missed the teapot by about six inches. I was really worried, she could cause herself a really serious injury, and told her so. She told me that she was going into hospital soon, to have an operation. John and I were to go to a friend of hers, after school each day, then walk home in time for Dad's return from work. I referred to Mum's friends as her 'Holy Joes', and this particular one was not one I cared for much.

She told me she would be in hospital for about three weeks. I thought, 'Oh God no, not three weeks of him.'

19

Suffer the Little Children

We were given our instructions, and Mum went off to the hospital, Dad took her on the bus, and saw her settled in, then went back to work at Carfin.

All that day in school I could not stop thinking about her, and was scolded several times for not paying attention. When the teacher finally yelled at me to go to the front of the class, I burst into tears.

She escorted me out of the classroom, saying, 'Therr, therr, whatever is the matter with you the day?'

I blurted out that my Mum had gone into the hospital for an eye operation.

She put an arm around my shoulders, and consoled me. 'Now, now, don't fret, it will all be fine, you'll see, she will be as right as rain.'

I sobbed, 'Ah'm no' worried aboot the operation.'

'Then what?' she asked, a trifle irritably.

'It's my Dad,' I wailed, 'I don't want to be left with him.'

She stared at me and said 'I see.' As far as I was concerned, I felt she could not 'see' at all, how could she know he was a vicious, spiteful bully? It was like leaving King Herod in charge of a crèche.

She told me to dry my eyes, and if anything went wrong, I was to tell her. After all, I had my brother to keep an eye on things, she argued.

All had gone well for the first few days, Dad actually cooked some not bad dinners for us and he was in his 'jovial' mood.

The first weekend he had been to visit Mum, we were not allowed to go as Dad told us children under sixteen were not allowed into the ward. 'Besides,' he remarked, almost absent-mindedly, 'yer mam 'as bandages over 'er eyes, so she could

117

not see yous.'

On Saturday he had returned from his visit in a foul humour, and on the Sunday he was pacing the floor cracking his knuckles. He did that by pulling out each finger individually. It made me squirm to see him do that.

I took refuge under the dining-table, armed with an egg-whisk, one of those double-wheeled efforts with a turning handle, it was the nearest thing I could grab. He knew my weakness and started to pick on John who totally ignored him. He cuffed John's ear and I yelled at him to leave him alone.

He snarled at me, 'W'at will YOU do about it – eh?'

For a reply, I began to bash the ornamental legs of the table with the egg whisk, leaving dents in the wood carvings.

He shouted, 'All right, all right, but come out from under there.'

As I emerged, John got up from his chair announcing that he was going out, and made for the door. I thought about following him when I noticed Fluffy curled up asleep by the hearth. If I left, Dad would ill-treat the cat

'You're going nowhere,' he snarled at me. I ignored him and he shrieked, 'Answer me w'en I speak to you!'

That made a change from, 'don't answer back, you.'

I said, 'I don't want to go out, anyhow.'

Then the tirade began, it was to be the first of many. This was something new, but better than the flying fists or the Karate type blows on the legs.

He got nowhere with the physical brutality, it was time for emotional battering, it worked on Mum.

I sat down on a chair and stared at him, mesmerised by the flow of verbal abuse that came from his mouth.

I heard it often enough later to remember the gist of it, which was that I was a millstone around their necks and that I was not wanted. I was an evil child of Satan, oh yes, I had brought poltergeists, and all manner of evils into their 'ome. He went on and on about how wicked I was, and as he droned on, the pitch and tone of his voice changed. As the pitch got higher, I could not help thinking about a Movietone film I had once seen, of Hitler at a rally in Germany.

As I watched him, I began to feel afraid. He had an odd 'far-away' expression on his face, and it seemed almost as if something was operating his mouth. I thought, 'Jesus Christ, who has done this to him?'

He was very agitated and seemed to be exhausting himself of both energy and abuse. The cat, who had been asleep on the fireside rug, had moved to a crouching position, and was staring at him, almost as if in disbelief.

His high-pitched tone whined on, 'I'm the 'ead of this 'ouse.'

He always dropped his Hs, and had difficulty with a lot of pronunciations. His French was perfect, but English with his Manchester accent posed difficulties. He seemed hardly to draw breath as he continued, 'I will be obeyed, you will do as I say at all times. 'Onour thy father and thy mother.'

I thought, 'Oh no, he's gone on to the bible now, we get enough of that from Mum.'

'The meek shall in'erit the earth.'

He droned on, as the pitch dropped, and he had stopped shouting, probably tired himself out. He wagged a finger in my direction saying, 'You must show respect for your elders and betters, you are a disobedient, wilful daughter of the devil. If it was not for your mother interferin' I would thrash you senseless.'

That did it, I had taken all the abuse I was going to take and my temper flared.

'You touch me,' I yelled, 'an ah'll git a polis, yer just a bully, like yer pig o' a faither.'

I screamed at him, 'Yer aff yer heid!'

He stopped short as if he had been slapped in the face, then moved towards me, slowly. The look on his face was one of pure hatred.

I was used to having to move fast and I got up from the chair. The cat let out an awful yowl, and before I realised what I was doing, I picked him up and hurled him straight at Dad.

The fur stood on end, and the splayed out claws found their mark. He landed, spitting and yowling, on Dad's chest, and clawed and howled at him, until he broke free and fled for the door.

We reached the door at about the same time, and Fluffy fled out, then into my room. I was half-way down the stairs when I heard a strange sound. At first I thought it was Fluffy, then realised it was Dad.

I crept back into the sitting-room and was dumbstruck by

the scene I looked in on.

Dad was hunched up in the chair I had vacated, head in his hands, sobbing as if his heart would break. It was a pitiful scene to witness, and I was at a loss what to do.

I went in and stood near him, at a safe distance, poised once more to escape, and waited for the flood of tears to subside. I had never seen anyone weep so bitterly.

When the sobbing got quieter. I ventured to speak to him, saying, 'It's all right Dad, it's all over now.' He looked at me like a small lost child, the demons that had tormented him were gone. He began to shake violently, his false teeth chattering, and I wondered if that was what shell-shock did to a person. I took hold of a hand, and just held on to it, I did not know what else to do.

There was a loud knocking at the flat's main door, which did not stop until I went downstairs to open it. I thought it might be John, but a flustered looking Mrs Mac from downstairs was standing there.

'Ur ye aw richt?' she enquired. 'We heard an awfie racket frae upsterrs.'

I told her Dad was not well, he had had an attack, caused by his shell-shock.

She thought for a minute then asked, 'Is he OK noo?'

'Yes, he's quiet now.'

'Whaur's yer mither?'

I told her she was in hospital, and she asked how we were managing.

'Not too bad, so far.'

'Hm,' she said, 'ah'll see yer faither noo,' and with that she made her way up the stairs and along the passageway, with me trailing after her.

Dad was in the chair where I let him and was still trembling, but seemed much calmer.

Mrs Mac went straight into the kitchen after only casting a glance in his direction, announcing that she would 'mak' him a cuppa.' I hoped there would be enough gas. She asked, 'Whaur's yer tea caddy?' opening a cupboard, then 'Hus he no' got nae messages* in?'

I wanted to die of shame, there was about half a sliced loaf,

---

* shopping

120

about one third of a packet of margarine, half a packet of tea, a messy looking bowl of sugar and four used up jars with a little jam in each.

Mrs Mac closed the door, without comment, then shuffled out of the kitchen.

'Ah'll bring ye's a cup up, when ah mak' oors.'

I thanked her, and closed the door as she left the flat, now I had to go back and face Dad.

He had not moved from the chair, so I went into my room to see if Fluffy was there, or had he gone out of the fanlight window?

I found him huddled under my bed, emitting low growling sounds. I managed to coax him to come to me, and I cuddled him and told him I was sorry I had thrown him. He just purred in my ear, and let me fuss over him.

The tea arrived for Dad, along with toast, and there was enough for three. I thanked Mrs Mac, and she told me to return her tray when we had finished.

John had returned, and asked what the tray was in aid of, and I told him Dad had not been very well.

I went into our kitchen, with the tray of things, to wash and return them, and Dad followed me. I was ready to bolt, but to my surprise, he put his arm round my shoulders saying, 'Thanks fer not tellin', I don't know w'at comes over me sometimes.'

It was the first time he had ever shown me even a hint of affection, I did not bother to reply.

Mrs Mac did not say much when I returned her things, but as I made to leave she said, 'If he starts again, yer tae bang oan the flair, an' ah'll be up.'

I nodded and left, wondering what Mum would think of it all, God only knew what she had to put up with from him.

We had gone to Mum's 'Holy Joe' friend on the first day. John arrived very late, and I knew that he too would rather be elsewhere. When I arrived, and knocked on her door, she opened it saying 'Oh, there ye are,' as if I had just materialised on her doorstep. She looked me up and down, with obvious distaste, and I thought she looked like someone who always had a bad smell under their nose. It was evident that I did not pass muster. When John eventually turned up she announced to no one in particular, 'Huh, the other yin's here.'

121

She lived in a terraced cottage, that had one large room downstairs, and two smaller ones upstairs. The downstairs room incorporated a kitchen area, by the main door, with a cooker unit and a sink. The lavatory was outside. I informed her with malicious glee that I had never seen anything quite like it. Even in our various lodging places, the toilet was never outside nor the sink in the living-room. I was delighted to see that I had touched a raw nerve, and told her snootily that Mum had warned me there were a lot of slums around Lanarkshire. She went purple with rage, as I sniffed, adding, 'You would not believe it was 1950.'

No wonder she hated me, but the feeling was quite mutual.

On our way home that evening John declared hotly that he was never, never, never going back there. He never did, he went to a class-mate's home, until it was time for Dad to return.

It quite spoilt my days at school, during those first few days, knowing that I had got to go to 'old mother Matthews', but I eventually ducked out of it also. An elderly lady lived next door to her and I would call into see her. She had a German shepherd dog, like the one I had known in London some years previously, and I played ball with him in her garden. His company was preferable to Mrs Matthews'. I had turned up one afternoon, just prior to Dad's attack, to find a beautiful doll's pram in her front room, complete with doll, pillow and covers. Our toys, such as they were, had arrived from Corsham. Fluffy was using the doll's bed to sleep on – I had no doll, anyway. A doll I once had, had been given away as they were considered 'worldly'. The tiny cottage I had was kept on the floor by my bed.

I stood looking at the pram and its contents when Mrs Matthews snapped, 'Dinnie you touch that.'

I replied, 'I was only looking.'

'Aye well,' she continued, 'it's no fer the likes o' ye, it's fer ma grandchild.'

I seemed to be forever being told that this or that was not 'for the likes of me'. I wondered what on earth was wrong with me? I replied angrily,

'Do you think I will soil it or something?'

'You jist lave it alane,' was her only response. I went out to play in her garden, until it was time to go home. She was one of

Mum's 'Holy Joe' friends, and she was giving a present to her grandchild. My mother had told me that presents were not allowed. I decided that my mother was a liar, but we never seemed to have money for food, let alone presents, so why tell lies?

I wandered off to the end of the garden, the old lady was out, so I could not play with the dog. There was a tall hedge at the end of the garden, and a wooden latched door, leading on to some fields beyond. The nearest field had a public right of way along the edge of it, and most of the gardens had access to it. A deep ditch flanked the field, so they all had improvised bridges across it, usually an old door. This path was a constant source of irritation between the local residents and the farmer who owned the field. He was wont to put his old bull in the field, with no warning. There was a stile over the gates at either end of the path, and 'WARNING BULL' notice on each gate.

He was a docile enough brute – the bull, not the farmer! – but very few people dared to chance their luck at getting through the field unmolested.

Curiosity got the better of me, as I unlatched the door and stood aside as it swung inwards. I found myself staring at the wrong end of Angus, who was parked on the footbridge happily chomping at something in the ditch. He flicked his tail, snorted at me, and continued chomping contentedly.

I did not tarry but quickly closed the door, realising just how flimsy that barrier was, one shove from Angus would demolish it. I thought of the fun he could have amongst Mr Matthews' vegetable plots, and toyed with the idea of leaving the door unlatched. I thought better of it, when I realised there were sometimes small children playing around those cottages.

I went back into the cottage and told Mrs Matthews that old Angus was by her back gate. She muttered something I prefer not to disclose, then exclaimed aloud,

'Wan day, that brute'll git somb'dy.'

Being the sweet child I was, I hoped it would be her.

Some weeks later, the farmer had disobeyed a court order, forbidding him to let Angus loose near a public right of way. Angus was in an ugly mood, and it took three men to rescue the farmer from under an old shed, where he had taken refuge from the bull's rage.

His blatant disregard for other people's safety had been

repaid.

When Mrs Matthews told me it was time 'to git aff hame,' I thanked her in my best 'pan loaf' voice. I knew that always irritated her, so I laid it on really thick. I informed her that I would not be back, I preferred to go to someone else, and added rudely, that I did not like her any more than John did.

She had not bothered to ask where John was, or how my mother was faring in hospital. Mum was forever going on at us to choose our friends wisely, I felt that it was high time she practised what she preached.

20

Visitors

Dad was quiet for a few days and hardly spoke to either of us. John had a paper round in the mornings and as he did not have a bicycle he had to leave very early. Both he and Dad were gone by the time I got up for school. There were sometimes cornflakes for breakfast or bread and marmalade. If the penny in the meter had not been used up, we could toast the bread under the grill. Our school dinner tickets were paid for monthly, so I had to just queue up on Monday mornings to collect the week's supply. The children who were on welfare had to form a separate queue, and that one was always longer.

There was to be a summer fete at school with fete queen and attendants. Naturally, every girl in the school wanted to be chosen, but I was not fooling myself. In the unlikely event of being chosen, My mother would soon put paid to that, I could just hear her: 'not fer the likes of you'.

John came home one day with a toy pistol he had swapped some comics for. He was always reading cowboy comics such as Gene Autrey, Tom Mix, Lash Larou, Gabbie Hayes, Roy Rogers of course, and his blasted horse, oh, we got them all, so he did not swap them easily.

Dad went berserk when he saw it and railed on at him like someone possessed.

'Thou shall not kill,' and then a lecture about the danger of firearms.

John reminded Dad somewhat sarcastically that it was only a toy and that set him off again. He got the 'elders and betters' speech, after which Dad confiscated the toy.

I had similar problems with a toy Gracie loaned me. It was a plastic trick ring with a small rubber pouch you filled with water. We had fun with it, using it on each other, one would make a great show of admiring the ring and ended up with a face full of water, whilst the wearer collapsed in fits of giggles. Gracie let me borrow it to get John with, but he had seen it before and besides, he was busy playing his own pranks.

Mum had bought some paper flowers from a gypsy at the door, John sprinkled pepper all over them and was trying to get the unwary to sniff them.

I was sent for a bath, so it was a perfect opportunity to play with the ring and I had fun squirting the walls with water. When I had finished and wiped out the bath, I went off to bed. I wanted to keep out of Dad's way as much as possible. About ten minutes after I had finished, he came storming into my bedroom, grabbed at an arm and dragged me towards the bathroom. He pushed me through the door, roaring, 'Did you do that?'

He was pointing at the wall that was damp, as they all were from the steam of the bath, and I was puzzled.

'Did you?' he roared.

'I said, 'Well, yes, but what is wrong?'

He pushed me and yelled, 'Ah'll tell you w'at's wrong girl, you've bin playin' with that stupid ring, 'aven't you?'

I nodded, he thrust out his hand.

'Give.'

I started, 'It's no' mine, it's Gracie's.'

'Give!' he roared again, so I went and fetched it from my window-sill and gave it to him. He snapped the plastic ring, tore off the rubber pouch, then opened the door of the coal store and threw the bits into the dusty darkness.

'There,' he said triumphantly, 'that'll stop yer silly games.' I was then told to 'git tae yer bed, an' stay there.'

It was about seven in the evening and there had been no food. He had not allowed me to go out to play when he was around and I knew Mum would not be back for a while.

I was hungry and feeling just a bit sorry for myself, how could I explain to Gracie about her toy?

John had been told not to speak to me or else. I had plenty of time to think and I began to wish that the poltergeist we had in Corsham had come with us. Boy, would I put the wind up Dad. He had called me the Devil's child, if I were I would wreak havoc on him!

Instead I imagined a playmate for myself and we would play

126

together. I decided I should have an angel playmate, one who would guard me, I was sure heaven could spare one for a while. Fluffy would watch solemnly from my bed as we 'played'. I used an old suitcase for a stage and would sing or dance for my strange audience, always remembering to bow at the finish. Oddly enough, I never gave my 'angel' a name, after all he was only on loan.

I was allowed out to the toilet and I would pretend that I could sneak out without my friend knowing, and when I returned, I would then have to seek him out of his hiding place. I took him to school, but kept him secret. There was a girl in my class who had a 'friend' she called Clarence, and a boy who had an imaginary dog called Scruff, but I kept my angel secret. It was to be a long time before I outgrew him, we spent many hours together in a world where grown-ups were not welcome.

Gracie had knocked on our door several times asking for me to play and had been sent away. She sought me out in the playground to ask why I did not come and play with her. I told her I had to stay in my room when I got home after school, but it would be all right when my mother returned. She asked me why, and I told her I did not know, but my Dad wanted me 'out of his sight', as he put it.

I could not go out and raid the nearby allotments at the weekends, so sometimes I felt quite hungry.

On the afternoons that I did not go to my class-mate's home, I would wait for John on the outside doorstep, for he had a key to let us both in. We would do whatever homework there was, then tidy the flat and set the table. When Dad got home he usually had something with him to cook for tea, or to heat up, but one evening he came home empty-handed.

He barked at us, 'Couldn't you get something ready?'

John replied, 'There isn't anything.'

He then snapped, 'Well, you'll just 'ave to go without.' He had a perfect knack of making things always seem someone else's fault. He peered in the pantry cupboard where there were about three slices of bread, left from a cut loaf.

I had had the last of the margarine at breakfast and there was no jam or marmalade.

Dad got out a soup bowl and broke up a slice of bread into it. I thought 'Oh no', I had given the last of the milk to Fluffy who had it with a slice of bread broken up in his dish, with a sprinkling of sugar on it. It was about all that cat ever got, apart from scraps I had seen the neighbours giving to him.

Dad went to the table, sat down and started to spoon the dry bread out of the bowl. I realised then that the next food John and I would have would be our school dinners. There were nearly always 'seconds' and John and I were usually amongst the regular crowd that went up for them. We still had the third of a pint bottle of milk at the morning break. This was collected from crates in the playground with the janitor keeping an eye on things. There were always a few bottles left over and I would hang about hoping to get another. The janitor would call:

'Come oan Bobbie Eriksson, hae anither yin, ye're far ower wee.'

John and I just sat and watched Dad, not daring to say a word. I was told to 'clear off' and so I went to my room where my 'friend' was waiting. The two old suitcases we had were in my room and I used to play on them, in them and around them. It is amazing what can be done with two old suitcases and a lot of imagination. I would be a housewife in a smart bungalow, or a shop assistant, a clippie on the buses, once even a circus performer. Nearly broke a leg with that one! One need never feel lonely with a bit of imagination and a few props.

On the second Friday of Mum's stay in hospital, we had a visit from three of Mum's 'Holy Joes', an elderly man with his son and daughter-in-law. They arrived just before Dad did and I invited them in. Dad seemed a bit put out when he saw them, then started acting the big 'I am'.

Oh yes, Nancy was fine. 'Was she hell,' I thought.

Dad got his tray purse out of his pocket, an act that always embarrassed me, and fiddled about in it. He produced a five pound note and I wondered who he had tapped for that. Dad told John to go and fetch fish suppers for everyone. I wondered if he had lost his reasoning, for we never saw the colour of his money and he certainly never bought us fish suppers before.

The chip shop was a good fifteen minutes' walk away and there was bound to be a queue, being pay day and all. Poor John had difficulty walking as he was still waiting for his operation to stretch a ligament. How he ever managed a paper round I will never know, but at least he got to keep the few shillings he got for doing it.

I volunteered to lay the table and brew a pot of tea, then realised we only had four cups and saucers. I thought about it for a few minutes, then had an idea. 'If you all sit at the table, John and I can sit by the hearth,' I said.

Dad bellowed out, '*I* will say who sits where and not you.' He then remembered that he had an audience. He smarmed at the Browns, simpering 'It is easier to send John for fish suppers than to cook when Nancy is away.'

I thought 'you lying toad' but said wickedly, 'Funny, I don't remember having fish suppers.'

Dad just grinned, everybody's Mr Nice Guy. He ordered me, 'Fetch the suitcases, you,' and when I had dragged them both in, he put them next to the chairs around the table.

I knew that there would not be enough gas to boil a kettle and warm the plates in the oven, so I beckoned Dad into the kitchen.

He said irritably, 'W'at now?'

I whispered, 'There's no' enough gas.'

He looked heavenwards, then got out that ridiculous purse and after fumbling in it, handed me two pennies.

'NOW, for goodness sake, shut up.'

The pennies seemed to make a dreadful noise when I put them into the meter. I could just reach the slot, for the meter was about a foot higher than I stood and I had to struggle to turn the lever of the wall-mounted unit. Luckily we had six plates and I put them into the oven to warm.

John returned with the food wrapped in newspaper. The newspaper was put on the fire, the food and inner wrappings were put into the oven.

Dad made the tea and I was allowed to dish up the food, with Dad carrying the plates to the table. I managed to break a piece of fish off my portion to put in Fluffy's dish with a couple of chips. Luckily Dad did not notice, but he saw my greasy fingers and niggled, 'Can't you wait?'

Our guests were called to the table and I was told to sit.

'Where?' I asked.

'On there,' said Dad, pointing to an upended suitcase. John had difficulty in clambering onto his and he was taller than me.

'Can I just stand?' I asked.

Dad got up from his seat, grabbed my arm viciously and yanked me round. He started to hit the backs of my knees with

Karate type blows, really hard with the edge of his hand, I could not keep standing as my legs buckled under the blows, so he kept yanking me up by my arm.

The Browns watched aghast, then Brown senior got to his feet and shouted, 'That's enough! Whit on earth dae ye think ye are daein'?'

Dad seemed to have forgotten that we had visitors. He blustered, 'She is a wilful, disobedient child and she needs constant disciplining.'

I was sobbing and stayed on the floor where I had fallen, the pain in my legs and arm was making me dizzy. I had difficulty breathing between sobs.

Brown junior lifted me up saying, 'Ye hae ma seat, ah kin manage that case.'

Brown Senior was still standing up, gazing at the spectacle in utter amazement.

'Guid grief man!' he exclaimed, 'Whit ur ye tryin' tae dae, cripple the bairn?'

I got 'Shut up and eat.' from Dad.

I had so looked forward to that chip supper, but it was all I could do to eat it. All through the meal convulsive sobs kept escaping from my throat and I could hardly swallow. My arm was throbbing and the pins and needles in my legs were almost unbearable. I could not seem to control my breathing or the sounds that escaped from me.

Brown senior went on at Dad, 'Therr's nae need fir that, if ye must hit a child, therr's a way. It's no' her fault she cannie climb oan that case.'

Dad ignored him and poured out the tea which looked rather stewed. Mrs Brown asked me if I was having any. I shook my head as another hiccup came. I thought for a moment that I was going to be sick, but it passed.

The Browns left us about an hour later and I was told to clear the table.

As I carried the plates into the kitchen I found that I could not straighten my legs and had to walk with my knees slightly bent. The pain shooting up and down my legs was making me feel ill, I thought I was going to faint.

Dad took the plates from me saying, 'Ye git tae yer bed, ah've 'ah enough of ye fer one day.'

Fluffy followed me into my room and I got ready for bed. I

130

crept out as quietly as I could to go to the bathroom and managed to return without being seen.

I had gone under the bedding so as not to be heard. Fluffy thought I was playing a game with him and kept poking me with a paw. I cried myself to sleep, with Fluffy snuggled up near the pillow.

I had hoped that on the Saturday we would be taken to see Mum, but was told 'NO'.

Dad had left no food in the flat and had not done any shopping, or left us any money to get anything. There was nothing we could do but await his return.

John went out after Dad left for the hospital and I sat on the stairs outside, with the door lock on the latch.

Gracie came round, saw me and asked me if I wanted to play, but I told her I was not feeling well, so she left. Shortly afterwards she returned telling me that her mother wanted me. I wondered what for, was I in trouble again? I wished my mother would come home.

I walked into their kitchen after getting a 'come away in' answer to my knock, to find Mrs Mac was cooking lunch for her family. She was laying another place at the table and when she saw me she said,

'Och, there ye are, ah've cooked ower mony chips an' ah wondered if ye'd help me oot eatin' a few?'

Well, would I! I did not need to be asked twice.

'Oh yes please,' I replied, trying not to sound too eager.

'Whaur's John?' she asked.

I told her I did not know, but he had gone out. It soon became obvious to me that she had not cooked too much by accident, for I had sausages and egg also. I felt a bit ashamed for I was sure that John had not eaten and Fluffy just had the scraps he could forage. I wondered what Mum would think of it all if she knew, I could just hear her whine, 'I have my pride.'

Dad returned from the hospital once again in a bad mood and I wondered what it was about the hospital that made him so cranky. He had bought some fish cakes along with a bag of groceries which we had for tea with a slice of bread. We never saw vegetables or fruit and only occasionally had potatoes, I suppose we never had the gas to cook them.

I remembered what I had tucked into earlier and felt quite

guilty. When Dad was not looking, I slipped one of my fish cakes on to John's plate and dropped half the other one on the floor where Fluffy was loitering. If I was seen, nothing was said, although Dad saw Fluffy eating something off the floor.

The evening passed without any problems. John liked to listen to the radio, it was a work of art to get it to function and it crackled when it did. He had the valves and innards out several times to try to improve the reception, but the radio had seen better days. No one dared to speak when *Dan Dare, Pilot of the Future* was on, or Paul Temple. I used to remind him when it was time for 'Dan Dare, pilot of the poocher'. I liked the big band sound and the brass bands. When we first moved to Newarthill and were with the Maxills, there would be a brass band parading through the streets most Sunday afternoons and I loved to watch them. I think it was a colliery band and the children used to follow them around the streets.

Worker's Playtime on the radio was fun and I also liked *Housewife's Choice*. The radio usually managed to conk out right at the vital part of a plot or right in the middle of a song I was trying to learn.

The newspapers were full of stories about two men called Burgess and MacLean. I thought they were a music hall comedy duo. The Festival of Britain was on, not that we saw anything of it.

Dad informed us grumpily that Mum would not be home for another week. John and I exchanged looks that said 'OH NO!'

21

The Showdown

The King was ill, Dad said it was because he smoked too much. Guy Burgess and Donald MacLean were spies, I thought, 'how exciting, who says nothing ever happens?' John declared that they should be shot, and Dad said that was not a very Christian attitude. The papers were full of stories about the Nuremberg trials. I did not know what they were about until John told me that people who had committed crimes during the war were being taken to task for them.

'Quite right too,' I told him.

Dad had gone off to one of Mum's meetings, probably to make sure we got no more visitors and I attempted the family laundry. I had to use cold water and household soap, and my efforts were not very good; the things did not look any cleaner, only very wet. I squeezed as much water out as I could, but they were still dripping wet, I spread them out on the pulley hoping that they would not crease too much, as our electric iron was broken, and hauled up the pulley struggling to wrap the rope around the wall-bracket. There were ominous 'drip drip' noises, and the floor soon had numerous puddles. I mopped up the water, then put newspapers on the floor. I knew that would mean trouble for they were needed to kindle the fire each morning.

Dad went mad when he saw the soggy papers and I explained that I could not manage to wring much water out.

He told me irritably that I should leave it to Mum. I told him that she should not come home from hospital to a load of mess. I got slapped and told not to answer back at my elders and betters.

He was pacing the floor once more and I felt like a trapped animal. I wanted to run away, but there was nowhere to go.

John returned from playing and was told off for being out. We had some bread and jam for tea, being told 'not too much jam' as usual. Sometimes, on a Sunday, we would have a joint of beef, with roast potatoes, gravy and carrots. Dad always loaded his plate up with lots of gravy over it all. When he had eaten the meat and vegetables, he would fetch a slice of bread to mop up the gravy, slurping all over it. His tables manners were quite appalling. Food particles that were trapped between his dentures and upper palate were dealt with in the most off-putting fashion. Out would come the offending dentures, regardless of who was seated around the table. He would hold them while he fumbled for a handkerchief from his pocket, then flick off the bits of this and that usually all over the table. I had to avert my eyes to avoid baulking.

Slurping soup was inevitable; all hot liquids, especially tea, would be held in their containers about an inch from his lips. He would then suck the contents into his pursed up mouth. If it had not been so disgusting, it would have been funny.

On this particular Sunday it was bread and jam. After tea I asked Dad if he would replait my hair for me. My hair was very long and I could not manage to get tidy plaits. Nancy from downstairs had done it for me a couple of times, but I did not like to keep bothering her.

I was told, 'No, git tae yer bed.'

I got washed and into my nightdress. I was feeling really depressed and missing Mum, in short, feeling really sorry for myself. John seemed to be ignoring me and things in general were just a bit much. The last straw was when Fluffy sunk his teeth into my hand, the floodgates opened. I sobbed uncontrollably, stuffing a corner of the sheet into my mouth so I would not be heard, but it did not work.

Dad came storming into my room, shouting,

'W'at's up wi' you? Stop that silly noise, or ah'll give ye summit to snivel about!'

I sobbed, 'I can't help it.'

With that he came over to my bed, grabbed my hair rolling me over onto my stomach. He then rained slap after slap on my bottom with the flat of his hand.

'There,' he sneered, 'that'll give ye summit to snivel for.' With that remark he left.

The cat had fled when he opened my door, so I was alone. I

felt on the edge of hysteria, but somehow I knew I had to be strong. During one of his ranting sessions he had told me that I should be destroyed, is that what he was trying to do, destroy me?

It seemed a long time before it got dark, although the curtains were closed, they were thin. I had heard children playing outside, and also the sound of the birds. I could not stop the hiccups that came and I had a strange headache. I wedged myself into the corner of my bed, which was against a wall, making a cocoon of the blanket and drifted off to uneasy dreams.

I must have been dreaming, for I awoke with a start to find Dad in the room in the dark.

'W'at's up now?' he asked.

He was standing there in his underpants, he did not wear pyjamas and I thought I was dreaming.

'Ah've to get up fer work in the mornin',' he niggled.

'I must have had a bad dream,' I replied.

'Well, c'mon into my bed, an' shut yer noise. Let's 'ave a bit o' ush.'

I started. 'Ah'm OK, ah want tae stay here.'

He grabbed my plaits, snarling, 'Move.' As he pushed me into his room, he said, 'Ye learn to do as yer told.'

I climbed into the parents' bed, which was also against the wall and he got in after me, pulling up the blankets saying, 'Settle down now.'

He started to move my nightdress and placed his hand on my bottom.

I went rigid.

'Stay still,' he said. I whined, 'Leave me alone.'

'Lay on yer back and open yer legs,' he snapped.

I moved away from him, but the wall was in the way. He pushed me on to my back, leaning his weight on one leg as he pushed aside the other one. He held them apart with his left hand as he pushed two fingers of his right hand into me.

I gasped with pain.

'Stop that, stoppit!' I cried as I tried to squirm free.

'You 'ave to be punished,' he intoned, 'you will 'ave to get used to this sort o' thing.'

'No, no, it's not right, leave me alone.'

I was getting desperate, trying to wriggle free. As he moved

135

his fingers in and out, he droned,

'I am your father, I will do w'at I like. This will be your punishment now, you are the devil's child, you must suffer.'

I screamed 'NO!' and heaved him aside. He was quite slightly built, but I was amazed at how easily I had pushed him over. I stood up in bed in the dark, then fled over the end of it and out of the room.

He was up and after me. No use going into the bathroom, the bolt was missing. I just ran, making the mistake of running towards the kitchen instead of getting out of the flat. I was trapped. He followed me into the kitchen, snapping on the light. He looked really angry, and as he moved towards me fists clenched he snarled,

'Make a sound, an ah'll finish you.'

I panicked as he moved by the door, barring my exit. I was standing up against the sink and as I edged away from him, something on the draining-board moved as I brushed against it. It was the breadboard and knife, still left out from tea-time. It was not a proper breadknife but a carving knife with a long pointed blade.

I picked it up, brandishing it towards him.

'You wouldn't dare,' he sneered as he edged forward. I hurled it at him. He ducked as it went into the soft thin plywood panel of the cupboard behind him and then clattered on to the floor. I leapt on it like a cat as he made a grab for me. I crouched on the floor and held the knife point upwards with both hands on the handle.

He hesitated, I got to my feet standing about four feet away from him.

I pointed the knife at him still clutching it with both hands and said through chattering teeth,

'You – ever – touch me again, ah'll kill you.' He stood stock still, his face a mask, then spluttered,

'No need for that, no 'arm done.' I continued, 'Touch me again, ah'll kill you, somehow, sometime, ah'll get you!'

I knew for certain that had he made one move, I would have used that knife.

He backed out of the door still spluttering,

'You, you best get tae yer bed, there's school in the mornin'.'

He left and went into his room closing the door. I stood there for a few seconds, then, leaning on the cupboard, I sank to the floor still clutching the knife. I began to shake uncontrollably, but somehow could not loosen my grip on the knife handle. My teeth were chattering like a monkey's, and I seemed to sit there like that for a long time.

I heard a noise, it was Fluffy coming in through the fanlight window. I got to my feet and went to put the knife on the draining board. On second thoughts, I picked it up again to take it into my bed. Fluffy followed me and made himself comfortable on my bed.

Fluffy had long since given up sleeping on the doll's bed, he preferred to share mine and I was glad of his company. He was like a purring, furry hot-water bottle, but if I moved about too much, I got poked by a paw.

I was very agitated and afraid that Dad might sneak back into my room as I slept. John had once shown me how to jam a chair against a doorknob to hold fast the door, but these doors had car-door type handles so I thought that would not do. I collected as many bits and pieces as I could find and made a heap just inside my door to act as a booby-trap. No one would get into the room in the dark without tripping over that lot.

I placed the knife under my pillow, then made a cocoon around myself with a blanket and tried not to sleep. Fluffy purred contentedly at my side. I wondered why he did not leave and find himself another home, I wished I could.

I felt my angel playmate had gone. John never seemed to be around and I was left to get by as best I could.

In the darkness I promised myself that no one would ever make me do anything I did not want to, ever again. I would build a wall around myself that nothing and no one would ever penetrate. If I was to survive and remain sane, I would have to do it alone, somehow I had to be strong.

I was eight years old, going on fifty. Years later I still had an aversion to long-bladed knives.

I drifted into uneasy dreamless sleep and awoke to hear Fluffy scratching at my door to be let out. Obviously no one had looked in or Fluffy would have been gone. I had lain hunched up in the top corner of my bed against the wall, had a stiff back and a crick in my neck. I had no idea what time it was, but everything was quiet. Fluffy had gone through the open sitting-room door, no doubt to leave the way he had entered via the kitchen window.

John had gone on his paper round and would probably go to school after that, of Dad there was no sign.

The electric clock in the sitting-room was the only one we had and it told me I was late. I rushed to get dressed, no time to wash or do anything with my plaits, I just brushed back the wisps of loose hair and hoped it was not too bad.

I put some milk and bread into the cat's bowl, drank the rest of the milk and then let myself out of the flat. It was as well that I was so rushed for it gave me no time to think about the night before. I ran as much of the way as I could. There seemed to be nobody about who should be around at that time of the morning and so I was sure that I was late.

The school bell was being rung as I raced through the gates, then up the main entrance steps. We were supposed to line up class by class on the rear playground, and then file in. I thought that I could just tag in on at the end of my group if I nipped through the main building. Needless to say I was seen and sent round the proper way. I arrived just in the nick of time gasping for breath. If you were late, you were kept in after school and got a lecture about timekeeping.

Our teacher was in a good humour and informed us gaily, 'This morning we're to do something new.'

Miss Simms came from Aberdeen and had a lovely sing-song voice that somehow always made me want to laugh. Instead of the usual boring English lesson that would take us up to the mid-morning break, we were to learn how to do a play. We were to see what could be done with a school version of *A Midsummer Night's Dream* by William Shakespeare.

I had read little snippets of his works in some of John's books and could not see it going down too well with a class full of scallywags and dunder-heids. The Brothers Grimm were more their style, but give Miss Simms top marks for trying.

All went fairly well until it came to casting, I just knew that there would be trouble. I was dying to know who would play Bottom – probably me with my track record of stage disasters. I rather fancied being Puck, the mischievous elf. The play was adapted for junior school children and had fallen victim to poetic licence, as there were more than the necessary number of fairies.

Jimmy Watson was being difficult, which was nothing new,

138

and as soon as he realised what it was about he hollered,

'Geez, it's a bloody fairy story, ah'm no' bein' a bloomin' fairy.'

He was dispatched to stand in the corridor.

'And close that door,' sing-songed Miss Simms. That got rid of him, but the damage was done. We had a boy in our class who lived with his grandparents whilst his parents were working abroad. His home was in London and he had a real cockney accent which stood out against the Lanarkshire twang. We called him London Tony as there was another Anthony in the class. He was swaggering about full of his own importance after being given a lead part. After Jimmy's departure, London Tony suddenly exclaimed, dumping his cardboard crown that was lovingly made by Miss Simms,

'No way, no way ah'm bein' a king o' the fairies!'

Titania was pleased, she hated him anyway. We all hated Titania, horrid teacher's pet!

I was to be a fairy – Cobweb.

'Huh, bloody spider, more like,' sneered London Tony, so I smacked his ear.

'Children, children,' chided Miss Simms, who by this time probably wished that she had never heard of William Shakespeare.

We got through a few lines and scenes when it became obvious that Titania was bored stiff. She stood at the front of the class which was used as the stage, yawning and digging in her left ear. My lines did not come up for ages and so I was back to 'people watching' – great for passing the time.

Miss Simms called softly 'Exeunt.' Then louder, 'Exeunt.'

Titania continued to excavate her ear but was galvanised into action when Oberon, played by Lizzie as the boys would have none of it, yelled at her;

'Tha-at means git aff the stage, ye glaikit doobit*!'

Very Shakespeare. I cannot imagine what Wills would have thought of it, but Miss Simms had had enough. She must have decided that we were not ready for culture as she sighed heavily, saying,

'Get out your poetry books.'

As the day wore on I began to worry about what might

---

* stupid idiot

happen later on at home. I had developed a very bad headache and was fighting to remain awake. I had been told several times to 'sit up and pay attention' and was eventually told to remain in after time.

When everybody had left I was beckoned out to Miss Simms' desk. She stood up and came to meet me asking,

'Whit on earth is wrang wi' you the day?' I looked away from her and she continued,

'Well, ur ye goanie answer me or no'?' She had had a bad day and was getting irritable. I did not know what to say and blurted out,

'It's ma Dad.'

'Whit aboot yer Dad?' she asked warily. I stared at the floor, replying,

'He made me get in his bed last night an' stuck his fingers between ma legs.' I heard a sharp intake of breath and looked up to add,

'He hurt me, so he did.' She raised her hand and slapped me hard across my face, shrieking,

'Ye wicked, wicked child, hoo kin ye say sic'a thing?' A sob escaped as I drew back from her, my face stinging and she shrieked again,

'You dirty little bitch!'

I sobbed, 'I'm not, not,' then turned and fled from the classroom.

Almost blinded by tears, I ran down the stairs and into the cloakroom, Mine was the only coat left, so I snatched it and ran out of the building without putting it on or stopping to look back. I ran across the back playground towards the main entrance, down the steps and out of the gate. I did not stop until I had gone up part of the main street where the shops were. I had a stitch in my side and so I waited for a few minutes outside the baker's shop until I got my breath back. A woman came out of the shop and when she saw me standing there, she asked,

'Ur ye aw richt hen, ye're looking' fair pechled*?' I nodded and she peered at me saying,

'Here, hus someb'dy hit yous in the face?'

I told her I was all right and mentally wished she would

---

* out of puff

leave me alone. I just wanted to run and run, but where to? Was there no one I could turn to? I had run up the main street, instead of turning into a back entrance footpath to the housing estate. That way I was less likely to be seen by someone who knew me. I spotted a class-mate with her mother and they were both coming in my direction. She had been to visit the dentist, but I did not want to be seen.

I went into a church doorway, hoping they had not seen me. After a few seconds they went past and I made to leave. I noticed it was a Catholic church, I had always been curious about the place and my curiosity led me into the main building.

It seemed a bit dark at first, but my eyes soon adjusted to the dimness, enough to have an impression of the place. I gazed about me taking in all the adornments on the walls. On the far wall was a huge crucifix above what seemed to be an altar. There were small booths down one end, and all around the other walls were pictures of Jesus on his way to the cross. The odour of incense filled the air and I noticed that there were several people in the pews who appeared to be praying.

So many times I had wondered about that building, but had not dared to ask Mum – she would have a fit.

I was thinking how fascinating it all was, when something brushed past me which made me start. It was only a nun in her long robes, I had seen her before out on the street. I had seen nuns once at Carfin where there was a grotto, oh, how I longed to go in there! John and I had once peered through the wrought iron gates into a beautiful garden with many paths, all leading to different statues. There was a tiny chapel of rest where a light burned whenever it was occupied. Near the entrance to the garden was a life-size statue of the Virgin Mary. John told me that on Good Fridays they could make it look like it was weeping, for there was a water pipe underneath. I thought that was an awful swiz.

The nun smiled at me as she passed then I heard a voice ask, 'Can I help you, child?'

22

Father Murphy

I almost jumped out of my skin, and as I turned, I saw a tall man in black robes, a priest. His accent was different to the local ones and I guessed that he must be Irish. I shook my head, contemplating a dash for the exit. He must have sensed that I was poised for flight, for he pointed to a pew saying,

'Let's take a pew.'

I was not too sure about that, but went and sat down where he pointed. I noted that he sat at the end of the pew, thus blocking my means of escape, and thought 'this one is crafty.'

He looked me over, then said,

'Ah'm thinking, ye're not of our faith.' Before I could reply, he continued, 'Would ah be right in thinkin' ye're in some sort o' trouble?'

I looked away as I felt the colour creep up my neck and face, and said,

'Aye, sort o'.'

He paused then asked, 'Would ye be wantin' tae tell me aboot it?'

I shook my head violently and felt very close to tears. He added, 'Ye should talk aboot whit ails ye, things ur nivver as bad as they seem.'

I thought 'Oh God, how can I tell him, of all people?'

He pleaded, 'Wid ye tell Sister Ignatius?'

'Sister who?'

'Ignatius.'

'NO,' I replied vehemently.

'Ye know, folks tell me all sorts. Ye know whit confession is?'

I nodded and he went on,

'Well, ah hear all their dark secrets, an' if they have sinned, ah ask God tae fergive them.'

After a pause, he asked, 'Huv ye sinned, child?'

'NO, I huv not,' I yelled at him, then whispered, 'not really,' and started to cry.

He patted my shoulder, coaxing,

'Go on, jist let it aw tumble oot, ye'll feel better, ye'll see.'

I wiped my face with a handkerchief I had up my cardigan sleeve. I was clutching my coat, like it was a life-line. Slowly, falteringly, I told him all that had occurred the previous evening. I could not bring myself to look at him, I felt so ashamed. I did not stop until the part where I dodged into his church, so as not to be seen by a friend in such a state.

For several seconds he remained silent and I stared at the floor, then he took hold of my hands saying,

'Well noo, that got that aff yer chest, an'ur ye feelin' better?'

I nodded, but said nothing. He asked if I thought anything further might happen at home.

Despite myself, I laughed and told him,

'Ah hope no', ah've still got that knife under ma pillow.' He smiled and asked,

'Whit's to do if someone is wanting tae slice bread?' We grinned at each other as he added,

'Put it back lass, an' trust in God, ah'll pray fer ye.' I looked at him and said,

'Ye hud better shout, ah think God is a bit hard o' hearin'.'

He wagged a finger at me, saying,

'God knows everything.' Then he added, 'Should ye be needin' me, ye know where tae find me.'

As I left, he caught me unawares saying, 'Ye're Bobbie, ur ye no'?'

'Yes, how dae ye know?'

'Ah ha,' he said, putting a finger to the side of his nose, 'Now, don't ah know all the bairns here aboot?'

'Will ye help me?' I whispered.

'Aye lassie, 'tis whit ah'm here fer, onytime.'

'It hus tae be a secret,' I warned.

' 'Tis safe wi' me,' he said, and I left.

I walked out of that gloomy church into the sunshine feeling as light as air, not a care in the world. I was invincible, nothing could touch me ever again. I had a friend, someone I could turn to, and he was my secret. As I skipped up the road to the housing estate, I could not believe how I felt. I had been desperate, in the depths of despair, now I knew there *was* help.

John was looking for me as I walked down Gowkhall, and rushed up to me saying,

'Where the hell huv ye been?'

I laughed and laughed, oh, if only he knew! I told him I had walked home the long way, and had found a new friend. One should never lie, but one can always rearrange the truth.

I thought about what had happened and realised that I did not know the name of the church, or the priest. I had heard the local children call him just 'faither', so, because of his Irish lilting voice, I decided to call him 'Father Murphy'. I had no homework that evening, which was just as well, for in my haste to escape from the class-room I left everything behind. I had snatched my navy blue raincoat off the peg in the cloakroom, breaking the hanging loop. I rummaged in the sideboard drawer for a needle and thread and after finding only black thread, I set about trying to repair it.

John was seated at the table doing his homework and when he finished, he announced that he was going out. He had given no indication that he knew about the previous night's happenings and I wondered whether I should tell him. I decided against it, he seemed so remote and distant to me I often wondered if I had strayed into the wrong family. Knowing John, I guessed that he had slept through it hearing nothing, that boy could sleep through the Apocalypse.

I was left to contemplate Dad's return. Fluffy had crept in as John left and was fussing around my feet. I picked him up to cuddle him, I had nothing else to give him. I cleaned and refilled his water bowl and he jumped on to the draining board to purr and fuss around me. I offered him the bowl of water and he meowed plaintively. I told him that if I had some place else to go, I would take him too. I could hear his soft purring in the silence of the flat, then I heard the outside door being unlocked. I listened to the stomp, stomp of Dad's footsteps on the stone stairs, then the clump of his tread on the passageway linoleum. My heart was thudding like a sledgehammer.

I always recognised his footsteps as he was a bit flat-footed. He used to buy heel attachments for his shoes, they were circular rubber pads, screwed into the heel of the shoe and they looked really stupid. The idea was that when one edge wore

144

down, you simply turned the pads round a bit, but they never really worked. More often than not, the round rubber heel-pad worked loose, leaving a gaping hole in the heel. They added about three eighths of an inch to his height and apart from looking ridiculous, seemed to make him walk with an odd, flat-footed gait. Once he fitted a pair to my shoes and I kept tripping up. After about two days I used a screwdriver to remove them and threw them in the rubbish bin. Mum gave me two shillings to call in at the cobblers and have stick-a-heels fitted. If Dad noticed he said nothing.

I went into the kitchen as he came through the sitting-room doorway, wishing John was back.

He breezed in with, 'Oh, 'ello, w'at, no table set yet? Where's John?'

I blustered, 'Oh, em, he's out, an' I didn't realise what time it was.'

'Well c'mon then,' he continued airily, 'ah'll light the oven, an' brew a cuppa, ah'v some chips 'ere fer us.' As he bustled around, he niggled,

'Go on, you set the table, this'll get cold.'

He was putting on his 'Mr Nice Guy' act and I was as nervous as a cat in a violin workshop. He stuffed the news-paper-wrapped chips into the lighted oven, telling me to put the plates in also. I hoped the paper did not catch fire, but said nothing.

He was pushing pennies into the gas meter on the wall, and as I watched him, he announced,

'We'll give John ten minutes, then ah'll brew a cuppa.' I watched as he unpacked some groceries from a brown paper carrier-bag, putting things in the cupboard that had the snick from where the knife dug into it. There was a tin of cat food and I asked if I could feed Fluffy. I could not manage the tin opener, so Dad did it for me. Puss must have thought it was his birthday, for he usually only got bread and milk sops, and was purring noisily between mouthfuls.

My heart was still hammering, but Dad seemed to be in a good mood, no one could have guessed what had happened a few hours previously.

He took an uncut loaf out of the carrier-bag, placing it on the breadboard. Just as he asked, 'Whaur's the knife?' I realised it was still under my pillow.

I said quickly, 'I know whaur it is,' and dashed off to my room to retrieve it. When I returned, I laid it on the draining board.

There was an odd expression on his face, as he gave an odder little laugh, then quipped,

'W'at were you doin' with it, cuttin' toe-nails?'

I could not believe my ears, so that was his game, pretend it never happened. Well I could not!

I heard John return and as he came into the kitchen Dad announced,

'Oh, there ye are, mam's comin' 'ome this week.'

'Oh dear God,' I thought, 'I do hope so.'

The evening passed without any trouble and I went to bed early. I was very tired and had a weird, dizzy headache, the start of many such headaches, I had nightmares about school and awoke feeling like I had not slept for a week. My ordeal was not yet over.

Dad had tried to act as though nothing had happened, but I still had to face my teacher.

I went off to school in dread of what awaited me and slunk into my class with a group of children, hoping I had not been seen. Miss Sims saw me and beckoned me out to her desk. I felt sick with apprehension and wished I could disappear like a ghost. My knees felt wobbly and although I wanted to run for the exit, my legs seemed to have a will of their own.

She did not seem to be angry and gave me a feeble smile as I approached her warily. She leaned over her desk and looking down at me whispered,

'Ah'm sorry aboot yesterday.' She even sing-songed when she whispered, and went on, 'It wiz jist such a shock, ah should no' huv slapped ye, am ah fergiven?'

I gaped at her, then nodded dumbly.

'Bide here,' she continued, 'when Miss Lee arrives, we've tae go tae the heidmaster.'

I thought I was going to faint and then heard her say from what seemed a long way off,

'Nothin' tae worry aboot, ah'm comin' tae.'

Miss Lee, who was the headmaster's secretary, arrived as the last child filed in. Interested stares were aimed in my direction as Miss Simms called the class to attention, informing them that Miss Lee would call the register and then give them a

146

spelling test. Amidst groans from her pupils she told them that she and I were to see the headmaster. That got their attention! 'Eh, what – trouble?'

Miss Simms quashed their curiosity by stating simply that we were to discuss what Bobbie did for lessons at her last school. That was too boring to contemplate further and they turned their attention to the nervous looking Miss Lee.

I wondered what it all meant, obviously Miss Simms discussed my revelation with the headmaster. Did they think I was lying?

By the time we reached the headmaster's office I was feeling quite ill. Miss Simms took hold of my hand and quietly knocked on the door before going in.

We were motioned to two chairs, placed just in front of his desk, and he smiled at us as we took our seats. He sighed then said, not looking at me,

'Well Bobbie, Miss Simms has told me about your trouble at home the other night.' He paused, then added,

'Is that right?'

I immediately felt that they both believed, or hoped, that I was lying. I felt very angry as I replied,

'It was all true, I did not lie, Father Murphy believed me.'

They looked at each other and the headmaster asked,

'Father who?'

'Oh that is not his name,' I said quickly, 'at least I don't know his name, I just call him Murphy because of his Irish accent.'

I felt a bit foolish at being caught out on my secret. Miss Simms said, 'But you are not a Catholic.'

'No,' I replied, 'but I ran into his church when I left here.' They both stared in amazement and I felt my face colour up as I continued,

'I went in there for a bit of hush an' he found me. He did not think I was lying.'

The headmaster said gently,

'Neither do we, Bobbie, but this is a very serious matter. Is your mother out of hospital yet?'

I told him that she was due home at the weekend.

'Does she know what goes on when she is not around?'

'I don't think so.'

Miss Simms asked, 'Will you tell her?'

'Good God, no!' I exclaimed. 'She has enough to worry about.'

'What will you do if it happens again?'

I looked from one to the other and said, after a pause,

'I will kill him.'

I saw the look that passed between them and the silence in the room was deafening. I told them quietly,

'Father Murphy says I'm to go to him if there is any more bother, he'll sort it out.

'What will *he* do?' asked the headmaster.

'I don't know,' I replied, 'maybe he can find me a home.' They remained silent for what seemed like ages, then the headmaster told me to return to my class. As I stood up to leave, he cautioned,

'You mind you tell us if anything else happens at home, don't be afraid.'

I nodded and left, wishing Father Murphy was with me, he would know what to do. One thing was clear in my head, I was not alone, there was help after all.

Miss Simms returned some fifteen minutes later, looking very subdued. I had the sneakiest feeling that for some reason she could not look me in the eye, but the rest of the day was uneventful.

I was quizzed during break about my visit 'tae the heid', but remembered what Miss Simms had told the class about the previous school, and they soon lost interest.

There was a girl in my class called Elsie, who was a very quiet girl and always seemed to be on her own. No one seemed to pay her any attention as she crept about like a wraith, a pale, thin, wisp of a child. She was taller than me, but then everyone seemed taller than me, all except Carol who was tiny. Carol had a heart defect and was not allowed to run around much. She used to seek me out in the playground and I would seek out Elsie, together we made an odd trio, but somehow we got something from each other.

Carol was often ignored at playtimes, because she could not join in tag, skip-a-rope or risk any rough and tumble. Carol would get upset and frustrated because she could not run around, she was very cosseted at home, but Elsie had very different problems on the home front. I often felt that Elsie would like to roll into a ball, or better still, become invisible.

One afternoon we three decided we would go into the playing field which was allowed when the weather was dry. We found a corner to sit down and Carol and I made ourselves comfortable. Elsie who had been especially quiet all day, just stood there. I patted the grass beside me, saying,

'Come an' sit here, Elsie.'

'I cannie,' she replied, 'ah've a sair back an' legs.'

'Whit's wrang wi' yer legs?' asked Carol.

'Thurr jist sair.'

Carol got to her feet, asking,

'Is thurr a bruise, whit's up wi them?' she grabbed at Elsie's skirt, saying, 'Ah cannie see onything.'

'It's the taps o' ma legs,' Elsie replied.

Undaunted, Carol made to look and from my seated position on the grass, I saw the wide, white, swollen weals on her thighs. I thought 'Oh no' as Carol gasped, 'Whit's that?'

Elsie sighed and said, 'Ma faither hit me wi' his belt.'

'Is yer back like that an' all?' asked Carol, shocked.

'Aye, all ower.'

Carol gaped in disbelief before exclaiming,

'My, but that's awfie!' Then after a pause she asked,

'Whit did ye dae tae git that?'

'Nuthing,' said Elsie, 'he jist gits drunk an' I git the belt.'

I asked, 'Did yer mum no' try an' stop him?'

'Oh no, she gits the belt tae, when ah hear her howlin' ah ken ah'm tae git it next.'-

Carol and I were shocked. Carol was never hit in her life and I had never been abused like that.

'Ye should tell the polis,' said Carol angrily.

'Somb'dy should pyzen the pig's beer,' I snarled, 'he wants lockin' up.'

Elsie, who had been watching us both, sighed and said quietly,

'Ma twa brithers arrived hame frae the airmy unexpected like, an' they beat him up an' chucked him oot, we dinnie ken whaur he is noo.'

'Bloody guid riddance,' said Carol vehemently, 'guid riddance tae bad rubbish.

I was worried. 'Whit happens when yer brithers huv tae go back to the army?'

Elsie thought for a minute, then said,

149

'Ah expect he'll come back, he aye diz. Ma brithers pit his belt in the bucket*, so that'll stop him.'

I had my doubts, more likely he would just find something else to beat them with, but I kept my fears to myself.

My problems at home seemed paltry compared to hers, but I told her that she had to learn to stick up for herself, no one had the right to treat a person like that.

'But he's ma faither,' she replied lamely.

I knew that there was a lot of child abuse and cruelty, it was not unusual to hear gossip about the 'cruelty man' being called in to so-and-so. However, no one wanted to admit that it went on in their street, the social stigma kept a lot of it secret. What went on behind closed doors was none of their business, they would 'tut tut' about it to each other, but do nothing to help the child victims.

One afternoon I was waiting for John to return from school to use his key to let us into the flat. Gracie came round for me to play, but I thought I had better not, as Dad did not want me to be outside. I told her to wait until my mum got back and I would be allowed out to play.

Dad was late, we were getting hungry and just a bit worried. He had been in a good mood the previous evening, but that could change at any time, his moods were totally unpredictable. I heard the main door open, then the sound of voices. He called up the stairs,

'Ah'm 'ome, an' look 'ooz 'ere!'

John went to the sitting-room door and said, 'Mum!' I leapt out of the chair and ran into the passageway. Sure enough, there she was with her little suitcase, it was Dad's attaché case that he usually took to work. It only ever had his sandwiches in and I thought it was just a touch of swank to make him look important.

I felt so relieved to see Mum standing there that I burst into tears – you would think that she had been gone for years. There was so much I needed to tell her, yet I dared not and so I cried even louder.

'For goodness sake!' I got from John.

'There, there now, I'm back,' Mum comforted. She peered closely at me, then said,

---

* rubbish bin

'Tch, look at that hair, when did you brush it last?' Obviously the operation had helped, she was seeing too darned much!

Dad fussed around her, fetching her a cup of tea – it was quite touching and clearly he had missed her. John and I just watched, I cannot remember what I was thinking, but once again, I felt just like an outsider who had intruded on someone else's life. I sneaked off to my room and left them to it, with Fluffy cat following me as usual.

I was called in for tea shortly afterwards. Mum commented that I was pale, and had I lost weight? Dad shot me a look when she asked me why I was so quiet, so I told her I did not feel very well, which was true, in fact I felt really ill. The headaches and dizzy spells persisted and I seemed to have no energy at all. I would be hungry, but when I ate I felt sick and had to fight to keep the food down.

I went to bed after tea and Mum came in to say 'good night'. She had not done that since I was very small, could it be that she had missed me too?

Dad came in as she left and I went rigid, he hunched down by my bed to whisper,

'It's nice to 'ave Mam back, isn't it?'

I replied 'Yes', but thought, 'you'll have to watch your step now.'

He continued, 'We don't want 'er ill again, do we?' I ignored him and he went on, still in a whisper,

'Not a word about our bit o' bother eh?'

I still ignored him, so he went on,

'It will be better if we say nowt, mustn't worry 'er.' He got to his feet and made to leave my room. As he reached the door, I said to him,

'It would be better if you left.'

He wheeled round, staring at me white-faced. I looked at him for several seconds then told him,

'I have already told several people.'

He went red, then paled once more as I added, 'You try anything again and I'll see you leave – for good.' I knew I had him worried, but I got no satisfaction from my malice. There was a nagging fear at the back of my head that I tried to eliminate, but it kept on nagging – there was something really wrong with my Dad.

151

23

All of the Monkeys are not in the Zoo

At half-term holiday, Dad took some days off work and we enjoyed being together as a family. Both parents seemed to be relaxed and carefree. Mum explained that her operation, whilst not a failure, was still not quite right and she would need another to resolve the problem. She had glaucoma and had been at risk from a detached retina in one eye. It all seemed quite frightful, but she seemed very calm about it all, and totally resigned to face another operation in about eighteen months' time.

I thought, 'Oh God no, not again', but then I would be that much older. I remembered what Dad had told me about his father and how he consoled himself by thinking,

'I won't always be small.'

Mum would always joke about her eyesight, she would laughingly say,

'Nothing wrong wi' my eyes, I jist cannie see,' and 'Never mind, I've one good eye.'

One day Mum overheard a couple of neighbours tattle as she went past them,

'Pst, that yin's blind, dae ye no' ken.'

Mum turned round to them, saying,

'Half blind, but ah'm no' deaf.'

We were informed one morning, after being woken up early, that we were bussing into Glasgow for a day out. John and I were both excited about it, we both found that city utterly enchanting with its trams, barrow boys and general hustle-bustle. For me, I loved the Glasgow people, a more cosmopolitan bunch you could never hope to find, and so kind-hearted. They had a unique sense of humour that I have never found anywhere else.

At that time, just after the war, there were a lot of Polish people in the area, refugees from war-torn Europe. The Poles who had learned to speak English must have thought they had arrived in the wrong country once they got to Lanarkshire. Their text book English was of no use there. Poles who understood little fared much better. Mum always thought it was hilarious to hear Glasgow 'twang' spoken with a Polish accent.

Once, when she was in a greengrocer's in Motherwell, she overheard a Polish man ask the shop assistant, oh so politely, for 'A pund o' green aiples.'

The assistant exclaimed,

'Jings, but it's jist great the way yous 'uv picked up English.' She went on, 'Tell ye whit, yous teach us Polish, an' weez'ul teach yous English.'

Mum laughed out loud, saying,

'Oh my, I know who'll get the best o' that bargain.' They all looked at her like she had just fallen off a Christmas tree.

I always enjoyed the bus journeys in and around Glasgow, there was always so much going on to keep a 'people watcher' amused. On that particular day, I was watching a girl of about my age tucking in noisily to a large red apple. I had never seen anyone make such a mess, or make so much noise. As she chomped and slurped her way into it, I nudged Mum, saying,

'Git a loady hur, she's lik' a pig.'

Mum shushed me and inclined her head towards the seat on the other side of the aisle, where the adoring mother was glaring murder at me.

I was getting bored, it was a longish journey, we had first got on a bus from Newarthill to Motherwell, then another for Glasgow. To ease the monotony, I began to sing. When the bus was moving, I was loud, but when it stopped for traffic lights or passengers, I lowered the tone – literally! I gave a lusty rendering of a childish local ditty, to the tune of *She'll be coming round the mountain*, that went:

'Ye cannie shove yer grannie aff the bus,
No ye cannie shove yer grannie aff the bus,
Oh, ye cannie shove yer grannie
Fer she's yer mammy's mammy,
Ye cannie shove yer grannie aff the bus.'

When I got tired of that, I gave voice to another ditty. There were also a lot of Italians in the area, who came in for more than their fair share of leg pulling. The ditty went,

'There wiz a wee Tally* who lived doon oor alley,
Who gied me some wallies†, tae build a wee hoose,
The wee house got started, but wee Tally farted
An' blew aw the wallies, away in the sky.'

I got a dig in the ribs from Mum's elbow and a muted 'Wheesht!' There were sniggers from John and Dad who were seated behind us, but Mum sat there with a face the colour of boiled beetroot.

There were a lot of people getting off and on the bus at most of the stops, so there was plenty to see. One very large lady lumbered on to the lower deck, I thought, 'she'll never mak' it up them sterrs' and she sat in front of us, taking up most of the seat. Most of the other seats were occupied, so when a tall thin man came up the aisle after her, he was obliged to sit on what little space she had left. As the bus rounded a corner, he had to cling on for dear life to the support bar of the seat in front.

It was all too much for me and I collapsed in a fit of giggles. Mum was shaking with silent laughter. When the conductor came to collect fares, he spoke to the large lady,

'Hello Mrs Johnstone, huv ye paid fer thae twa sates?'

'Dinnie be sae cheeky you, orrul skite yer lug,' she said, chuckling.

I noticed he passed by without collecting her fare. After a few stops, the lady looked at the man seated precariously beside her and said,

'This is ma stope.'

There was no response, she tried again.,

'Ah've tae git aff here.'

The man looked at her puzzled, and she must have guessed he was Polish. She must also have thought he was stone deaf, for she yelled at him,

'Shift yer bumski!'

Message received and understood. He grinned broadly at her, stood up in the aisle, and bowed her out with a flourish.

---

* Italian
† tiles

154

The fat lady lumbered out awkwardly, then waddled off down the aisle, muttering,

'Tch, furriners.'

Mum and I were still giggling when it was our turn to alight, several stops further on. As Mum made to get out of her seat, I giggled, saying,

'Shift yer bumski.'

We got off at Sauchiehall Street and made straight for George Street, where the famous barrow market was held. I gazed about in awe, of all the places I had been or was destined to go, nothing could compare with the feeling of delight I got in that city.

There were barrow boys selling their wares from hand carts all along the kerb. The nearest one was selling vegetables, his cart laid out like a harvest thanksgiving display. There was a boy of about John's age, who was yelling out something I could not understand. I watched him juggling two small cabbages and was mentally willing him to drop them, the noisy show off.

After a few seconds he stopped, looked at me, then asked, 'Whit ur ye gawpin' at?'

I looked him up and down, replying nastily,

'Nuthin'.'

He sneered, 'Ur ye wantin' a cabbage fer a heid?'

'You need a big yin fer yer gob,' I replied rudely. Mum put paid to further discourse by dragging me off, niggling,

'Can't you keep out o' trouble?

We had to find a tram stop, so all thoughts of cabbages and barrow boys were forgotten in the excitement of having a ride on a tramcar.

'Whaur ur we goin'?' I asked.

'You'll see,' I was told.

We bumped and rattled along in the tram, I was half expecting it to blow up, and wholly hoping it would not! Just as I was getting used to it and deciding that I quite liked it, it was time to get off. Dad gave me the tickets as a keepsake, much to John's annoyance, but then he told him that he could have the ones from the return journey.

As we waited to cross the busy road, I realised that we were going to the zoo. We had been taken to London Zoo some years before, but I did not remember much about it, only an elephant that had my name.

155

I could hardly contain my excitement as we went through the turnstile after paying our entrance fee. The first thing that struck me was the beautiful flower beds that I had not expected to see. I do not know what I expected, but it was all so marvellous. John and I got a lecture about wandering off, or speaking to strangers, and I could not help thinking that it would not do if we were to enjoy ourselves too much.

The memories of that zoo visit were something I would never forget. The playful monkeys with their comical antics seemed to delight in having an audience. I could not help thinking how like some people they were.

There was the usual collection of big cats and I wondered what Fluffy would have thought of that. Mum and I had lingered to admire the Bengal tigers, when something furry brushed up against my legs. I looked down to see a small grey tabby cat and stooped to pick it up. I was having my face lick-washed and was generally fussed over by the cat, when Mum said,

'Goodness, would you look at that tiger watching you.' It was the most amazing thing I had ever seen from a wild animal. The tiger was rooted to the spot, literally staring at me, almost as if in utter amazement. It moved nearer the wire enclosure, still staring. I moved forward, still cuddling the cat, until I reached the spectator barrier. I said to the tiger,

'Ah couldnie cuddle ye like this, could I?'

Mum laughed, saying, 'He'd huv ye both fer a snack an' still be hungry.' The cat jumped down and strolled off, getting a disdainful look from the tiger, and we moved on.

We found John and Dad in the reptile house. I was not too keen on snakes, but there was a man in there holding a large boa constrictor, inviting children to come and touch it. I went up for a closer look and gingerly put my hand on the snake's body. I was surprised to feel it warm and dry, the very opposite of what I expected. However, I went right off it when I heard the keeper tell one boy that the snake ate live mice and chicks.

John was peering into a glass case, so I went to see what was so interesting. Mum refused to look, Dad had walked away and I just had to see what it was. I should have known that it was a large spider. 'Tarantula,' said John. I told him I thought tarantula was a dance.

'Don't be daft.'

156

I said it was beautiful and John said, 'Yuk.' I had a sniggering notion to sneak it home and put it in the parents' bed. Next stop was the marine collection. The only big fish I had ever seen had been covered in batter dished up on a plate with chips, or laying in pieces on the fishmonger's marble slab.

Once John had come home with a small minnow he had caught with a net and put it in a jam jar full of water. He caught it in a nearby burn (stream, to those who have never ventured north of Hadrian's Wall) and Mum insisted it was a trout, so it was called 'Tammy' after a character on radio children's hour. He fed it on ant's eggs, brought with money from his paper round. As Tammy grew, he had to have a goldfish bowl, but he kept trying to leap out. A couple of times we found him floundering on the sideboard but we managed to plop him back into the water in the nick of time. Mum told John to return Tammy to the burn, giving him a lecture about removing things from the wild. Before John could be persuaded that it was in Tammy's best interests, Tammy made a bid for freedom when no one was about to plop him back into the bowl and we found him dead on the sideboard. I was surprised Fluffy had not eaten him, but probably the cat did not know what it was. There was no burial in what passed for a garden, the means of disposal of the dead fish is left to your imagination.

The zoo specimens were something else, huge flounders that seemed the width of our dining-table top, ugly sharks and terrifying eels. The octopus gave me bad dreams for weeks after, but I had to return for just one more look. Dad came after me and clipped my ear for wandering off. It really hurt and made me feel giddy, he had caught me with a back-handed swipe that almost bowled me over. He made to grab my arm but I dodged away from him, leaving the dark building to go and find Mum. Dad joined us some minutes later complaining to Mum,

'She was in there 'anging about.'

'I knew where she was,' said Mum irritably, then added, 'Look for a place to sit, we'll have our lunch.'

There were groups of people, some with picnics, on most of the grassed areas, but we found a space and sat down. Mum rummaged in her bag and brought out a pack of sandwiches. There were two slices of bread each, spread with margarine and meat paste.

'Wot, no jam?' I asked, getting a threatening glare from Dad, some people just have no sense of humour. The sandwiches had been wrapped in margarine papers, then put into a brown paper bag. With the heat and the fact that they had been made several hours previously, the sandwiches resembled something that had been found in an archeological dig. I was hungry enough not to care as we ate in silence, watching what was going on around us.

I noticed that two elephants and a large camel were being used to give children rides. They had been fitted out with special seats with six children on each elephant and four on the camel. I did not like the looks of that camel, it seemed to have a permanently superior smirk on its chomping face, as if it knew something nobody else knew. I mentioned that to Mum and she said that all camels look superior and smug, for they are the only creatures on earth that know all of God's names, and thus are disdainful of everything.

I would have liked a ride on an elephant, but knew better than to ask, my ear was still ringing from the last clout it got.

There were a lot of children about, I suppose because of the half-term, and they were running around having fun. There were numerous animal keepers and other staff about, so there was no danger for children, or chance of mischief. A small girl came running up to where we were seated and invited me to play. I looked up at Mum and she shook her head. As the girl walked away, I asked Mum,

'Why not?'

I got the 'I don't you want you mixing with those sorts' speech. I did not for the life of me know what she meant by 'those sorts'. People were people, they could not all be the same, so what did it matter what 'sort' they were' We all breathed the same air, but then I thought animals stick to their own kind, could that be what she meant?

Dad got his fourpenny worth in, by giving me the 'disaci – disassociat, what's it, disassociation – there I said it' speech. I looked from one parent to the other, thinking, 'who the hell do they think they are?'

John went to look for a drinking fountain and I asked if I could go too.

'You shut up,' I was told by Dad. I turned to Mum, saying,

'I am thirsty too.' She sniffed and replied,

'You'll just have to get on with it.' Dad bellowed, 'Ah'll give you a good 'iding if you don't stop pesterin'!'

I thought, 'Oh Lord, he's in one of his moods.'

He went off for a drink when John returned and had told him where to find a fountain. When he returned I hoped that Mum would not go off and leave us with him, instead she gaily suggested we split up, and she and I could go and look at what we fancied, while he and John went their way. She was making a brave attempt to rescue what was in danger of becoming a bad situation, but poor John was lumbered with Dad.

Dad snarled, 'We stick together,' so we all went into the aviary for a look round. I was getting a headache and was desperate for a drink. As we left the aviary, I noticed some public conveniences across the path. I nudged Mum, saying, 'I need the lavvy.'

'No you don't,' snapped Dad.

Well, I had had just about enough of him, and I raged at him, 'Dae ye want me tae dae it whaur ah stand?'

'Be quiet,' he snarled.

'Whit is up wi' you?' I yelled at him. People were beginning to look as Mum took charge.

'Stoppit both of you,' she turned on Dad and snapped, 'For goodness sake, will you leave her alone?' and to me she said, 'Go on, off you go, we'll be in there.' She pointed to the building marked 'APE HOUSE'.

I thought, 'How appropriate.'

Luckily the cubicle was free, or I might have done 'it' where I stood! I emerged and went to wash my hands in one of the row of basins. I sloshed cold water all over my face and was about to drink from cupped hands, when a woman who had been watching me called out,

'Dinnie drink that hen, thur's a fountain in the wall yonder.' She pointed, and I saw a drinking fountain similar to the one in our school playground. I used a none too clean roller towel to dry my face and hands, then went to the fountain and drank my fill.

I found Mum in the gorilla house, but there was no sign of gorillas. She said,

'Oh, there you are, nuthin' in here, let's go.' There were two large, very secure looking cages that went the full length of the building and were each about fifteen feet wide. As we made to leave, I heard a noise and turned back to look. There, standing upright in the nearest cage, was the biggest, hairiest creature I had ever seen. It stood, with what looked like hands, on the bars behind a steel mesh and peered at me with glittering eyes.

I went for a closer look and was amazed at the sheer power of the thing. For its part, it seemed just as interested in me. We indulged in mutual admiration for some seconds, before a gnarled looking finger-nail poked through the mesh. I could not get too close because of the spectator barrier. I noticed a plaque saying,

'DO NOT GIVE CIGARETTES TO THESE ANIMALS'

I wondered who in their right mind could even think of harming such a wonderful creature.

'Aren't you wonderful,' I told it and watched as a smaller gorilla came out of the loft in the adjoining cage.

Another plaque informed me that they came from Africa. I decided to give Africa a miss, as I did not want to happen upon one of those, wonderful as they were.

I heard Mum return and when she saw me she said,

'Come on Bobbie, let's – Oh my God, oh, oh.' I said, 'Hush Mum, you'll scare them back into their lofts.' For some reason, she seemed to think that was very funny.

We moved to the next enclosure to see the orang-utans, who were showing off to their audience. I said that it must be hot under all that hair, but Mum said it was a lot hotter where they came from. Next were the chimpanzees, but so many people were crowding round that we could not see much. I caught sight of one wearing a party frock and I did not like that at all, it seemed to be an insult to the animal.

John and I wandered off to watch, once more, the mischievous monkeys, before our parents told us it was time to leave.

Dad announced with all trace of his earlier ill-humour gone, 'We'll get some chips on the way 'ome.'

I wondered if it was just me, or my presence, that annoyed him so irrationally. I always tried to keep out of his way, but it seemed not to make much difference.

The return journey was uneventful. In Motherwell we went into a chip shop near our bus stop, before the final lap of our journey to Newarthill. We had to eat them sitting on a bench, as Mum said we could not get on a bus reeking of vinegar.

I was looking at the newspaper the chips were wrapped in, reading a column that ran a story about Scone. I thought it was a tea cake and asked Mum what the 'stone of scone' was. She thought for a moment, then said,

'Scoon, not scone.'

The legend has it that on this stone Jacob had his dream of angels ascending the ladder to heaven. The Stone of Scone had been used for ancient coronation rites in Scotland. How it ended up in Scotland is anybody's guess.

'It's in Westminster Abbey now,' announced Mum.

'Not any more it's no',' I said, 'some bugger has jist pinched it.'

'Bobbie!' Mum said angrily, 'Where do you pick up such things?'

'It's in this paper,' I said, waving it at her.

Mum laughed, saying, 'You know what I mean.' I read out the story which said that the stone had been found dumped in Arbroath Abbey.

'Humph,' said Mum, 'they should'uv dumped it in the sea.'

'Very patriotic, I don't think,' said Dad.

24

Pals of the Right Persuasion

Apart from playing with Gracie from downstairs, I did not venture very far on the estate. The residents were predominantly Catholic, and to happen upon one of those children meant facing a barrage of questions about one's religious persuasion. I usually managed to keep them guessing, by saying that I was neither Catholic nor Protestant, that really got them wondering.

One large girl called Flora, who I always felt should have been named 'Weed', informed me imperiously that it did not matter what I was, as I was not a Catholic, I would go straight to Purgatory, whatever. I told her, just as imperiously, that if Heaven was to be full of folk like her, I would prefer Purgatory.

'You'll gaun tae the bad fire,' she screeched at me. 'Good grief,' I thought, 'what *do* they teach those bairns.'

Flora had a younger sister, who was my age, and Mary attended the Catholic primary school. She delighted in reminding me endlessly, that whilst she could go to any school she liked, I could not go to her school, sinners were not allowed. We would meet on the playing field on the estate, where there were swings and a couple of roundabouts. At one end of the field stood two huge greyish black rock formations about twelve to fifteen feet high. They were like giant-sized lumps of charcoal, all pitted with holes and crevices.

Local tattle believed they were meteorites, but no one seemed to know for certain where they had come from. They were wonderful for climbing on, but a bit sharp in places, and it was quite a feat to reach the top of one and get back down with the skin on your knees intact.

Mary would call out to me, as I climbed,

'Goan Bobbie, git richt tae the tap. Het's the nearest ye'll

162

get tae Heaven.'

We had an unpleasant little incident, shortly after our arrival at Gowkhall. A brick had been lobbed through the sitting-room window, with a scribbled note tied to it with twine.

The note read, 'PRODDIES OUT.'

We were not the only non-Catholics in the immediate area, but I guessed it had something to do with Mum's door knockings. Luckily we were out when it happened, but arrived home to find the brick on the floor, and broken glass everywhere. Mum was upset about it, and I was sent to fetch a policeman. There was a station in the main street, I think, but I found one walking his beat and he said he would be along soon. He arrived about half an hour later, on his ancient 'sit up and beg' bicycle, to inform us that, 'This sort o' thing happens now an' again, huv ye offended or upset onyb'dy lately?'

I thought, 'Heck, my mother does it fer a livin'.' We had no idea who could have done it, and were told enquiries would be made. He told Mum that a 'bloke frae the cooncil' would be round soon, to replace the pane of glass.

It was around this time that I hinted to Flora and Mary (John always reckoned they should be called Flora and Fauna) that no, I definitely was not a Proddie.

Mary came to me one afternoon after school and proudly told me that I could 'cry on her' whenever I liked. I was puzzled at first, then it dawned on me what she meant. I had seen and heard some of the local children go to a friend's door, and instead of knocking, they would call for whoever to 'come oot', until they got a shout of 'cummin'' or 'no' cummin' oot'. I thought it was ridiculous, but everyone seemed to do it.

It was so demeaning, to stand at Mary's back door hollering 'haw Mary', but it seemed to be the expected thing. I was a bit apprehensive, for the sisters had warned me to steer clear of their place, as their parents hated Proddies. I was just beginning to suspect that I had been set up, when Mary opened the door, saying,

'Haud yer wheesht, ma mither says ye're tae come in.' My heart was doing its sledgehammer routine as I entered the kitchen. The elder brother, who was about seventeen, made a hasty exit when he saw me and I had a feeling he knew more about our brick episode than was good for him.

We had had a visit from a priest, not my Father Murphy, a much older man. On his departure, Mum declared hotly that he knew who the culprit was.

Mary's mother scrutinised me for several seconds, then remembering her manners said,

'Come awa' in hen, sit ye doon,' she peered closer and then asked, almost conspiratorially,

'Yer no'a Proddie, ur ye?'

It was more of a statement than an enquiry and I felt it was prudent to reply in the negative.

'Oh no,' I told her, 'we belong to one of the fringe religions, neither one nor the other.'

She seemed relieved, but somewhat puzzled, then thankfully changed the subject, by saying,

'Yer awfie pan loaf, ur ye no'?'

Mary ventured, 'She lived in England fer a while.' Her mother gazed at me and said, clicking her tongue, 'Tch, pair wee sowell.'

There was a new girl in class, and she was to sit next to me. I knew it was rude of me, but I just stared at her, she was not at all like most of us; she was tidy, no, she was immaculate. Her navy blue gymslip was crease perfect, her school blouse white, not 'offish', and her navy blue cardigan was shop new. Her hair was cut in a collar-length bob, with a full fringe, a style that was fast becoming popular.

'Bobbed hair bandits,' Mum called them, when I pleaded with her to have my long plaits cut.

Her socks were white with no holes, and her shoes were mirror shiny. She looked like she had just been lifted out of a box.

I managed to collect my untidy self, enough to say 'hello'. She smiled saying,

'My name is Sofia.'

She pronounced it So-fie-ah rather than So-fee-ah. I thought 'oh for a handle like that', and begrudgingly told her my name was Bobbie.

'How unusual,' was her only comment.

'Polite too,' I thought.

In the playground at mid-morning break, she asked if we could be friends. I could hardly believe it, I had never had a friend of my own before, except for an imaginary one, so with

Elsie and Carol, we became a foursome. Even John called me 'tag-along', which just about summed me up.

At dinner-break, she informed me that she was to stay at her grandparent's house for a while, and it did not occur to any of us to ask why. It turned out that her temporary home was a few doors away from where I lived. Her grandmother lived in a semi-detached house at the top of Gowkhall, and I could not believe my luck. Elsie and Carol both lived on an estate at the other side of Newarthill, so I only saw them at school.

Gracie was fun, but she was younger than me and Nancy was older; to have a class-mate just up the road was too good to be true.

Sofia was a lovely child, well brought up, her lifestyle was far removed from mine. Perhaps the opposite was the attraction, but it was doomed to failure.

Sofia had never ever shinned up a tree, swung on a gate, or kicked a tin can in the street and she most certainly never played with rough boys. She was aghast at some of the japes I told her John and I got up to.

I explained that dark, windy evenings were perfect for playing pranks on the neighbours, especially 'chicky melly'. She listened agog, as I told her you got a length of twine or strong thread, then made it into a loop about four feet in length, placing a button in the centre, before fastening the loop. One end of the loop was attached to a window-ledge whilst you kept hold of the other end. You needed to choose a window that afforded a good hiding place, then you tip-tapped on the window, until someone came to investigate the noise, when you would lower the button and twine out of sight. You had to be ready to make a run for it, when you were discovered. Snowmen built on doorsteps was another favourite, or snow balls hurled at a door from a safe hiding place.

Sofia listened in wide-eyed amazement, before informing me lamely that she was not allowed out after dark. I introduced her to the delights of pavement art, using her coloured chalks, until her grannie came out with a bucket of water and a scrubbing brush, and made me clean it all off. The gable end of our staircase to the flat was covered with graffiti, so I chose her path – unwisely.

Some of the songs I taught Sofia did not go down too well either! By venturing further into the estate, I met other families. There was Morag, also a classmate, she wanted to play doll's house and doll's hospital all the time, and I soon wearied of that. I did not have a doll, as they were considered idolatrous by Mum, and mine had been disposed of. Cops and robbers, cowboys and Indians were more up my street, but I missed my threadbare old Ted, who had met a sorry end from a Jack Russell terrier.

Then there was Kirsty and Gordon, both very much younger than me, but tremendous fun. I adored Gordon, he was the sort of little boy you could just steal. He did not mind that I was rough and ready, and we spent a lot of time together. He loved to hear about all the things I did, and the places I had lived, and I liked to play with his toy cars. They had a television set, something rare in those days, at least rare on that estate. Andy Pandy was Gordon's favourite, but if anything happened to Andy Pandy Gordon would cry, he was such fun to be with. Kirsty was a tom-boy so she was fun as well, never a dull moment with those two.

John laughed at her one afternoon as he was coming home from school. It was pouring with rain, and there was Kirsty, outside in it, dancing around. She did not want to get her hair wet, so she had hitched up the skirt of her frock over her head. Her mother had come out as John passed, yelling at her, 'Come you in Kirsty Freeman, the whole street kin see yer knickers.'

Sofia had started walking to school down the main street, instead of through the back of the estate. Our seating arrangements in class were changed regularly, so I no longer sat next to her, and I got the feeling she was avoiding me. I cornered her in the playground at break one morning, and asked why she did not want to play with me any more.

She seemed very uneasy, and blurted out that her mother and grandmother had forbidden her to play with me. I was a bit taken aback, and asked her, 'Why?'

She looked near to tears, and I had no wish to see her cry, so I just walked away, saying, 'Never mind.'

I was hurt, but deep down I had a pretty good idea why she was warned off and I could not blame her. As we filed back into class at the end of break, she prodded me and whispered,

'I'm sorry.'

'That's OK,' I whispered back, but I felt terrible. I had

166

heard my mother say often enough 'I have my pride', and I was beginning to understand what she meant. My pride had just had a kick in the teeth and it was not funny.

At lunch-break we sat at the same dinner table in silence, and afterwards I wandered off into the playing field alone, I could not even face Elsie or Carol. London Tony came rushing up to me, breathlessly saying,

'Come on Bobbie, yer needed fer rounders,' then raced off calling, 'Come on!'

'Oh well,' I thought, 'why not? I'm too rough for girls.'

Elsie and Carol came running to fetch me after about ten minutes, Sofia was in tears, would I come? When I found her and asked her what was the matter, she told me she wanted to play with me, but had been ordered not to. Again I asked, 'Why?'

'Because, because,' she faltered, 'you're a hooligan.' I was hurt, but knew exactly what her mother was afraid of, and as she wailed, I decided to make light of it. I had always been infuriated by Mum's 'pride', it was time to swallow mine, and it hurt!

'Oh, is that all?' I quipped gaily. 'Jings, fer a minute ah thought it wiz summit serious.'

She gave a nervous little laugh and I told her we could be friends at school, her folks need never know. I told her I almost always had only boys to play with, and you have to be rough to survive.

I was still smarting when I got home from school and told Mum what happened. I got no sympathy, just a lecture about the company one keeps – very profound, but it made me think it was high time I changed my image.

We were to spend the last few weeks of term in an annexe nearby as the decorators were in, so I ended up sitting next to a girl called Margaret. She lived on the same estate as Elsie and Carol, so we gained another member in our group. I noticed that Elsie and Carol went off together a lot and Sofia tagged on to someone else, so I was mostly around with Margaret, which seemed to annoy Sofia.

We were to have our annual class photograph taken, so Mum made sure that I was dolled up for the event. I had to endure those hateful ringlets again and was warned to keep clean and tidy. The front of my hair was waved and had a ribbon in it. A lot of girls wore hair ribbons, mostly made from parachute silk bought from the Glasgow 'barras'. I managed to arrive at the school gates without any mishaps, just as a few class-mates arrived, including Sofia. She came running up to me and when I saw the huge pussycat bow in her hair, I almost laughed, but then who was I to laugh with my daft ringlets? She peered closely at my hair, saying 'very nice', then proceeded to ruffle up the waved bit at the front with both her hands.

I saw red, my mother would be livid if I was a mess on that photograph, so I caught hold of Sofia's ribbon and yanked it out. She howled with rage, but she had been seen ruffling my hair into a mess by a mother at the school gate, and the woman said,

'Serves ye richt, ye messed up her bonny hair, ye spiteful wee besom.'

Long hair was something Sofia had never been allowed to have and mine was too much, but for all that the eventual photograph was passably good.

The school doctor paid a visit prior to the end of term, so we all had to be examined and I was one of several who were referred to the family practitioner. I could only recall one visit to a doctor years before, when we were supposed to be going to Ceylon as it was then called, and I was not that bothered.

When it came to my turn, she scared the life out of me. She was one of those women who looked like nature had just changed its mind, when she should have been a man. She was a huge woman swathed in tweeds, lurking behind heavy thick-rimmed spectacles, and had her grey hair cropped short.

I was weighed, measured and prodded.

'How old?' she boomed.

'Nine in October,' I told her.

'Hum,' was her only response, as she scribbled on a piece of notepaper, pushing it into an envelope and practically swallowing it as she sealed it shut with a huge lick.

She flicked it across the desk at me and peering over the top of her spectacles, then she boomed,

'Take that home, see yer mither gets it – NEXT!' I fled before she could change her mind.

Mum struggled to read the scrawl and after several attempts left it to Dad to decipher. All he could make of it was that I must see the family doctor – I did not know we had one, but Mum seemed to be forever going off to see a doctor. If we had any ailments we were told to 'get on with it' or 'keep it 'till it's better', and she seemed to be annoyed at being told to take me to a doctor.

The evening I had taken home the note was the evening for Mum's 'meeting' and she did not intend to miss it. I was informed that I need not think I could get out of it, I was to go also. I was feeling unwell, but did not want to be left with Dad. We were a bit late, what with 'all that nonsense with the note' and the tea being late. As we walked down the hill towards the bus stop, Mum heard a bus pull up and told me to hurry. I was feeling really ill and a wave of dizziness made me fall over, hitting my head on a lamp-post as I went down.

'Oh for goodness sake!' Mum exclaimed irritably. 'Get up or we'll miss the bus.'

My head was swimming and someone helped me to my feet as the cobbler came out of his house to help. Between them they got me to the chip shop by the bus stop and I was given a glass of water. Someone asked Mum if she needed help getting me home and she replied she could manage, adding irritably,

'Oh, it really is too irritating, she's always the same.' I had not managed to eat much tea and was feeling ill, my head throbbed as a wave of dizziness washed over me. Someone said, 'Ye'll hae tae git that bairn hame.'

How I got home I will never know, but once there, Dad got the whole sorry tale about how I stopped her getting to her meeting. I was amazed as Dad let fly at her, telling her that I could hardly help being ill, or banging my head when I fell. He told me to go and lie down and minutes later brought me a cup of tea. I thought I was dreaming until he told me I looked terrible, that was more like Dad. As he left the room he said,

'You're tae get tae the doctor's.' Mum came in with a cup of soup and some bread, saying,

'Git that down ye.' There was no 'how are you?' or any other sympathy, and as she left she added,

'Ye're coming wi'me tae the doctor's, so no need tae get up fer school.'

The doctor sat reading the note and informed Mum that he also had a letter from the school medic.

'What does it mean?' she asked haughtily.

He looked at her for some seconds, then picked up a piece of paper. It was the report from school, he told her.

'Well?' demanded Mum. She could be unbearably snooty when she thought there was trouble brewing. He waved the piece of paper saying,

'Your daughter is underweight, undersized and undernourished.'

'Well, really!' exploded Mum.

He lost his temper and proceeded to lecture her about nutrition and diet, ending by yelling at her,

'An' get that damned hair – CUT!'

Mum blustered, 'I don't think –'

He cut her off shrieking, 'Get it cut!'

They both tried to control their outbursts as he added, 'How would you like to lug that lot around?'

He got up, came round his desk and lifted up one of my plaits.

'No wonder she has dizzy headaches, that lot is sapping her strength.'

He ended the consultation by telling Mum to bring me back, in one week, minus some of my hair.

'Get some food into her,' he said to Mum as we left the room.

Later that day there was a big consultation at home, I stayed well out of the way.

Nancy from downstairs had had very long, thick plaits. Her mother had arranged for someone to come to the house to cut her hair and Nancy was very upset over it. It had been cut shoulder-length and Mrs Mac made her go on an errand to the shops afterwards. I saw poor Nancy running up the road, sobbing her heart out. I could not wait to see my hair hit the floor.

I was taken to a salon on the main street where a hairdresser told Mum that my heavy hair could be thinned out and just the broken ends cut off, so I ended up with less hair but it was still long. The girl told Mum it was a sin to cut such hair, so I did not get my wish.

Back at the surgery one week later, the doctor jumped to his feet as we walked into his consulting room, saying,

'That hair.'

Mum stopped him in his tracks announcing,

170

'It has been thinned out – look.' He came round to inspect and declared that it was much better.

I was to have cod liver oil and vitamins. I thought 'ugh' and he told Mum that he had made me an appointment for an eye test.

25

Stick That In Yer Gob, and Sook It

I was worried about that eye test, what with all the trouble Mum was having with her eyesight. I was taken to the clinic in Newarthill and was seen by an elderly man wearing a white coat, who positively reeked of stale cigarette smoke. The fingers of his right hand were badly stained with nicotine and I thought he was just disgusting. I did not want him near me and the examination was a disaster, with me refusing to do anything he asked.

He turned to a female assistant, saying, 'Och aye, I expect she hus her mither's trouble.'

That nearly scared the life out of me, but I was amazed to see that he was filling out what looked like a form for spectacles, which he then handed to the assistant, saying to Mum, 'She's tae wear thame, ah kin dae nuthin' fer her.'

The assistant told Mum to wait, frames had to be tried. She then told Mum curtly that we would be told when to collect the spectacles.

When we left to walk home, Mum bristled with rage, saying that she had never seen anything like it in her life. She ranted on, 'It's all slapdash and that'll do.'

We were summoned to collect the wire-framed pink monstrosities one week later. They were plonked on my face with a 'Howzat?' I replied, 'Cannie see a blessed thing, the walls are aw bowed oot.'

I was told tetchily, 'You'll git used tae thame.'

Mum was told equally irritably, 'See she wears thame.'

As soon as we were on the street I removed the spectacles, because with them on, I could not see where I was going, and misjudging the position of the kerb I fell over. I told Mum that I thought glasses were supposed to help your vision, not render you helpless.

'Shove them in your pocket, therr as much use therr as on yer face,' she said adding, 'Ah'll take ye tae a proper optician.'

Back at school, Miss Simms was doing her 'bit' by ensuring that all children were wearing their prescribed spectacles. She asked me where mine were and I told her, 'In my coat pocket, Miss.'

'Well go and fetch them,' she sing-songed.

'No point Miss,' I told her, 'therr in bits.'

She demanded to know what I meant, so I told her I had put a note from my mother on her desk.

'So why are they in bits?' she persisted.

'Ah stamped on them.'

'Ye, whit!' she exclaimed, getting to her feet.

'Jist read the note, Miss.'

The note informed her that as I was short-sighted I should be allowed to sit nearer the blackboard and not wear glasses that bevelled the walls.

She sat motionless for a few seconds, and I swear she smirked.

'Right then,' she addressed the class, 'who's goanie swap seats wi' Bobbie, so she kin be nearer the blackboard?'

I had been sitting next to Margaret and she looked a bit put out about it all. A girl called Anne, who sat at the front, put up her hand saying, 'Me Miss, me.'

'Verra well,' said Miss Simms.

I realised to my horror that I would be seated at the same desk as the dreadful Isobel, the class tyrant and bully, and next to London Tony, the class show-off.

The spectacle saga ended with a visit to an optician in Motherwell, who confirmed that I was short-sighted, but not enough to need remedial treatment. He warned that I may well need glasses when I was older, and thirty or so years later, I did!

The whole purpose of Isobel's life was to be a pain in the neck. She got into so many fights after school that her mother had to collect her every day, much to Isobel's chagrin. Next door to the school was an old stone-built detached house, the lower part of which was converted into a sweets and tobacco shop. It was run by an elderly couple, the lady was nice, but the man seemed to hate all humanity. He had poor eyesight, so

173

he would dash the coins on the wooden counter to ensure that they were real. Once he got hold of a coin, he would tell the customer to 'clear orf', it amazed me that anyone ever ventured into his shop. The local children called him Fagin and it certainly suited him.

Dear Isobel would hang about outside the shop doorway, waiting for someone smaller than herself to emerge with their purchases and then she would pounce. A scuffle would ensue with Isobel grabbing what she could before pushing her victim over.

She tried it on me once.

I spotted her from the shop window loitering by the door, so I was more than ready for whatever she had in mind. I pocketed my halfpenny chews before I left the shop and pretended to carry something in my hand. She pounced and I punched, catching her a wallop on the side of her face.

All afternoon in class, she kept nudging me saying, 'Ah'm goanie tell of you,' until I told her to shut up or I would wallop her again.

By the end of the afternoon she was developing a 'keeker' of a black eye and, as we left the playground, she ran out to her waiting mother whining and pointing at me, 'She did tha-at, she did it, her.'

Her mother rounded on me, with Isobel giving me that 'now yer for it' look, and demanded to know, 'Did ye bla-ack ma Isobel's eye?'

'Yes I did,' I replied, then slipped into the vernacular, 'an if she tries tae pinch ma sweeties agin, ah'll bla-ack the ither yin tae.'

I intended to stand my ground, but Isobel's mother turned on her, shrieking, 'Whit huv ah telt ye aboot tha-at, whit, whit?'

The poor girl got slapped and yelled at all the way down the road, I almost felt sorry for her, but she never pulled that stunt again.

Mum would sometimes give John and I a threepenny bit each for sweets, you could get a lot for threepence. One afternoon, I brought Mum a lollipop known as a 'tooth-breaker', a pink and yellow ball on a stick that was as hard as concrete. It lived up to its name, for Mum broke one tooth off her dentures. It was never repaired, I suppose because it was a back tooth and it was years before she got new ones.

For a penny you could get two large gob-stoppers, which changed colour as you sucked through the layers. It was nothing unusual to see children popping them in and out of their mouths to check on the colour changes. They lasted for ages and were too large to crunch until almost three quarters gone. That meant that it was sometimes necessary to put them into a convenient pocket to go into class, but later it was not too difficult to pick the fluff off the sweet before popping it back into the mouth. If our teacher took a while to come into class after break and we were brave enough to sneak one in, we could have an impromptu game of boules on the wooden floor. When your turn was over, you had to rub off any grit etc. on your cardigan sleeve before popping the sweet back in your mouth. The sweet was popped out again when your next turn to 'hit' came round. Nobody knew the meaning of hygiene! There would inevitably be a whiny child who would plead, 'Gies a sook o'yer gob-stopper,' but somehow that did not appeal to me at all. If a person was being told something that ought to give them pause for thought, the discourse would end with an admonishment, 'stick that in yer gob an' sook it,' being the variation of 'stick that in your pipe and smoke it'.

Chocolate was something of a luxury and a thing we rarely had. I was pea-green with envy when John had to go to the hospital for his ligament stretching operation. I almost cried when I saw him in traction, but lost all sympathy when Dad gave him four half-pound bars of chocolate. Surely I could have some, but then John was bound to give me a piece. Did he thump! He just sat there gloating over the chocolate and I secretly hoped it would make him sick.

He had been taken into New Stevenston hospital and when he was shown where his bed was, the parents were told to leave. Visiting was strictly limited and, 'would you please not telephone, this is a busy ward'. The ward was like a prison camp with a tyrannical ward sister and an even worse matron. Dad had called it Stalag 17, but I expect people made sure they did not stay there any longer than they could avoid. I think the hospital motto must have been, 'Get your patients well, make their stay hell'. God help any child that had an untidy bed, Matron ruled the roost and the staff were terrified of her.

John survived the experience for two weeks in Stalag 17,

then he had several weeks in plaster and a leg-iron. He had to endure taunts from local kids of 'toe dancer' and 'hoppalong', but he had heard it all before. His main gripe was having that contraption on during his school holidays and, of course, not being able to do his paper round. When the plaster came off there seemed to be very little improvement and Mum declared that he was not going to go through that ever again. Years later it was discovered that his hip and spine were out of alignment and nothing was wrong with his legs. When I hear of doctors practising, I think I know exactly what they mean!

We had an odd assortment of pets, for brief spells thanks to John's comic swappings. We had an albino rat with the colouring of a Siamese cat that we called Ratty. He was used to being handled and we loved to watch his antics. For his part, he enjoyed human company and was fond of viewing his world from a human shoulder. He would endlessly fuss and preen his fur and whiskers, and was very particular and proud of his tail. It was the tail that almost put me off, but anyone who thinks that rats are dirty just does not know them. I expect it is the places the rats frequent in the wild that are dirty. Fluffy took a dim view of it all and we realised that if we kept Ratty, his days were numbered, so John swapped him for another pile of comics.

The next 'critter' we had was a goldfish, got from a rag-and-bone man who exchanged him for a pile of old newspapers.

Local parents had to be vigilant when his blue van appeared on the estate and he rang his bell. He had goldfish and balloons for exchange and no scruples whatsoever. It was not uncommon to see father's best 'Sunday' suit being sneaked out, to be retrieved by an irate parent, and a glum looking rag-and-bone man taking back his balloon. That would be followed by sounds of whacks and yells coming from the offender's house.

If you exchanged for a goldfish, it usually lived until the next day, but John was luckier, his survived for a few weeks. Happily it was still swimming around its bowl when John returned from the hospital and no, we had not overfed it, or done this or that!

However, one morning John had rushed off to school, not noticing (we thought) that Goldie was floating on his side. Mum gave me a florin to call in at the pet shop on the main street on my way home from school, for a replacement. I was to

176

try and pick a goldfish that looked the same. I usually got home before John, but it would be a rush and I hoped that the shop had some goldfish.

I was sure I was the first out of school that afternoon and I ran nearly all the way to the shop. By the time I reached it I had a stitch in my side and stumbled into the shop gasping for breath. The shopkeeper peered at me over the top of his spectacles, saying,

'Crivvens, is auld Nick efter ye, hen?'

I explained between gasps that I needed a goldfish quick, before my brother got home from school. I had to explain why – seemed he had all the time in the world, I had not. I looked into a glass tank that held about twenty goldfish and pointed to one. A notice leaning against the tank read, '2s. each'. He caught one and I said pointing, 'No, no, not that one – that one.'

About six fish later when the shopkeeper was getting a bit fraught, he caught a goldfish that seemed to fit the bill.

'Michty me,' he grumbled, 'whit diffrince diz it mak' which wan ye hae?'

'It hus tae look lik' the wan that's deid,' I told him.

'Guid sakes, whit ever nixt?' he declared.'Oh do please hurry up,' I begged.

'Huv ye a jeely jaur*?'

'No,' I replied, 'ah've jist come frae skale.'

Before he could decline the sale, I ventured, 'Lend us yin mister, ah'll bring it back.'

'Oh, aw'richt, but mind ye bring het back.' I thought he would never hand the jar over, I gave him my florin and fled, up the main street, on to the road past the allotments, up the farm road then down Gowkhall like, as the man said, 'auld Nick' was after me.

I reached our path, no sign of John – good. I rattled our letter-box knocker expecting an immediate response. 'Oh no, she can't be out,' I thought, 'not after what I've been through.' Mum opened the door and I rushed in.

'Oh good,' she said, 'you've got one. Hurry up or he'll be here soon.'

I dashed upstairs and went to the bowl on the window-sill at

---

* jam jar

the top of the stairs. Mum had removed the 'departed', cleaned and refilled the bowl ready for me to plop in the new arrival. I told Mum I had to return the jam jar and she told me to do it on Saturday morning when she would find some more jam jars to give to the man.

We had about five minutes to spare, so I collapsed into a chair, with Mum and I in fits of giggles. Typical John had dawdled home with a friend and arrived about twenty minutes later, by which time we were bored with the whole thing. We eventually heard him use his key to get in, I giggled and Mum said, 'Shush, now.'

He paused at the top of the stairs for what seemed like ages, then rushing up the passageway he burst into the room saying, 'Goldie, huv ye seen Goldie?'

'What about Goldie?' asked Mum as I smothered a snigger.

'Well,' he said in disbelief, 'when ah left this mornin' he wiz floating on his side – deid.'

Mum let out a howl of laughter, exclaiming, 'Halleluia, another miracle!'

I nearly fell off the chair laughing.

John said rather huffily, 'Whit's up wi you twa?' then stomped off to his room. We never did tell him how Goldie recovered, but I think he had his suspicions.

Dad had been very subdued, we rarely saw him and when he was home, he busied himself with 'do it yourself' jobs. Mum said he was waiting for the news to go into a military hospital near Edinburgh, for help with his shell-shock trouble. It was a hospital for 'war damaged' people who came from all of the armed services. Meanwhile Dad indulged in causing mayhem with a set of tools that consisted of a hammer, saw, set of screwdrivers, hand drill, nails, tacks and far too many staples! The staples were huge ugly black things about half an inch wide, mounted on insulating tape. When Dad discovered insulating tape, he used it and the staples all around the flat. Dad's attempts at electrical installations would give even the most hardened safety officer nightmares.

Mum refused point blank to plug in, or switch on, anything Dad had fiddled with. He installed wall-lights either side of the fireplace, 'who needs rawlplugs when a six inch nail would suffice?' He used quarter-inch heavy duty cable (I think he wanted to link up to the national grid) which was fixed to the wall, at two inch intervals, with the aforementioned staples. This installation went down the wall, all along the top of the fireplace then down to a plug and socket. He joined the two lengths of cable by twisting the wire ends together and covering them with insulating tape. They might not work, but they certainly would not fall off the wall like the ill-fated bookshelf did. It was all the cat's fault, he kept jumping onto the bookshelf with his big clumsy paws!

I could not understand why we needed a bookshelf, we had a few of Mum's religious books that were useful for steadying wonky furniture, drawers full of dated magazines and tracts that no one read, so why put up a great, ugly, slightly askew shelf? Dad manufactured the shelf from one of the old tea-chests that had come from Corsham, every home should have one! The holes the shelf left when it came down were big enough to put books in.

Mum kept fretting about what the man from the council would say about the damage. When the rent collector came, he had to be left at the door, Mum did not want him to see what had been done.

I was given the dubious honour of doing the grand 'switch on' of the wall-lights. I expect the parents had discussed it and decided that I would be least missed if they blew up. I did not care, I plugged in and switched on with a flourish – nothing! We realised that the lights had a pull-cord at the side, so Dad pulled the cord nearest him and one set of the wall-lights came on. As neither of us had gone up in smoke, John pulled the other cord and the other set of lights came on. It was a pity really, for it boosted Dad's confidence and there was no stopping him. It was not long before we discovered that we could have the ceiling light or the wall-lights on, but not both. We also discovered that the wall-lights could not be switched on for very long as the smell of burning rubber was just too awful.

His next triumph was a bathroom electric fire. It was a wall-mounted one, with a pull on-off cord. Again the cable and staples, but this time he excelled himself. It had come all down the wall, from about four feet above the bath, along the bath edge, stapled to the wall, then down to the skirting-board level. He complained of there being no socket in the bathroom, but never mind, he could knock a 'ole into the kitchen and use the

179

socket there. He miscalculated the positioning of the socket he wished to use and ended up with three holes. The holes that were of no use he bunged up with newspaper, then he hit a snag.

'There's always a snag,' he informed me.

The stupid gas pipe was in the way, it was no use, he would 'ave to ease it over a bit. That was the last straw for Mum, no way was he touching the cooker or the gas pipe. So be it, he would just 'ave to go round it.

The cable, of course, was not long enough, so he just had to make one of his twisted wire joints covered with the black sticky tape. It was just amazing what he could do with a roll or four of insulating tape. The cable came through a hole that the cat and one of his pals could get through, then was stapled at about four-inch intervals along the skirting board then up the wall near to the socket. We all had to view his handiwork, how clever it was!

'See, nowhere near that dratted gas pipe,' he informed Mum, who was eyeing it with suspicion.

I pointed out that, as the plug was in position when the cable was stapled to the wall all neat and tidy, it was impossible to remove the plug to use the socket for the kettle or iron.

'Always findin' fault,' he niggled.

Mum sniggered and I left the room. Dad solved the problem by yanking out the two top staples together with some plaster from underneath and we gained two more holes.

When he wearied of converting the flat into a war zone, he turned his attention to outdoor activities and bought himself some gardening tools.

Mrs McKissock from next door had complained at length about the weeds and tall grass, so Dad set about tidying up the strip of ground between our path and her beautiful front garden. He informed her, after her 'aboot time' comments, that he could not manage the back as it was too much, it would need a mechanical digger. It had been left untouched by the builders, with heaps of soil and rubble all over, and nature had taken over.

I was relieved that he was not going to touch it for that was my favourite play area, my jungle, and was a haven for all sorts of wildlife. I found wonderful things in there, huge grasshoppers that made Mum shriek when I showed her them, and a large toad that was very friendly. His favourite perch was on my shoulder, but I had to stay still. I would sit amongst the long grass with the toad in my lap. I once carried him off to show to Mrs Powell, who lived next door to Mrs Mac. She laughed and told me I should kiss it, it might turn into a handsome prince. I told her I would rather keep the toad.

'Verra wise, verra wise,' she said laughing. One afternoon during my school holidays, I found a large spider, so I went off to ask Mum for a jam jar. 'No, no,' I said as she offered me one, 'ah need a big yin.'

'What for?'

'Somethin' ah found in ma jungle.'

As I left the kitchen, she called out to me not to bring it indoors – whatever it was.

It was ages before I found the spider again and I managed to coax it into the jar so I could have a closer look. It seemed not to mind being examined and I wanted to show it off to someone. Mrs Powell always seemed to like my 'finds' so I would take the spider to her before I freed it. I knocked on her back door and Mr Powell answered. I was told 'his missus was oot and what was it I wanted?'

'To show her this,' I said, holding aloft the jar.

Mr Powell went as white as a sheet, then to my horror slumped to the floor. I went next door and hammered on Mrs Mac's door. Mr Mac opened the door with, 'Whit's up wi yous, ur ye on fire or summit.'

'It's Mr Powell,' I spluttered, 'ah think he's fainted.'

I was still clutching my jam jar and Mr Mac peered at it then gasped, 'Geez, ye didna' show him tha-at, did ye?'

'Aye,' I replied lamely.

'Nae wunner he's oot cauld, huv ye nae mair sense lassie?'

'Ah'm sorry,' I whined.

Mr Powell began to come round.

'Be off wi'ye,' said Mr Mac, 'an tak' that thing wi' ye, afore he sees it again.'

I took my prize specimen back to where I found it and watched as it scuttled off. I wondered how a grown man could faint at the sight of a black furry thing that had eight legs.

John heard about the incident from Mr Powell's son, Charlie, who also told him that his dad had been a prisoner of war in Korea for some months, and he was tormented by his guards with large crawly things. I felt really awful about it and told Mum, who insisted I go and apologise. It was the following day when I went to knock on Mrs Powell's door again, this time without a jam jar. My knees were knocking and I expected a right telling off.

It was Mr Powell who opened the door and when he saw me he said, 'Oh, it's you, ye huvnie got onything in a jeely jaur huv ye?'

I replied in the negative and he went on, 'The missus thocht it wiz dead funny, she says ye're aye gettin' things oot o' that waste groond, cry it yer jungle.'

I told him it was bung full of wonderful crawlies.

'Aye, weel, ah'm no wantin' tae see ony mair o'thame, thank ye verra much, so be aff wi'ye.'

When I returned to our flat, Mum wanted to know what Mr Powell said. I told her that he did not want to see any more of my 'finds'.

She replied, 'Aye, him an' me both.'

To give Dad his due,he worked really hard to clear the strip of ground next to the fence between us and Mrs McKissock. The fence was a stretched wire one and I liked to sit on it to admire her garden, which was immaculate. There was always a lovely display of flowers and the lawn was like a bowling green. Fluffy liked her garden too, much to her annoyance. She would yell at me from her front window, 'Yous git aff that fence, an' git that moggy aff ma gairden!'

Dad had removed bucketfuls of stones and rubble and managed to level off the ground. He sent me off to the hardware store on the main street to get a bag of grass seed, saying I could keep the change from a half-crown. There was fourpence left, so I bought a packet of flower seeds, night scented stock. He left a small patch by the gate for me to plant the seeds and by the time they were through and ready to flower, he had gone.

He had been admitted to a military hospital in Fountain-bridge, near Edinburgh, and would be gone for three years. We would be told when we could visit him.

At last school was out, it was to be a glorious summer, the best of my entire childhood.

Because of Dad's D.I.Y. disasters, we nicknamed him 'Bodger' from a cartoon series in the daily newspaper. It was a nickname that remained with him for the rest of his life.

26

As Dad was to be away for a while, arrangements had been made for his wages to be paid directly to Mum, with a small allowance going to him. It was unbelievable, Mum had never had money from him, and the small wage she had got from her job at the school in Corsham went on housekeeping. She had to eke out every penny. Heaven only knows what he spent his money on, but it was certainly not his home and family, at least, not his legal one. We had suspicions about his 'goins on' for years, but he was too clever to be found out. We hardly knew ourselves, we had regular meals, even the cat gave up foraging, and John and I got pocket money. Mum was forever asking, 'What did he do with his money?'

She began to stock the larder and the coal cupboard. We had things like tins of fruit in the pantry, and could have fresh fruit also. Oranges were not allowed when Dad was around, as he could not stand the smell of them. Seems he had made himself ill, pigging them, on a visit to Gibraltar whilst he was in the Navy. He informed us that they were a waste of money. I once asked him if we could have apples or bananas, his reply was, 'Nope, I don't like 'em, never did like fruit.'

John sometimes bought apples with his paper round money, but Mum and I never had them.

We rarely had salads or greens, seems Dad did not like them either. Mum said he liked only a honeymoon salad – lettuce alone.

Mum was like a school girl, I had not realised she could be so much fun, and I had never seen her look so happy. It was as if a ray of sunshine had broken through a black cloud.

We had been learning a song at the end of term, 'There's

nae luck aboot the hoose, there's nae luck at aw', there's little pleasure in the hoose, when oor guid man's awa'. I sang it for her, changing the last line to, 'there's little pleasure in the hoose, when oor man's no' awa'.' Even John was behaving like a human being once more, no sulks or gloomy silences, he could be such a sullen boy, it was good to see him having some fun.

I actually enjoyed going round with Mum on her door knockings. We spent a lot of time around different parts of Motherwell, amongst the families of colliers and steelworkers. As school was out, there were plenty of playmates, and Mum was content to let me go and play, whilst she went door-to-door. There was none of the 'I don't want you mixing with those sorts', and I met all sorts.

We spent one afternoon calling at a row of miners' cottages, so-called 'but an' ben' type cottages. Two main rooms, one for living, with a small kitchen area, and an alcove for a bed, and one room to sleep in. You washed in the sink of the kitchen area, and the lavatories, usually shared by two or more families, were outside at the back. To bathe or to do laundry meant a trip to the municipal baths.

Behind this particular terraced row of cottages were allotments full of vegetables and flowers, and the occasional garden shed known as 'faither's hut'. Immediately behind the boundary fence, about twenty yards from the cottages, was a huge ugly coal bing* that went the full length of the cottages.

A small boy came up to us, and asked Mum if I could go and play. He was grubby looking, covered in coal dust and I was sure she would say 'no'. I was wrong, she said, 'All right, but don't wander off.'

We went around to the rear of the cottages, past the gardens and along a track, to where a group of children were playing. They were taking turns at sliding down the bing, on old tin trays. I noticed a couple of them had pieces of corrugated iron, but it looked great fun. I watched them, two or three at a time, clamber up the skiddy surface of the black grime, to reach a ledge further up, almost half way up the bing. It was tricky, trying to place the tray on the ledge, climb aboard, and with a helpful shove, slide down precariously to the grass below.

---

* slag heap

185

A couple of boys who were using corrugated sheets looked like they were really enjoying themselves. The older looking one came over to me and asked, 'Hey you, wid ye like a shot oan it?'

I replied, 'Ah'v no' done that, ever.'

'Och it's easy, the wurst ye kin dae, is fa' aff,' he enthused, adding, 'ye kin git really clarty*, but ye'll no hurt yersel'.'

I followed his advice, the most difficult part was clambering aboard the sheet of corrugated; getting clarty was easy.

I spent the whole afternoon with those children until Mum came looking for me. She took one look, and exclaimed, 'Jist look at the state of you!'

I expected to get told off, but she just chuckled saying, 'You've obviously had a lot of fun.'

I told her excitedly what I had been doing.

'It wiz great an' ye can git really clarty.'

'So I see,' she said and laughed.

She had bought some socks and underpants for John and me. Normally when I played outside, I did not wear socks, sometimes no shoes or sandals either, just bare feet, as did a lot of children during summer. We could walk on hot coals with the hard skin we had on our feet.

It was quite a novelty for me to have knickers that could stay up by themselves, without the help of a safety pin, but somehow I never felt secure without that pin. Needless to say, my new white socks were as black as the bing I had been sliding down, and my plimsolls unrecognisable.

One girl had noticed my white socks and remarked, 'Jings, jist look at her socks,' then to me she said, 'We dinnie hae socks in summer, only cissies wear socks.'

I almost socked her. It was at this point that the boy had invited me up the coal bing, I noticed that he too wore socks and thought, 'we cissies must stick together.'

About one week later we returned to the same row of cottages to call again at the ones where Mum had left a magazine or tracts. I asked if I could go and play and was told, 'Yes, if you can keep clean. Ah'm no' goin' oan a bus wi' summit that looks like a chimney sweep.'

I promised to keep clean and off I went. It was a Saturday

* dirty

morning and I was surprised that I could not find a playmate, the place was ominously quiet. I returned to the door I had left Mum at and knocked. The woman who answered informed me, 'She's nixt door, hen.'

When my second knock was answered, I saw her sitting in the room as the woman told me, 'Come awa' in the noo.'

The room seemed very dark as there was only one small window, but my eyes soon adjusted to the gloom. The door to the 'ben' was closed and the curtains were drawn across the alcove. I wondered if it was perhaps because the bed was unmade. Although it was June, there was a fire in the grate and the lady was drying washing by it. Outside it was a beautiful clear day and I wondered why she did not hang the washing out to dry, but then, my mother never hung washing outside. The lady behaved as if I was either deaf or not 'all there' and enquired, 'Wid the wee lassie like a drink an' a piece an' jam?' Mum replied, 'I don't know, why don't you ask her?' She turned towards me and raising her voice asked, 'Wid ye like a piece an' jam, hen?'

Ever the opportunist, I replied, 'Oh, yes please.'

Mum usually bought pan loaves, the bread I was offered was from a tall white loaf with hard black crusts top and bottom. We used to have it when we first arrived in Scotland, I liked them but nobody else did, so we had pan loaves – tin loaves for those from S.O.T.B.!*

My eyes nearly popped out of their sockets when the bread was handed to me. The strawberry jam that looked home-made was about half an inch thick. I was used to a mere scraping, Dad would have a fit if we piled it on that thick, it was absolutely marvellous.

Mum asked if I had found a playmate and I told her there seemed to be no one about.

'Och no,' chipped in the lady, 'het's the miners' gala the day, therr a' doon toon fer the parade.'

'Oh,' I said to Mum, 'could we go?'

'No,' she replied, 'we are on the Lord's work.'

'Fiddlesticks,' I niggled, 'kin the Lord no tak' a day aff?' She flashed me on of her 'killer' looks and I shut up. She then asked the lady why she had not gone.

---

* South of the Border

'Oh, ma man's werkin' the day'n he'll be in fer his denner the noo.'

Mum jumped to her feet saying, 'Oh dear, you should'uv said, we'll no' keep you.' She was motioned back into her seat with, 'Och bide a while, ah'd like fine fer him tae meet yeez, we dinnie git mony visiturs. Himsel'll be hame soon, he's jist at the pit doon the road.'

'Himself' turned up about fifteen minutes later, covered in coal dust. I made a mental vow never to marry anyone who had anything to do with coal, the wretched dust seemed to get everywhere, he seemed to move in a cloud of it. He was obviously not expecting visitors and I got an instant impression that, like my Dad, he was capable of playing to the gallery with a 'Mr Nice Guy' act. He might hoodwink Mum, but he did not fool me, I was instantly wary of him. We were introduced and as I made to shake his hand, I noted that at least that was free of coal dust.

I watched as he seated himself down and opened his piece-box (lunch box to those from S.O.T.B.). His wife must have read my face, for she said as she poured him a mug of treacle-thick tea, 'He aye comes hame fer his piece oan day shifts.'

I was a bit puzzled for he did not give me the impression that he was the loving attentive sort, more likely he was keeping tabs on his spouse. I had only just met the man and I did not like him one little bit.

After some time he said to his wife, 'Gie the missus (Mum) a cuppa lass, an' the wean a piece an' jam.'

I was about to decline as I had just demolished a huge wedge of bread and jam, but decided it may be prudent to keep quiet about it. The lady seemed to be nervous in his presence, and I could smell a rat, a tall dark rat, covered in coal dust, wearing tackety boots. I considered that had he been an inch of a gentleman, he would have removed the said boots as he came indoors.

Being a 'people watcher', I was quick to sense an atmosphere in that room. If Mum sensed it, she was not letting on, but whatever it was, the room almost stank of it.

The bread and jam was handed to me on a plate with, 'Here hen, git that doon ye.'

I thanked her and had a feeling that she was relieved that I made no mention of my previous slice.

'Braw jam,' I quipped.

'The missus maks it hersel',' said Coal Rat.

I wondered how on earth I would manage to eat it, I was so full from the first one.

The adults were exchanging niceties and making small talk, so I got up and taking the plate with me, went for a wander around the room. I looked at the knick-knacks on the sideboard and spotted a framed photograph. It was one of the couple taken some years before, for the lady, who was smiling, had teeth. He was grinning his 'Mr Nice Guy' smile and was arm-in-arm with a slim, pretty girl by his side. Could it be the same lady?

I imagined her now to be in her mid-thirties at most. She was a large cumbersome person, absolutely toothless, with lank unkempt hair, that according to the snapshot, had once been long dark curls. She had what was locally known as 'tartan legs' from sitting too close to the fire. It was only the expression in her eyes that told you it was the same woman. How could someone so pretty let herself go like that?

I recalled something I had once read in a poem a long time before, 'beware the smile on the face of a tiger', and involuntarily shuddered. What would another ten years or so do to that woman?

I came to the curtained alcove and stopped, there was something unnerving about those closed curtains. I mentally rebuked myself, thinking, 'Don't be so melodramatic, probably the bed is just not made.'

Curiosity or just plain nosiness got the better of me, I just had to peek through those curtains. Oh, what a relief! No dead bodies or skeletons, just a bed that was made! I was about to withdraw my head when the senses went into overdrive, I was being watched!

I peered into the gloomy alcove which seemed to measure about ten feet wide by eight feet deep. The bed was at one end, with a small chest of drawers and a wicker chair in the opposite corner. I could not see much detail as it was so dark, but the feeling of someone being there was overwhelming. I say 'someone' for had it been an animal, it would have acknowledged my intrusion, by either fleeing or coming up to me.

I had decided I was being silly, when I saw in the farthest corner a huddled shape. I moved in behind the curtains, peering into the corner at a small human shape. All I could see clearly were the whites of the huge, staring eyes, I almost yelped with fright.

We had been in that cottage for almost two hours, and the lady had made no mention of a child, nor had there been any sound from the alcove. I peeped out at the adults who were deep in animated discussion, if I knew my mother, it would be her 'this system of things' speech, and how only her kind would inherit the earth. With what I had seen of the earth and its people, she was welcome to it, the rest of mankind would be destroyed. Only the righteous would enter the New World, she seemed to forget that Jesus died to save sinners, not the righteous.

I seemed to have been forgotten, so I withdrew behind the curtain once more. My eyes soon adjusted to the gloom and I saw the child, still huddled in the corner. I realised I was still clutching the plate of bread and jam, so I approached the shape, I now could see was a girl, and proffered the plate. A small hand reached out and took one half of the slice, and ate in silence. I thought she might be about my age, but when she stood up, she was head and shoulders taller. The large-eyed, sombre expression had not altered during her eating, or getting to her feet. She came close, staring at me, and I felt that there was something oddly menacing about her. I offered the remaining piece of bread, and she took it furtively. She reminded me of a scared little rabbit, as she nibbled through the bread, never taking her eyes off me.

I whispered, 'My name's Bobbie, whit's yours?' She placed the index finger of her right hand against her lips, shaking her head. The only sound that had come from her was the sound of her breathing, and it occurred to me that perhaps she could not speak. I whispered again, 'I'm here wi' ma Mum, she's selling religious magazines.'

It was no use, there was no response from her, and I supposed she must be deaf also. I wondered how I could communicate, and sat down on the edge of the bed. I sat on something hard, something I had not noticed in the gloom, and moved over to see what it was. The girl had moved up closer quietly, and was standing almost over me as I made to shift off the hard object. I pulled out a long, wide leather strap, which had been laid across the bed. I stared at it for some seconds, then it dawned on me why Coal Rat came home for lunch, and why the child had been huddled in the corner.

I turned to look at the girl and jumped in alarm. She was glaring at me with a look I could not understand. It was not hatred or fear, but something of both. Something of that girl's expression made me shiver as she towered over me. I got to my feet and left her in the alcove, still standing staring at me.

As I went through the curtains, going through the centre where they met, I called out to Mum, 'Mum, Mum, there's a girl in there!'

'Eh what?' then niggled, 'Don't interrupt.'

I had stopped her in full flight, right in the middle of her conversion tattle and she was annoyed, for I had quite spoilt the effect.

Undeterred I continued, 'There's a girl in there, we have been here ages and we did not know she was there.' Before Mum could comment I turned on the lady, who was looking very vexed, and demanded, 'Why is she there in the dark?'

She wrung her hands as she replied, 'She's bin a bad lassie, she's tae git the strap frae her faither.'

I turned on Coal Rat, 'So, that's why ye came rushing hame fer lunch.

He laughed as Mum said, 'Bobbie, stoppit.'

He laughed again and told us, 'She hud twa whacks afore ah left this mornin', ah'd nae time tae belt her right.' He laughed again adding, 'It'll keep, ah'm oan day shift.'

It was all I could do not to punch his sniggering face. Not satisfied with punishing the girl for whatever she might have done, he was terrorising her.

Mum coughed and flicking through her Bible whilst peering at it myopically, she said, 'Come now, we must get on.'

I was dumbfounded, a child was being ill-treated and brutalised and she could not care less. It was fairly apparent that it was not for the first time either. Mum continued to flick through her Bible, probably looking for Solomon's advice on child rearing, then said, 'Now, where were we?'

I was livid and wanted to wreck the room, so I had to get out of there before I broke something. Coal Rat was grinning, the caring mother was wringing her hands and the temptation to cram that book into my mother's mouth was unbearable, so I made for the exit.

For Mum's benefit I snarled, 'When ye've managed tae make thae twa intae God fearin' Christians, ye'll find me ootside.'

Before I slammed shut the door, I yelled, 'It could tak' furriver!'

I sat on the fence bordering the allotments seething with rage, there was no doubt in my mind at all that the child was being ill-treated. I suspected that she was a bit backward, possibly even deaf and dumb, it was too awful to contemplate. My mother's attitude to it all and the fact that she seemed to be totally unconcerned, was the turning point in my relationship towards her. Our relationship had never been good, but now I was going to give her hell. I was still seething when Coal Rat went past less than ten minutes later. He saw me sitting on the fence and called, 'Ah'm aff noo, yer mither'll be oot soon!'

I called after him, 'D'ye ever see Auld Nick doon that mine o' yours?'

'Oh aye, oh aye,' he said, laughing as he walked down the path.

I hollered after him, 'Ah hope he bites your arse!'

Mum emerged after about ten minutes and when she saw me, she said sweetly, 'We'll go for a bun an' drink, then home.'

'Jist hame,' I snarled at her.'

'Very well,' she replied.

I always enjoyed going into a cafe, but that was before all this happened, now I wanted none of her company or her silly chit-chat and I sure as hell did not want her damned religion. It was days before I spoke to her and then only because I had to. She asked in exasperation, 'Whit on earth is up wi' you?'

'Nuthin,' I snarled and then added, 'Ah've jist realised that it's thanks tae folk lik' you, the world is fu' o' atheists!'

She had not the slightest idea what I was talking about.

27

The Summer of '51
Door Knockers

There were many callers round the doors on the estate that summer and it was the first time I met an 'onion Johnny'. He was one of many who came from France to tour Britain on bicycles selling their wonderful onions. The onions were braided into long bunches and draped over the handlebars and the rear panniers of their bicycles. They always had time for a chat and Mum usually bought a few onions. I felt it was a pity Dad was away in hospital, for he would have been delighted to chat to them. He had spent a large part of his boyhood in France and to him it was like home, he would have loved a natter in French.

One very hot afternoon Gracie, myself and several other children were playing by the side of the road. We had sat in a row along the kerb to discuss everything in general and nothing in particular, when one of the boys leapt to his feet exclaiming, 'Quick, quick, rin an' hide, afore the bogeyman gits yeez!'

With that he was off running towards home, with his smaller brother in hot pursuit, yelling, 'Wait fer me, Jamie, wait fer me!'

'Dinnie look!' yelled Mary as she too fled homewards. She called to Gracie and I, 'Dinnie look, yeez'll turn tae stane!'

'Whit the hair-ile's up wi' thame?' I asked Gracie, thinking it was some new game.

'Het's the bogey man,' said Gracie, getting to her feet and adding, 'Ah'm awa' hame, ye cummin'?'

She shrugged when I replied, 'Dinnie be sae daft.'

I was left sitting on the kerb, so I got up to look out for the 'bogey man' – who ever heard of such a thing?

'Come you on!' called Gracie from her safe hiding place in the jungle.

'Awa' an' bile yer heid!' I told her.

All I could see walking down the pavement on the opposite side of the road was a small brown man, carrying a large suitcase. He was wearing western style clothes, but had a turban on his head. Bogey man, my Aunt Fanny! He was a door-to-door salesman, goodness knows there were enough of them around.

He crossed the road and as he drew level with me I said, 'Hello.'

He had been looking down at his feet as he walked, but looked up startled as I spoke. We exchanged smiles and neither of us turned into stone!

I asked, 'Ur ye selling brushes an' things?'

He replied, 'No, haberdashery.'

'Whit's tha-at?' I asked, never worried about displaying my ignorance.

He laughed and replied putting down his suit case, 'Let me show you.'

He opened the lid out flat to display all sorts of sewing implements, threads, mending wools. It was a portable Aladdin's cave to me, with objects I had never seen before.

He watched me peering at the contents of his suitcase and asked, 'Do you like them?'

'Oh aye, ah've nae money tae buy onythin', but if ye gaun tae ma mither she'll buy somethin'.' I then added absent-mindedly, 'Ah'm aye needin' elastic.'

I declined to explain why!

He looked puzzled and I realized I had quite forgotten to drop the vernacular, so I repeated, 'If you call on my mother,' I pointed to our door, 'I am certain she will buy something, we always seem to need elastic.

He grinned, replying, 'Thank you little lady,' and closed up his suitcase. He went to our door and sure enough Mum was buying something from him.

When the scaredy-cats reappeared, awestruck, they were amazed to find that I had not turned into stone, even after talking to the 'bogey man'.

'Wur ye no' feart?' asked one of the boys, 'He's a bogey.'

'Dinnie be sae daft,' I told him, 'he's no'a bogey, he's a wee

194

Paki' sellin' haberdashery.'

He gaped at me and then asked, 'Whit's haber-haber thingy?'

'Good grief,' I replied haughtily, 'don't you know what it is?' and swaggered off to find what Mum had bought. As I walked away from him I overheard him tell his brother, 'Sometimes that yin talks awfie queer.'

Mum had bought some reels of thread, a needlecase and, of course, some elastic! I looked at the coloured threads and remarked, 'They'll mak' a change frae huvvin' tae mend aw'thing wi' black or white threed.'

She replied with one of her glares, guaranteed to turn milk and confound the mighty.

Answering a knock on the door was quite a novelty during that summer. Usually we had to keep quiet and pretend were out as it was most likely to be someone for money Dad owed them. Nothing ever seemed to be paid and Mum could hardly show her face in the shops on the main street, so I was sent on errands. She had been quick to notice that when I went to the fishmongers for two shillings' worth of white fish, I came out with considerably more than she ever did. She was not the one to miss out on an opportunity and her infamous 'pride' was noticeably absent when a visit to the local chippy was planned; Apart from being quicker than John, the lady serving always piled on the chips for me.

We had all sorts of salespersons call on the estate and late one afternoon a man in a small van came ringing his bell calling, 'Pears, get your honey pears!'

I thought June was an odd time to be selling pears, it would be September before local pears were ready, but Mum gave me a florin and told me to go and see how many I could get for that.

I had to chase half-way across the estate to catch up with the van and I wondered if a bag of pears was worth having a heart attack for.

I asked breathlessly, 'How much?'

'Fower fer twa boab,' I was told.

'That's expensive,' I complained.

'Well,' said the man pulling a face, 'they've come frae Sooth Africa.'

'Ah'll hae a shuftie, afore ah buy ony.'

195

He held aloft a large yellowish pear which seemed to be all right, so I nodded saying, 'Ah'll hae four o' thame and ah'll see them as ye pit them in the poke*.'

'Oh my my,' he sneered, 'bin aroond huvn't ye?'

'Aye,' I replied, 'an' so huv thae pears.'

I had been gone about twenty minutes and on my return Mum greeted me with, 'Where *have* you been?'

I told her I had to chase the van half-way across the estate.

'Hoomph,' was her only response.

That 'hoomph' was her masterpiece. Her response to anything she had no reply for. A sound of dissent used for any number of little aggravations, and I seemed to be a constant aggravation.

She lifted a pear out of the bag, peered at it then exclaimed, 'There is no honey in this!'

I could not believe my ears but the look on her face told me she was not joking. I yelled at her, 'Ur ye daft, of course thurr isnie ony honey in them, how the hell could thur be?!'

She niggled on. 'Only four, only four!' she shrieked.

:'Well,' I told her, 'ye telt me tae git whit ah could fer twa boab. Ye should go yerself, then ye couldnie moan.'

She glared at me and I waited until she had taken her first bite before I suggested she should first wash it – another glare. She had eaten almost half of it with John and I watching her. I thought how funny it would be if a fat maggot popped out of it, brandishing an African spear. I smothered a snigger as she barked at us, 'Well, go on, have one.'

We did not have to be asked twice, we had had tinned pears before, but that was my first 'real' one. It was rock hard and later gave me a bellyache, possibly retribution for that maggot wish.

The said bellyache gave me a day off from Mum's door knockings and I was left at home after a lecture on do's and don'ts. John went out saying that he would not be gone long and Fluffy and I were left in charge. John had left me his prized Dinky toy cars to play with, which was quite an honour as usually I was not allowed near them.

Fluffy started to pester to be let out, the kitchen window being ignored when there was a human about to open doors for

---

* paper bag

him. I followed him down the passageway, then down the stairs to the main door. We had almost reached the bottom step when there was a rat-a-tat at the door. I nearly tripped with fright, but remembered that opening the door was one of the 'don'ts.'

It could not be Gracie for she would have called out. Fluffy was mewing and scratching at the door, so I opened it enough for him to dart out. Having done that it seemed foolish not to brazen it out. By not opening the door, it would show that I was alone, I thought.

A tall young man with dark hair was standing on the outer landing. He seemed taken aback as I opened the door, but said, 'Oh, er, is yer ma in?'

I replied, 'Yes, but she is very busy, can I help?'

He stared at me and I realised I had forgotten the 'twang'. I wondered why it was, that people stared at me as if I came from another planet whenever I chose to speak properly. He gave me the name of the man he was looking for, adding that he had been given our address.

I realised he wanted the man who had lived there pre-viously. My mind was racing, thinking of the loose floorboards in my bedroom which had been his hiding place for stolen goods, and of the local gossip that had him in prison for his efforts. Should I tell, or not let on?

He announced that his name was Peter and he had been given two addresses to call on, adding with some embarrass-ment that he had just come out of prison. It was my turn to be embarrassed as I told him that the man he was looking for was, according to the neighbours, in prison himself. He roared with laughter and then asked if neighbourly gossip knew what he went 'in' for.

'Buggery,' I told him.

He stared at me in shocked disbelief, so I explained, 'He'd hidden all the stuff he had pinched under the floorboards an' the polis found it.'

He howled with laughter and burst out with, 'You mean burglary,' in between hoots of laughter.

He laughed so much that tears streamed down his face and I wondered what was so funny.

I was amazed to see that Fluffy had come back up the steps and was rubbing up against the man's legs. 'He must be all right,' I thought, for that cat was very particular about the human company he kept.

When Peter managed to compose himself, he asked me if I knew the other man. I told him I did not, but I knew where he lived, and stepped out of the doorway on to the landing to show him the house. It was in the next street, but we overlooked the back gardens and I pointed to the one he wanted.

'Oh, right, thanks,' he said and made to leave. I watched him go down the steps, two at a time and then walk up the path to the gate, thinking that he kept some odd company. The man he was now going to call on had been in prison, we had seen the police digging up his back garden searching for lead and they seemed to be at his house an awful lot. He had a thing about lead flashings and he simply could not bear to see them wasted on church roofs. Whenever another church roof let in rain, the police would be round to dig up his garden. Surely, nobody worth his salt would use the same hiding place twice! I wondered if the police had tried his floorboards.

Peter had just reached the gate when he about-turned, ran back up the path and bounded up the steps two at a time to ask breathlessly, 'Huv you an older sister?'

'No,' I told him, 'jist an older brother.'

'Oh shoot, wouldn't ye jist know it.' He grumbled, rummaging in his jacket pocket and producing a wrapped toffee which he handed to me with, 'Here kiddo, huv a toothbuster.'

That was another 'don't – take sweets from a stranger, but he seemed all right and he was not exactly a stranger. I knew his name and where he was going to live (he hoped).

He bounded down the steps once more calling out, 'See ya!' then stopped again.

'Hey whit's yer name?' he asked.

I told him and he said, 'Really?'

I nodded, he shrugged his shoulders then without comment waved and walked off.

I saw Peter several times during that summer, it was always, 'Hi kiddo,' with a rummage in his pocket for a toffee.

One evening Mum and I were coming down our path to go to one of her meetings, when Peter and the man he lodged with walked by. I got the usual 'Hiya kiddo' and to Mum he said, 'You got a nice kid there missus.'

Mum ignored him, but when the two men were out of

earshot, she asked a bit snootily, I thought, 'Do you know tha-at man?'

I replied, 'Aye awb'dy kens him, d'ye no'?'

She declined to comment.

The next day she carefully quizzed me about how I knew him. I told her how we met, leaving out the bit about the 'burglary'! She thought for a minute then said almost to herself, 'Hm, I don't know.'

'Don't know what?' I asked, getting just a bit rattled. Before she could reply, I told her that I knew of his reputation and how he was supposed to have an older brother in London who was a gangster. She opened her mouth to speak and I went on to tell her that it meant nothing to me, I liked the Peter *I* knew, despite whatever gossip was going around.

Mum gave me an odd look and said nothing.

Later that year he left the area and some months after his departure we left also. I never saw him again, but some years later we were to hear about him and his activities, which made national news. What we knew of him later made me feel very sad. One little incident reported in the newspapers convinced me that it was the man I had known so briefly. After one of his crimes he had stopped to open a tin of salmon to feed the household cat before letting himself out of the house.

I cried the day he died and Mum told me we would never know what made him walk down such a path as the one he finally chose. I never forgot him and somehow can never look at a wrapped toffee without remembering: 'Hiya kiddo, huv a tooth buster.'

Our only other caller worth remembering was another travelling salesman with a difference. Mum had gone to answer a knock on the door and I heard her talking to someone. She did not usually chat to anyone at the door, so I had to go and see who it might be. When she saw me at the top of the stairs, she told me to fetch her purse. I fetched it and saw that the caller was a man in his mid-thirties, very dark and quite handsome. He had a gold ear-ring in one ear and I supposed he must be a gipsy. He was selling curtain wires, stretchy type wire covered in plastic sleeving, for light-weight curtains. As he measured a length out for Mum, he reached for his wire cutters and positively gaped at me. He looked away quickly and fumbled in his box for the hook and eye attachments for the curtain wire. I watched his every move, thinking what an improvement it would be from the string across our window tops tied to nails at either end. Mum was telling him she would manage to fix it as he put the wire and fitments into a paper bag. As he handed the bag to Mum, he stared at me once again.

Mum said, 'This is Bobbie.'

We grinned at each other and he asked Mum, 'Does your child have the gift?'

'Dunno,' said Mum, adding, 'Ah jist know she knows too darned much fer her ain good.'

He stared at me again and said, 'My name is Leo, you know, like the lion.'

I laughed and told him, 'My name is Bobbie, you know, like the footballer.' We said our goodbyes and he left.

'What gift?' I asked Mum.

Nobody ever gave me a gift and I wondered what he had meant.

'Oh, he meant are you psychic,' she said.

'Oh that.'

'What a bore,' I thought, but went on to Mum, 'Most folk hae that, they jist dinnie ken they huv.'

'Hoomph.'

John and I did most of Mum's errands during that summer and one of mine was to go and pay for two bags of coal that had been delivered. She gave me a ten bob note, told me to fetch a receipt and off I went. I was to call at his house not the yard. I had not far to go as they lived in our estate. My knock on the door was answered by the son who was in my class at school. I felt very embarrassed when I saw him for I was sure he must have known that it was unusual to get payment from us. His father had called on several occasions in the past to collect payment and we had to pretend to be out as Mum had no cash to pay him. It was Saturday morning, so his dad was probably out and about on his lorry selling coal.

He had left the door open and gone off to his mother, telling me that she kept the books and would give me the receipt. I knew that he had three sisters, one older and two younger than him. I heard a door open and out came the elder sister. She was absolutely stark naked and it gave me quite a shock, as I quickly averted my eyes. She had seen me at the door and

200

wandered up the passageway to say 'hello'. I turned round not knowing where to look. She seemed to be quite at ease in her altogether, so I pretended not to notice. I only just managed to stifle the giggles that were threatening, but curiosity was not so easily quelled.

'Whaur's yer claes?' I asked her.

She shrugged, replying, 'Ma mither's washed aw'thing an' it's no dry yet.'

'Huv ye no' a nightie or summit ye could pit oan?' I asked, stifling another giggle.

'Naw,' she grumbled, 'she took that tae.' I never saw her mother but just heard her yell, 'Come awa' frae that door'n you in yer nuddy!'

I was thankful the boy's clothes had not been laundered that morning.

When I returned home I went indoors to give the receipt to Mum and she waved a letter at me, saying, 'It's from Dad, we can go and see him next week.'

28

The Summer of '51
Get Well Soon, But Not Too Soon!

I felt a pang of guilt as I had not given Dad a second thought and he had been gone almost a month. Mum told me we would go to Motherwell by bus, then use the rail warrant to get to Edinburgh. I rushed off to find John to tell him, but when I got outside our flat I realised I had no idea where he could be, so I sat on the fence to await his return. He would not be long as it was almost dinner- time.

Mrs McKissock knocked on her window, calling, 'Git aff that fence – you!'

As her window was shut and she could not hear me, I said, 'Awa' an' bile yer heid, ye auld crow.'

Charlie Powell came round from the back of the flats just then and when he saw me asked, 'Ur ye bein' cheeky tae Mrs McKissock?'

'Aye,' I replied, 'whit's it tae you?'

'Good fer you, hen, good fer you,' he enthused, adding, 'She's an auld witch so she is.'

I told Charlie excitedly that we had been told we could visit my Dad in hospital.

'Hospital?' shrieked Charlie, adding, 'awb'dy kens he's in the loony bin, he's aff his heid.'

It hit me like a bolt of lightning. I had often suspected that something was wrong with Dad, but to hear my worst fears voiced by someone who had obviously been listening to gossip was such a shock. I gaped at him speechless. My facial expression must have relayed my shock to Charlie, who had gone a deep pink colour as he stammered, 'Ah'm s-sorry, ah sh-shouldnae huv said that, het's no your fault he's daft.'

That did it. I got off the fence and screamed at him, 'You

wid be daft if ye'd seen half o' whit he's seen! Ye jist ask yer ain faither aboot the war, he'll tell ye, ye hateful fat scunner*!'

Charlie rose to the bait, probably his red hair had something to do with the fact that he was easily riled. I felt like punching him, but he kept his distance as he shouted back, 'Who ur ye cryin' a scunner, ye wee shite?'

I yelled back, 'You, ye great fat mingin' toley!'

Charlie's mother appeared on the scene at about the same time as John, who yelled at Charlie, 'Lave ma wee sister alane, you!' Charlie complained as he got a slap from his mother.

'Ah Ma, it's her, she startit it.'

His mother yelled at him, 'Ye deserve a skelp on the ear, pickin' oan a wee lassie, ye should ken better!'

He went off glowering as John asked me what was going on. He seemed as shocked as I had been about the general consensus of opinion on the state of Dad's health. We told Mum about it and she angrily told us never to discuss our business with anyone.

I cannot recall much of the journeys to and from Edinburgh, only the effect the hospital had on me. Everywhere I looked I saw people with limbs missing, people swathed in bandages, in wheelchairs or on crutches. I had difficulty in determining the sex of some of the people in the hospital grounds. It was a beautiful day and many patients had been taken outside either by staff or by their visitors. It was appalling to see their deformities.

We found Dad's ward and saw him before he saw us. He was perched on the edge of his small iron-framed bed looking thoroughly dejected. When he turned and saw us, he stood up and came to greet us with that old familiar grin creasing his face. I noticed how pale he looked and he seemed very frail.

There was an awkward silence that was broken when he said, ''Ave you 'ad a good journey?'

He seemed pleased to see Mum, but he only barely acknowledged John and me. They needed to talk, we were told, there was something wrong I felt, so I hovered close enough to hear their conversation without making it seem like I was eavesdropping.

It seemed that Dad was vexed about his salary being paid

---

* sickening person

directly to Mum, with only a small allowance for him. She had as yet received only one payment, but it would continue that way as long as Dad was in Fountainbridge.

I suppose he had hoped that he would be free of the responsibility of us whilst he was away and could do as he pleased with his money, which was what usually happened anyway. He was getting quite agitated, telling Mum that it was not right or proper for a wife to 'ave money or property.

I remembered his scrapbooks of newspaper clippings, especially the one about an edict passed in the House of Lords, stating that housekeeping money was the property of the husband as was any money saved from housekeeping. He had underlined it in red ink, before gumming it into his collection.

As far as I was concerned, I felt that each Lordly gentleman who had supported that edict should have his Lordly backside kicked by housewives like my mother, who rarely saw any housekeeping money.

Mum was retaliating, 'But we have to have something to live on, what d'ye want with money in here?'

Dad informed her pompously that 'e would decide w'at she needed, w'at she could 'ave and a wife 'ad no say.'

I wished that Mum would whack him in the mouth, but I imagined it never occurred to her, she just replied, 'Yes dear,' to his 'I'll provide', and added scathingly, 'Like you always do.'

Mum was never violent, but she had a tongue that could cut steel. By this time I was openly listening and John was hovering in the background. After an uneasy silence when both parents realised I had heard everything, Dad announced that we would take a stroll about the grounds. As we went off, Dad began to chatter about the hospital, but said nothing about his treatment. He was in a ward with about twenty other men of various ages and backgrounds. They were all shell-shocked or suffering from the effects of traumatic experiences. One man would dive under his bed at every little noise, another would have hysterics if he heard bells or sirens of any sort. The man in the bed next to Dad cried if anyone shouted at him. Dad went on to tell us that he was a 'trusty' which meant that he could bus into town for errands for other inmates. He had to wear a uniform and observe curfew times. I wondered if it was a hospital or a prison camp.

I felt sorry for Dad even though I had reason enough to despise him, but somehow that did not seem right. He could be very quiet and gentle, never loving, but sometimes very comical. He would sing and dance, fooling around like an overgrown schoolboy. I decided that he had never been shown any love, so he did not know how to respond to other people. I never once heard him speak ill of anyone, not even his own parents. When he spoke of them, which was rare, the things he told us were said as a matter of fact with no emotion whatsoever.

Somewhere along life's path Dad had been lost, he kept reaching out for help, but his reach was never quite long enough. There was a small frightened child locked in a man's body, we could never see or understand the shadows that haunted and tormented him. I hoped his stay in hospital would help him find his way.

I can never forget the way I felt walking about the grounds of that place, or the sights I encountered. To me they were the terrible and pathetic leftovers of mankind's inhumanity. When I read or hear of people glorifying war, I just think of that place and feel heartsick for them.

We had walked past a group of men, five in all, three in wheelchairs and two on crutches. Dad announced solemnly that they always went around together and only had three legs between them; for some reason John and I found that very funny.

We were still giggling some minutes later and as we followed two men who were limping, we imitated their walk. Mum, who was walking behind us, said not a word as she cuffed us both round the ear. We did not need to be told why we got clouted, her face said it all. Later, when we were back home, she told us it would be some time before we could see Dad again, the hospital authorities would write and let us know when we could visit.

John and I played happily around the estate and when I could not find a playmate, I would tag along after John and his friends, as I had done in Corsham. One afternoon we walked with some boys to look at the new television booster mast at Kirk o' Shotts. It was not very far and to us the mast seemed to be most impressive. There had been several car accidents caused by drivers peering up at it instead of watching the road.

I thought Gracie might like to see it, so some days later we set off on her small bicycle that had belonged to her sister Nancy. We had spent days wheeling up and down Gowkhall, I had got the hang of it and two skinned knees, but Gracie just could not seem to keep her balance. I pedalled the bicycle, whilst Gracie sat on the pannier, feet on the chain guard cover, clinging on to me like a limpet to a rock.

It goes without saying, really, that we did not get far. We had gone up the back road, past the farm lane and into a side lane to avoid the traffic, not that there were many cars then. As we rounded into the lane, there before us was an incredible sight, the sort of thing a roving camera-man or artist dreams about happening upon. It was a tinker's caravan, full of boisterous, sun-browned children. It was painted with many bright colours and had all sorts of pots and pans hanging from hooks around the door. Some children were playing on the grass verge where a very large shaggy horse had been tethered, just next to where the shafts of the caravan were resting, and some were leaning out of the stable type door of the caravan. They seemed only to speak Gaelic and I told Gracie that they could be Irish. She was very worried by them and was fretting to return home, so we gave up on the idea of an adventure to see the television mast, remounted the bicycle and set off precariously back the way we had come.

Another attraction was a disused mine-shaft on farm land about a mile from the estate. Some of the railway track for the coal waggons was still in place, but overgrown with weeds. A spider-work of metal supports still remained over the actual shaft, where the coal trucks would have been hauled to the surface by means of a pulley system, most of which had corroded away. The opening of the shaft had been sealed with huge wooden planks that looked like railway sleepers, but the passing of time and the elements had left the whole structure in an extremely dangerous condition.

Like all forbidden or known danger areas, the mine-shaft was like a magnet to inquisitive children. Looking back, I am amazed that nobody was injured or killed, for we spent hours playing around that area. There was always a daredevil show-off clambering up the spider-work to hang precariously over the gap in the woodwork covering the shaft. By leaning over the edge of the sleepers one could peer down into the cavernous

206

gloom. We would hurl boulders down into the gloomy darkness and then count the seconds until we heard a splash. John once told me that he reckoned it was a hundred and fifty feet down to the water level.

The dares got more and more outrageous and one afternoon a crowd of older boys managed to move a derelict coal bogie along part of the track. They heaved and hauled at it until it was just a few feet from the shaft entrance, then, with them all shoving from behind, managed to push it on to the rotten wood covering. It sat there for what seemed an eternity with some boys trying to push it further on to the sleepers, when we heard the creak of the rotten timbers giving way under the weight of the bogie. Two boys flung themselves clear as the timbers started to move and the bogie slowly descended along with the timbers into the now gaping cavity. There seemed to be an eerily long pause before we heard a tremendous splash. Nothing was said, as we all looked from one to the other and knew how near to tragedy those boys had come. We all realised that two or more of those boys could have slipped or tumbled with the sheer effort of pushing that bogie, and gone over the edge with it. John grabbed at me saying, 'We're going – now.'

All the way home he nagged at me never, never to go near that place ever again. He need not have bothered, wild horses would not get me near that place, I had nightmares about it for weeks.

Some days later we heard from one of the boys who had been involved, that the authorities had fenced off the whole area with barbed wire, putting up warning notices at intervals along the length of the perimeter. He had gone home and told his father what happened and he had called into the police station to complain about it. Seems there was quite a scene, the constable told the boy's father that he was responsible for the safety of his child and should keep him away from danger areas. The father argued that it was not good enough, he felt it was the responsibility of the coal board to render the area safe and the police to ensure that they did it. The tenant farmer whose land it was on added weight to the argument by saying that he did not want his sheep straying on to it in the dark. Mother-in-law yes, but not his sheep.

There were rumours about the shaft being filled in, but instead it was fenced off and forgotten about. The ground for miles around Lanarkshire must have been riddled with shafts and tunnels and probably still is. I wondered why they did not fill them in with slag and get rid of all those ugly coal bings that sullied the landscape. I once mentioned to Mum that one day one of those bings would slide, probably into a row of cottages.

'Don't be silly, dear,' she replied.

29

The Summer of '51
Meanwhile, Down on the Farm

It was the Glasgow fair, that time of the year when Glasgow closes for the last two weeks of July. There is a mass exodus to all points of the compass, anyone arriving in the city on the first Monday could be excused for thinking there had been a holocaust. If you were lucky enough to spot another human being it would most likely be another unwary tourist. Those Glaswegians who had not departed to get Scotland a bad name, would probably be holed up at home recovering from the weekend binge, financed by the two weeks' holiday pay, and could not be expected to surface before Wednesday.

Gracie had gone to Rothesay, to the seaside with her family. I had heard nothing else for weeks, but I was quite envious as I had never been to the seaside and could not remember anything of the sort from Rosyth. It seemed strange to me, living on an island and never having seen the sea.

There was a dearth of playmates so I had to find my own amusements. I had wandered up to the farm lane and noticed a small haystack near a large barn. It was a lovely summer's day and I fancied climbing on to that stack, but soon realised that it was not possible. It was just a heap of hay, like a stack that had collapsed. I walked around the end of the barn and almost into a man coming from the opposite direction. I had seen him before and recognised him as the farmer.

'Well hello,' he said grinning, 'an' who ur you?'

I blustered, 'Oh, ahm jist huvvin' a look see, ah'v no touched onythin'.'

He grinned again and I added, 'Ah've naeb'dy tae play wi,' 'cos o' the fair.'

'Zatright?' he asked, adding, 'Well, ah've yin lik' you at

hame, she's naeb'dy tae play wi' either, come oan and meet her.'

He motioned me to follow him. I was a bit wary as I had been warned about strangers, especially men.

He called again, 'Come oan, she's up at the hoose.'

I followed at a safe distance, all the way up the lane to the farmhouse. I thought it would be all right, I could wait by the door and if anything seemed amiss, make a run for it. I heard him call out to someone in the house and after a few minutes a girl came to the door, shyly peeping from within.

The man, who I assumed was her father, pushed me through the doorway to meet her, saying, 'This is Rita, whit's your name?'

I told her it was Bobbie, but she just stared and said nothing. She was as dark as a gipsy and I must have seemed very strange to her. My mother had told me I was pale as a wraith, so we were exact opposites. She was my height and build but she was two years younger.

Her dad invited me in to meet the rest of the family, a mother and Rita's two brothers. He told them he found me in the haystack looking for a pal and Rita laughed.

To make conversation, I told her she was lucky to have two brothers. She gaped at me, then exclaimed, 'You want them, ye kin tak' the wee buggers hame wi' ye!'

Her parents seemed embarrased so I ventured, 'Ah huv an older brother.'

'Dae ye like him?' asked Rita.

'Sometimes,' I told her, adding, 'Ah cry* him "big both-er".'

I do not know if it was the small brothers that prompted her, or the need to escape, but she blurted out, 'We've some piglets, wid ye lik' tae see them?'

The nearest I had ever been to a pig, the four-legged variety, was a slice of fried bacon on a plate, so I was keen to see them. They looked so delightful in pictures and I could not wait to see the real thing. I had heard that some of their little habits were less than endearing, but then, I knew several humans who were less than endearing!

We went off with her father round the back of the cow sheds

---

* call

into a smaller building. In what looked like a cow byre was a stall full of straw and recumbent upon it was a huge pink and black pig. She lay on her side with a look of contentment on her face, while a hoard of small pink squealing piglets jockeyed for a position at a filling post. I was enthralled, I kept trying to count them, but there was such a frenzy of activity, it was quite impossible. Rita's dad asked if I would like to hold one.

Every child at some time should be allowed to hold a piglet, it was utterly enchanting. The warm, pink, wriggling bundle emitted a series of alarmed squeaks until I snuggled it in my arms. Mother was totally unconcerned, probably because there were so many more, but Rita's dad replaced the cute baby, asking if we would like to feed the other pigs. Oh boy, would we!

We walked out of the building and went around the back to where there was a row of styes that had a stone wall all around and an entry gate. Inside was sectioned off with fencing into separate styes. I climbed on to the gate to look over the wall and found myself looking right at the most ill-natured boar you could ever wish not to come across. Rita's dad laughed, saying, 'Aye, keep well awa' frae that yin, he's a nasty bit o' work.'

He fed him first with a pail full of the most disgusting looking gunge I had ever seen, it smelt just awful. I could hear that ugly brute snorting and grunting and thought that it had once been a cute piglet.

The same applies to a lot of people, they start off nice enough . . . !

Rita's dad remarked, 'We've tae feed him furst, or ther'ud be an awfie stooshie*, it's no' ladies furst roond here.'

The 'ladies' created a lot of noise when they caught a whiff of that gunge, and knew that food was on the way. He came out of an outhouse carrying a metal pail in each hand. I wondered where all that gunge came from, but felt it was better not to ask, I was already feeling quite queasy.

'Your turn noo,' he quipped, placing the pails on the ground beside us.

He left us, and returned to the outhouse. The feeding area had troughs all around the fenced perimeter, with ranch type fencing, and it was a simple matter to tip the contents of the

* uproar

211

pails into the troughs – too simple!

I persuaded Rita to do the job properly and get inside the feeding area, that way she could fill up the troughs at the far end. Over the fence she went, as I handed her a pail full of grey, reeking sludge. I was about to warn her to 'mind yer feet', I had noticed the slimy looking surface of the paved area, when down she went, pail and all. She landed in a sitting position, legs akimbo, covered with sludge from the waist down.

'Oh dear,' I said.

What Rita said is best left to the imagination, I cannot spell half of it and could not comprehend the rest.

By the time her dad re-emerged carrying two more pails I had shinned over the fence to go to the aid of the unfortunate Rita. The pigs were showing too much interest in her for my liking. They were having fun, feeding time had never been such a laugh, and I swear those pigs were laughing.

When Rita's dad saw us he guffawed with laughter and had to put down his pails as he gasped, 'Michty me, ah'v twa mair pigs than ah thocht ah hud.'

He drew his sleeve across his face adding, 'That ud gie that crabbie auld boar a fricht, right enough.'

The pigs were crowding around us as he laughed and laughed, the tears running down his face.

Neither Rita nor I thought it was the least bit funny, my plimsolls and socks were covered in sludge. I did not like the way Rita was looking at me and felt that if I did not move, and quick, I would end up like her, covered in it. I made a hasty exit back over the fence, and as I cleared it, Rita yelled, 'Ah'm goany molocate* you!'

'Now, now,' said her dad, still laughing as he told us, 'Yer mithers'll murder yeez.'

He went towards the farmhouse, saying, 'C'mon yous, git cleaned up, yer mangkit†.'

We followed him into the house and he told us to stay by the door. By this time we were both giggling. It was a large house with stone floors and we were left in a part of it that was not being used.

Rita's mum appeared with a basin of water, towel, soap and

---

* batter
† filthy

a nailbrush. She really laughed when she saw us and we all stood there laughing fit to burst. She told Rita she had best get in a bath and she would put her clothes into a sink to soak, she then turned to me.

'Oh dear,' she said, 'whit'll yer mither think o' us? Jist look at yer gutties*.'

'Och dinnie worry,' I told her, 'it'll wash aff.'

I told them I should go home as my mother did not know where I was and I left.

I thought that would be the last I would see of Rita, but her dad came after me as I went up the lane. I expected to be told off, but instead he asked, 'Will ye come again?'

I did not know what to say, so he continued, 'She's hud a great time the day, an' she needs someb'dy tae play wi'.'

I replied, 'Aye, OK, ah'd like tae come again, but no' tae feed pigs.'

We both laughed, saying, 'Cheerio.'

When I arrived home, I found Mum in the kitchen.

'Whit's that awfie smell?' she asked as I walked in. I told her it was me, I had been feeding the pigs up at the farm and had found a new pal.

'It wiz a right laugh,' I told her.

'Good heavens!' she exclaimed, 'Did ye git in the trough wi' them?'

'Not quite.'

Rita and I spent many happy hours that summer playing in and around the farm. The fallen haystack provided hours of fun. We would clamber up the straw bales in the barn, cross over to the far end and from about eight feet up, leap off on to the fallen stack. Apart from a few scratches it was enough to keep us out of trouble.

One afternoon we lay sprawled in quiet companionship, when we both became aware of an odd noise. We both shushed each other to listen, sure enough it was a series of little squeaks.

'Mice,' I told Rita.

'Uh uh,' said Rita, shaking her head, 'Rats.'

'Rats!' I shrieked.

'Oh aye,' she replied quite unconcerned, adding, 'We're owerrun wi' them.'

---

* plimsolls

213

I stared at her and she shrugged, saying, 'Dad's aye pittin' doon pyzen, thurs nae shiftin' the buggers.'

'How awful,' I said. 'Ye'd better go and git yer Dad, he'll no want them in his barn.'

I had enjoyed my brief encounters with John's pet rat, but did not relish the thought of being overrun with them. We both set off to find her dad and came across him in the pig pens. The piglets had grown unbelievably fast, and I remarked upon that fact to be told,

'Oh aye, they'll soon be oan someb'dy's denner plate.' I thought, 'Who'd be a stockman?'

We told him about our 'find' and he said he would be along to deal with it. I preferred not to be around when he did, so I announced that I would be wanted at home. Rita told me that she would be away for two weeks, being mercenary I thought, 'Oh well, Gracie will be back soon.'

Rita's dad said to me, 'Ye'll be seein' her at the skale, she's changed frae her previous wan, too far.'

'Ah'm no gaun tae nae skale,' spat Rita.

Her dad laughed, saying, 'She's no' awfie plased aboot it.'

A string of expletives and obscenities came from Rita. I was shocked, but her dad shrugged, saying, 'Ah dinnie ken whaur she hears language like that.'

I laughed and told him, 'She'll no' ken hoo tae spell thae words, if she disnie gaun tae the skale.'

The look I got from Rita sent me hurrying for home. I did not see much of Flora or Mary and a lot of other Catholic children seemed not to want to play with a 'could be' protestant, there seemed to be a lot of ill-feeling between the two factions.

Just prior to the Glasgow fair, Mum had taken me into Motherwell where we were supposed to be going to visit someone she knew. We found the road we were looking for, full of people milling about and lining the kerbs. I noticed rows and rows of milk bottles and beer bottles lined up in the gutters. Mounted police were parading up and down the road, trying to keep the throngs of people from spilling over on to the road. I wondered if it was prior to a football match, but the crowds seemed to be waiting for something or someone. Most shops had boarded up their windows, so I guessed it must be a visiting football team's coach they were waiting for. Whatever,

214

I could not help thinking that it was a good place not to be!

I asked Mum what was going on and she said she was not sure, but we had to get across that street. She took hold of my arm and tried to steer me through the throng. As we pushed forward, a woman turned to Mum and said irritably, 'Haw Missus, ye shouldnie hae a bairn oot in this, d'ye no' ken whit day tiz?'

Mum ignored her and pushed me even harder. We had almost reached the kerbside when a policeman grabbed her and me, saying, 'Git that bairn oot o' here, ur ye mad, wumman?'

He pulled us both back through the crowd and pushed us into the nearest close*.

'Stay there,' he ordered Mum, 'until they've gone.' And with that he left.

Mum had started, 'Until who's gone?' then to herself, mumbled, 'Of course.'

I noticed that his police hat had been replaced by what looked like a riding hat and he was carrying a truncheon, obviously he was expecting trouble.

I could hear a band playing and as it came nearer, all hell broke loose as the crowds lining the street went wild. I asked Mum what it was and she shouted to be heard above the din, 'Orangeman's walk!'

Her attempts at further explanation were drowned by the noise from outside, whistles, catcalls, shouts and the sound of breaking glass. An assortment of missiles including bottles and bricks flew past the entrance as we huddled inside, it was all quite frightening. The screaming mob outside followed the parade down the street to the accompaniment of ambulance sirens. It was all over in about twenty minutes. The band miraculously had managed to keep on playing despite the flying debris, but there was an ambulance just outside collecting a sorry looking victim of the parade still clutching his banner. I heard one woman exclaim, 'Oh my, that wiz great fun, ah scored a hit wi' an egg.'

Then she told her companion, 'Ah dinnie lik' chuckin' bottles, ah'm no wantin' tae hurt naeb'dy.'

'Aye,' replied her companion, 'it was rerr.'

---

* entrance to a tenement building

I heard one man tell another, 'Och, it wiz nae wurse than an efternin' wi' the auld firm*.'

Mum said, 'That's it, Bobbie, we're fer home, c'mon.'

I asked her what it was all in aid of and she told me to wait until we got home, then she would explain. It was July twelfth, the anniversary of the battle of the Boyne, when Protestant Ulster broke free from Catholic Ireland. William of Orange was blamed for most of it, hence the 'Orangeman's walk'. In many parts of Ireland and Scotland, the flower 'Sweet William' is still referred to as 'stinkin' Billy'. I was beginning to understand why there was so much animosity between the two factions. I thought 'damned religion again', but said to Mum, 'They're aw daft, they worship the same God.'

Then I told her, 'Your lot are aw daft tae, they think they're holier than awb'dy else, an' ur the only wans gaun tae heaven. God must be fair seek o' the lot o' yeez.'

She gave me one of her withering glares as I got up to leave the flat, saying, 'Ah'm awa' tae find masel a wee Ca-athlick tae play wi'.'

I had found the Hever family who lived almost opposite us. From what I can remember, there was a teenage girl, a boy just older than John, a girl my age and two younger girls. I cannot recall any of their names and I never knew or cared what their religious persuasion was. It seemed not to matter and I was always welcomed at their house. The girl who was my age and myself would run errands for her mother. I had got to know her from going to the swings and the play area where the big rocks were. Their back garden overlooked the play area and she told me I could take a short cut home by climbing over their fence and going through the gap between the two houses. It was all right as long as her brother was not around, he used to chase me off, as we did not get on at all.

I had been outside their house, sitting on the kerb with his sister when he came along with a bag of marbles to show us. He was very proud of those marbles, especially the ones he had won. We were being shown the most prized one when disaster struck, he dropped the bag. Out rolled the marbles and one after another plop-plopped down the drain as we looked on aghast. He turned on us in his rage, it was all our fault, but we

* Rangers v Celtic football match

216

could not see how it could be. He swiped at his sister, then made a grab for me. His father who had been walking down the path behind us, yelled at him when he hit his sister. When his dad reached where we were standing, the boy whined, 'Well, they let aw ma boules go doon that condie*.'

The father sneered, 'Dinnie be sic' a big Jessie.'

I had to keep out of his way after that.

Gracie was back from Rothesay full of it. She made it worse by sneering, 'Did yeez no' go nae place?'

She knew fine that we went 'nae place.' She had brought me a stick of rock so I could not really be rude to her, but oh, the temptation.

We were perched on our usual place on the kerb and I had to endure every detail of her scrabblings in the sand.

'Ye ken, it gits aw place,' she informed me.

I replied, 'Really?' but spitefully wished she had got a lot of it in her gob.

She eventually got round to what I had done whilst she was away. That was my cue for revenge and I went on at length about what I did at the farm. She seemed quite put out by it all, I was supposed to have missed her to distraction.

She said huffily, 'Ah got ye a stick o' rock.'

I had already thanked her profusely for it, so I replied, 'Thurs nae rock at the far-rum, but ah'll fetch ye a neep† if ye like.'

She glared at me, replying with a sniff, 'No thank you, verra much.'

We lapsed into silence, broken when she signed, saying, 'Oh jings, only wan mair week an' it's back tae skale.'

---

* road drain
† turnip

217

30

The Summer of '51
Enter, Mac Sporran of Gowkhall

Mum announced one evening, 'It's up early the morn, we're aff tae Glasgow for the day.'

I thought, 'Oh great, the fair's over, the barras will be back.'

It was overcast and drizzling, but Mum said, 'Never mind, jist put on yer school coats.'

We had breakfast and got ready, but when I put on my coat, Mum laughed saying, 'Jist look at that coat, yer growin' ower fast.'

Well really! I was forever being told I was 'ower wee'. She went on, 'Tch, you'll need tae hae another afore winter.'

'Ah should bloody hope so!' I exclaimed.

'Bobbie!' she raged, 'Where do you hear such language?'

Before I could reply she niggled, 'It's that far-rum, that's where, you keep away frae there.' I thought, 'uh oh, better watch it'.

We set off to catch a bus into Motherwell, and then another for Glasgow. I hoped that it would stop raining, as it was such a trial to get my hair dry, and the hood of my coat was too small. Mum tucked my plaits inside my coat, but once inside the bus, I pulled them free. I sat with them brought over my shoulders, to hang down my front, where I could keep an eye on them. Once, after a bus ride into Motherwell to attend one of Mum's meetings, I found a lump of chewing gum, pressed into one plait. It had to be snicked out with scissors, but although it did little damage, I vowed to be more vigilant, those braids were too much for some people.

Mum declared angrily that it was probably done by a 'bobbed-hair bandit'.

By the time we alighted on Sauchiehall Street, the rain had eased off and a watery sun was peeping through the drifting clouds. We went straight along to George Street and the open market at Glasgow Cross, the 'barras'.

John had two half-crowns burning a hole in his pocket, and I had a florin a neighbour had given me for doing odd jobs, and fetching her messages*. Mum had given us a half-crown each, boy were we rich! We did not know which way to spend it.

Since Dad had been away, Mum had given us a half-crown each for pocket money every month, and this was the second time we were given it.

John had his paper round money, which he spent on odds and ends, comics and small toy cars. He would bus into Motherwell, spending threepence each way on the fare, then two shillings for each car. How I envied him that paper round. I earned some cash doing odd jobs, but mostly I was given food for my work. When we had our first pocket money from Mum, John took me into Motherwell with him, to the toy shop he got his cars from. Whilst he spent ages deciding which car to have, I wandered round the cramped little shop, gazing at the shelves of dolls. One particular doll caught my eye, a small, black, piccaninny doll, oh how I longed to have that doll! She was about twenty inches tall, with true negroid features and was wearing a red frilly frock. Her crinkled hair had a matching ribbon, and in her ears were tiny gold rings.

I had never before, or since, seen a doll quite like it. I asked the shop keeper, 'How much is the black dolly?'

'Six guineas,' he replied, without looking up from where John was poring over the cars on the counter.

'May I see it?' I asked.

He looked up, hesitated, then said with a shrug, 'Oh, why not?' As he reached up to fetch down the doll, he admonished, 'Be careful noo, het's real cheenie†.'

I held it very carefully, this was no doll to be played with. I gazed at it taking in every detail, so I could conjure up an image of it whenever I chose. I could never hope to have such a doll, but I could always remember it.

I worked out that if Mum continued to give us a half a crown

---

* shopping
† china

per month, it would take me four years and three months to save up enough money to buy it, by which time it would be long gone.

There was not much I could get for a florin, John was not keen on me buying a small car as I might choose the one he wanted, so I chose a small wicker basket.

The shopkeeper replaced the doll on the shelf, saying, 'Ye'll no hae the doll the day, then?'

I shook my head, I could hear a mental echo of one of Mum's favourite quips, 'it's not for the likes of you.'

At a later visit to that shop, I saw that the doll had gone and I wanted to cry. Instead I just vowed never to go back to the shop and I never did.

We were waiting to cross over George Street, when Mum grabbed me and started to frantically push my plaits inside my coat.

'Whit ur ye daein'?' I raged. It's no even rainin'.'

'Wheesht,' she snapped, 'just you keep that hair in yer coat.'

With that she propelled John and I across the street in unseemly haste, pushing us hurriedly into a baker's shop.

I turned to rage at her once more, but it was obvious that she was upset about something, she looked almost scared. There was a woman behind the counter putting something into a paper bag for a customer, but when she saw Mum she exclaimed, 'Ur ye aw richt, Missus? My, but ye look guy queer, is thur summit wrang?'

Mum went red in the face, blurting out, 'There's a man followin' us, oot there.'

'Geez, whit a nerve!' exclaimed the customer.

'Ah'm fetchin' a polis,' said the assistant menacingly.

'Oh no, if we could jist wait here a minute, ah'm sure he'll be gone.'

The shop assistant opened a door at the rear of the shop, I could see the staircase just beyond and she yelled in the direction of the staircase, 'Haw Harry, git yersel' doon here – noo!'

Harry dutifully appeared, all fifteen stone of him, wrapped in a vest and wearing trousers that were obviously prone to succumb to the force of gravity. Harry was not the trusting type, he was determined to defy gravity with the aid of both braces and belt. He stood sheepishly as he was told off, 'Tch,

220

huv ye no' a shirt tae yer back?' Before he could reply, he was told, 'Awa' and find a polis, this wifie's bin feart wi'a loony trailin her.'

Mum burst out with, 'Oh, it's all right, ah think he's gone, ah cannie see him noo.'

Harry asked, 'Whit frit ye Missus?'

Mum told him that she noticed a man following us as we left the bus station, she got agitated again as she added that he got a pair of scissors out of his coat pocket.

Harry exploded, 'Tha-at bloody swine wiz efter the bairn's hair.'

He pointed to my still partially concealed plaits.

'Is that no awfie?' soothed the customer and before anyone could comment, she went on, 'Ma lassie's a pal at the skale, wha hud wan pigtail snicked aff in the street.' She continued, hardly stopping to draw breath, 'Lang ginger wan, awfie bonny it wiz, pair wee sowell went hame in hysterics, so she did.'

We stared aghast as she continued, 'Her faither cut aff the ither yin an' jist tidied up her hair wi' the scissors.'

She laughed and almost talking to herself added, 'Selt that pigtail fer a fiver an' gied hur a quid, ye ken, hur hair wiz aw' curly wi' nae weight ahin it.'

When she stopped, presumably to breath, she peered at me and told me, 'Ye keep yer bonnie hair hen, dinnie let some useless ticket pinch it aff ye.'

Harry was convinced by Mum that we did not really need a 'polis', so he turned to the shop assistant and said, 'Gie thae weans a cream cookie, Senga.'

I thanked Senga, thinking that her name was as strange as mine, when John nudged me and whispered, 'That's Agnes, backwards.'

The payment Mum proffered was angrily refused, so we said our goodbyes to Harry and Senga and then left.

Once outside the shop, Mum niggled at us to take care not to get cream all down our fronts. I sighed. Could we never be allowed to enjoy anything without a veiled threat or grim warning from one or the other parent?

We eventually arrived at the open market with all its hustle-bustle. The day was almost ruined for me, for I was as wary as a cat and despite the watery sunshine, my hair remained hidden under my coat. Mum told me to 'stay close' and warn her if I saw anyone suspicious.

'Dinnie worry,' I told her, 'if ah see a man wi' a pair o' scissors, ah'll kick him in the goolies.'

'Really – Bobbie!' she exclaimed, but I noticed she was laughing.

John was missing!

'Oh Lord!' exclaimed Mum, 'Where *is* that boy?'

I got the weep, wail and gnashing of teeth routine. I could not help thinking that it was high time Mum changed her reading material, this was Glasgow AD 1951, not Babylon BC! She ranted on, 'Ah knew it wiz a mistake tae come here.'

I thought, 'Blast John, we will never be brought here again', and we never were.

I could not entirely blame John, for Mum just could not cope with the hustle-bustle. I knew 'big bother' would not be far, and 'tag along' knew where to find him even in a crowd.

'Find a pet stall, find John,' I declared.

Sure enough, there he was poking around a barrow that was alive with what looked like four-legged crusty meat pies.

'Whit on earth urr they?' I asked John.

'Tortoises,' I was told.

'Can I have one, mum?' asked John, adding, 'Thur five bob.'

Before she could reply he was telling her, 'Ah huv five bob, ah kin pay fer it masel.'

'All right,' she said, sighing.

I thought he would never finish choosing one, he must have gone over every one on the barrow. Not for John the liveliest or shiniest shelled one, oh no, he had to choose one that looked like it needed a home. Out of about thirty or so tortoises that looked fairly healthy as far as one could tell, John had to select one that was being climbed over and ignored. It was the only one with a damaged shell.

Mum asked, stifling a yawn, 'Do you *have* to have tha-at one?'

'Oh yes,' he replied gleefully, 'this wan is different frae all the others.'

The stall-holder let him have it for four shillings and sixpence as it was damaged.

222

We wandered around the market for some time, but John was anxious to get his pet pie home and Mum was beginning to look a bit frayed.

All the way home John fussed over the thing, but I had to admit the tortoise seemed happy to be off that barrow. I wondered what Fluffy would make of it, lucky it had a hard shell to retreat into.

Fluffy, as I had feared, was not amused or impressed, but discovered a new game. If he poked one of the six protrusions, i.e. head, tail, four legs, all six disappeared into a shell. He would sit behind the tortoise and patiently wait until it re-emerged only to poke it again. Torty had to have a name.

'Something grand,' said John. It would be 'Mac'.

'Huh, that's no' grand,' I sneered.

'Ah,' replied John, 'how about Mac Sporran?'

'Now that *is* grand,' I enthused, and giggling added, 'Mac Sporran of Gowkhall.'

We both giggled, but the look on the cat's face said it all, 'Blooming humans, huh.'

'Poor old puss,' I said, 'how about Fluffykins of Gowkhall, or Pussy Fluff the First?'

As John and I fell about laughing, Fluffy gave us a look of absolute disdain and with a flick of his tail flounced off to make his exit via the kitchen window, probably to raid a neighbour's bin. He was being fed regularly, but old habits die hard.

Mac, as he was to be known, was not averse to raiding the cat's bowl and was fond of milk sops, but only if they had sugar on them. John would return from his paper round with pockets full of dandelion leaves for his pet pie. We discovered that he liked harebells, small bluebell-shaped flowers that grow wild in Scotland, and we would scour the 'jungle' for them and all sorts of other goodies. I asked John how Mac would cope in winter, when there were no harebells or dandelion leaves and was told that by then Mac would be hibernating. He went on to explain what that meant and I found myself wishing I could hibernate and avoid the cold and hunger that seemed to haunt our winters. Maybe it would not be so bad this winter with Dad being away. Since he had been in hospital, we had had regular meals. Mum seemed more at ease and not so anxious to escape to her meetings.

I should have known better, as I had learned at a very early age that good things seldom last, the eternal optimist was in for yet another let-down.

31

Exit, the Summer of '51

The last few days of that summer, before school term restarted, were spent playing with Gracie or Rita, and spending time with Kirsty and Gordon. Something had gone wrong for Mum at her Motherwell meetings and she was bussing to Hamilton. They were a nice enough lot of people and we had some happy afternoons out with them at open air meetings held in the local parks. Someone would give a sermon, but most of the children, myself included, went off round the park exploring.

One Sunday we visited the park that had a miniature railway system, you had to pay for a ride on it, so that ruled me out. I stood and watched as the little waggons, fitted with bench seats, filled up with children, then off they went to chug round the track, the tiny engine's whistle pheep-pheeping at bridges and tunnels.

I was with a younger girl called Elizabeth, who had boarded the train with her grandmother. I wished that I had a grandmother. I had once met Dad's step-mother who seemed a sweet old lady, but I never got to know her. Mum's mother had died long before I was born, but Mum once hinted that the old lady I saw in a mirror in Corsham fitted her description. We had briefly met some of Mum's cousins whilst we were lodging with the Maxill family in Newarthill, but apart from those brief meetings we had no relatives we knew, or who paid us any heed.

I longed to have uncles, aunts, cousins and people I could belong to like so many class-mates, but when I questioned Mum why we knew no one, I was told with a deal of irritation that we had 'disassociated' ourselves from such worldly things.

I waited at the little entry gate for the train to return. When it did about five minutes later, Elizabeth squealed, 'Again!'

The grandmother called me over and told me to climb on behind Elizabeth. I told her I had no money to pay for the ride, but she replied, 'Git oan, ah'm payin'.'

I thanked her and climbed aboard as bid. We were off around the little track and with a blow from the whistle entered the tunnel, then over the bridge, through the second tunnel and back to the miniature station. I was not so rude as to say so, but it was all a bit tame after the real thing, it was hardly the record breaking *Bristolian* or the famous *Flying Scotsman*. I thanked the grandmother as Elizabeth squealed 'Again!' and made my excuses that my mother would be wondering where I was.

We went home shortly after the train ride, but heard at the next meeting that poor Elizabeth had come a cropper on that model train. She had not kept her feet up as she was told to, and a foot had been trapped under the train as it moved off, breaking her ankle. Some days later we visited Elizabeth to commiserate with her at her grandmother's home, which was one of a group of Nissen huts. They reminded me a lot of Rudloe Manor in Corsham, where we had lived in the ex-RAF Nissen huts, and for some odd reason I was overwhelmed with a longing to be back there.

Mum found me collapsed in a fit of sobbing, 'I want to go home, home,' I wailed.

'Oh for goodness sake,' she niggled, 'we'll go home soon.'

'To Corsham?' I asked.

'Don't be silly, dear,' she replied, but she had a really strange expression on her face and for a moment I thought she would sit on the grass beside me and howl too.

I returned from playing at the farm one afternoon to tell Mum that there was a strange man hiding out in the barn. I told her that Rita seemed to know who he was, but would not tell me, indeed she looked like him so maybe he was related to her.

Mum was not really listening for she was poring over a letter that had come in a buff envelope, but she answered me almost casually, 'You stay away from there, you hear? Anyway ye'll be back at school next week.'

Her thoughts were obviously elsewhere or I would have got third degree questioning, instead she waved the letter in the air, saying, 'We've to see yer Dad again.'

I thought 'oh no', and John voiced my thoughts when he said, 'Do we *have* to?'

I daresay it was a bit unfair and disloyal, but neither of us could be blamed for not missing him.

We went off dejectedly to Edinburgh, not knowing what to expect. We found him seated on a bench in the grounds of the hospital, sunning himself like a tourist. He had a hanky on his head knotted on the four corners and I thought he looked really funny. He came to greet us, grinning from ear to ear, full of bounce and vitality. He wanted all the news and what we got up to when he was not around. We told him about the eventful trip to Glasgow, about the tortoise and all the little this and thats of domesticity.

He seemed animated when Mum asked him how he was faring, were they helping him at all?

She was told, 'Fine, fine, flyin' colours.'

I groaned inwardly, I had seen it all before, this was the 'Mr Nice Guy' side of his personality, preferable to his 'Hitler' routine, but he did no fool me for one minute. 'Surely to God, I thought,' he cannot fool clever, experienced doctors?'

We journeyed to Newarthill in total silence, all absorbed with our own thoughts. Mum pale-faced, John was sullen, me – I just wanted to scream. A nagging fear would just not go away; he was not going to be away for the advised three years and no one could force him to do so, at least not without a deal of trouble for all concerned. The summer was fading along with my hopes for a normal, happy family life.

The school term commenced with very little fuss, we met our new teacher and were told where to sit. I was next to a new girl, Margaret, we already had two Margarets in our class. Some new houses had been added to the estate and her parents had been allocated one. I thought she was very lucky, a lovely new semi-detached house, almost opposite the play park and only a short walk to school.

Our teacher was middle-aged, tall and slim, with silver grey hair that she piled on top of her head. Whenever her spectacles were not precariously perched on the end of her nose, they hung around her neck on a chain. She looked like a dowager duchess from out of a fairy tale. She reminded me of pictures I had seen of Queen Mary. As far as I was concerned, she was a lady and I liked her at once, something rare for me as I usually needed time to get the measure of a person.

She went through her register of almost forty names, calling out each one individually. We had to stand up when we heard our name, so she could identify us. I thought she must be clever to remember every one. When it was my turn to stand up, she asked if I was the sister of John Eriksson. I wondered what on earth she could have heard about me and blushed to the roots of my hair.

When I replied in the affirmative, she commented, 'Well, miss, you do as well as him, we'll git on jist fine.'

As I made to sit down, she added, 'I like your hair, it's lovely.'

I blushed once more and thanked her.

She had something agreeable to say to every child and I mentally confirmed my original opinion of her, she was a lady.

I noticed that Elsie was missing and her name had not been called out, so at break time I asked Carol if she knew where she was. They lived quite near to each other, so I was sure Carol would know if anything had happened.

'Oh,' said Carol, 'wan nicht they did a moonlight flit, naeb'dy kens whaur they went.'

She noticed my worried expression and added, 'Dinnie worry, they skidaddled afore her faither got oot o' the clink, he'll no' find them.'

I stared at her as she explained, 'He got sozzled as usual, an' beat someb'dy up, he wiz aye gettin' in fechts.'

I changed the subject by informing her that my Dad was in hospital.

'Oh, whit a shame,' she consoled, 'nivver mind, ah'm share he'll soon git hame.'

'Good God, I hope not!'

'Oh right,' she replied, giving me a funny look.

As the bell rang for the end of break, I saw Rita in her class queue further down the playground and resolved to find her at lunch break.

On Monday mornings we had to collect and pay for our lunch tickets. I noticed that the 'welfare' queue was much longer than the other where tickets were paid for. There was one girl in the welfare queue who, at playtime, had been boasting about her family's new television set. I thought, 'Whit a nerve, I must ask if she gits TV on the welfare.'

She had just turned to one companion in the queue to say, 'You kin git tae watch it,' then turned to prod the one in front of her to sneer, 'But no you, ye're no gettin' tae see it.'

As I walked past her to return to my desk, I nudged her to say, 'If yeez kin afford the TV, ye should pay fer yer denner tickets, no' scrounge aff the state.'

'Ah'll tell of you, ah'll tell ma faither!' she shrieked.

'You *do* that,' I snapped at her, adding, 'If ah hear ye bummin' yer load* again, ah'll tell the whole skale.'

After dinner, I found Rita standing alone in a corner of the playground. I went up to greet her, but before I could, she turned on me like a cat, spitting obscenities with adjectives one might hear at a football match amongst the losing supporters!

'Whit's up wi' you?' I dared to ask.

A child, who I supposed must be in Rita's class, came up to me to say, 'Keep awa' frae her, she's got a clarty mooth.'

That brought another string of obscenities from Rita.

The child went on, 'She's hud a smack frae oor teacher, an' she's tae git the belt frae the heid maister, if she does it again.'

'Oh Rita,' I whined, 'kin ye no' keep oot o' trouble?'

'You bugger aff.'

On Saturday morning I went up to the farm to find out if Rita was all right, and if she had settled in her class. Her dad confided in me that they were at a loss as what to do about her, but added that arrangements had been made for some of her class-mates to visit her at the farm.

I felt that I had been a complete failure and could not help at all, but I still called at the farm most Saturdays.

Our class was to have an outing to the Empire Theatre in Glasgow to see *Peter Pan*, the cost would be five shillings for the ticket and coach fare. I raced home that afternoon to ask Mum if I could go, our teacher had told us we could pay sixpence per week, starting that week. We were to go at the end of October, to a Wednesday matinee.

Mum listened in silence as I told her all about it and when the silence continued, I asked, 'Well, kin ah go?'

'Well,' she started, 'I don't know, you know how I feel about these worldly things.'

I panicked and pleaded, 'But Mum, the whole class is going,

---

* bragging

they will all be discussing it and I, as usual, will be left out.'

She whined, 'You have neglected your studies lately.'

'Whit ur ye talkin' aboot?' I asked, knowing very well that she was using blackmail to promote her crank beliefs.

'Ma teacher thinks ah'm doin' jist fine.'

She sniffed and fiddling with her hair replied, 'Ye know what I mean, your spiritual studies.'

I looked at her for a deliberately long time, then told her, 'That is your choice, not mine, all the threats and blackmail in the world could not force me to believe the garbage you spout.'

She opened her mouth to speak, but before she could, I said, 'If you want a fight, so be it, but one day I will make you pay for all the misery you cause John and me.'

As I made to leave the room Mum stood up from where she was seated. She was white-faced and gaped at me as I said, opening the door, 'If you had said you had no money, *that* I could understand, but to use religion to inflict your will is just disgraceful!'

Shaking with rage I slammed out of the flat and sat down on a step outside, hidden by the stair wall. I thought about what had just happened, how I had addressed her with no 'twang' and only a hint of accent. When I got angry, I could be as vicious tongued as her. I wondered if I had a split personality like Dad, or had she pushed me too far?

I had always felt that I was the cause of Dad's unbalanced moods, but could it be her? I realised with some dismay that I did not like either of my parents, but consoled myself with the belief that that was not so unusual.

I wondered what could be so wrong or wicked about wanting to go to the theatre, or having some fun out of life. Was it a sin to be happy?

On several occasions when I questioned Mum's beliefs, she had told me in anger that I was the Devil's child, wilful and unworthy. If I were the Devil's child, what did that make her – my mother! Dad was wont to tell me how evil I was and how I caused our poltergeist activity. When I refused to pander to Mum's religious whims, she would shriek in rage, 'Be it on your own head!'

Oh dear, oh dear, I had a lot to answer for!

John came along and I slid across the step to let him pass.

'Whit's up wi' your face?' he asked.

I told him, 'The wicked witch of the west is in wan o' her moods.'

He grinned and used his key to enter the flat. About half an hour later John opened the door and finding me still sitting where he had seen me, said, 'Ye're tae come in, tea's ready.'

Mum glared at me and snapped, 'Wash your hands.'

As I did, I thought, 'She talks to me like I was a dog.'

I thought it was sniggeringly funny, how, when we had 'words', I spoke very precisely, hardly a hint of accent, but when I was with her 'holy Joe' friends, you could cut my accent with a knife. She used to squirm with embarrassment and once she commented to one of them, 'Tch, you'd think she came out of the Gorbals.'

'At least thae folk dinnie behave lik' they jist came doon the Clyde oan bikes,' I replied.

We ate our meal in total silence, if I had looked at John, I am sure I would have burst out laughing.

Mum snarled at me as she started to clear the table, 'You kin go to your darned theatre, an' be damned.'

When I did not reply, she added, 'Have your bloomin' sixpence a week, an' see where that gets ye.'

I looked at her mean, pinched little face and replied, 'Thank you, it would be nice, just for once, to be able to actually enjoy something.'

I got my sixpences along with prophesies of hell fire and damnation. I was warned not to try to dodge out of any meetings, seems she just did not get the message. Never mind, I could always use a good laugh and there is nothing like a religious crank for a good laugh.

Gracie was pea-green with envy, she would have to wait until she was up two more classes before she could go on school trips. I told her that she could go anytime she wanted with her parents if they liked – they did not, so I had to endure her complaints and whines:

'How kin ah no' go?' and 'Dinnie go, dinnie go, ah dinnie want ye tae go.'

I pulled her leg, telling her she really could not go as it was *Peter Pan* and you needed to be able to fly.

She gaped in astonishment.

'Whit, ye kin fly?'

'Oh aye,' I swaggered, 'learned ages ago.'

A couple of days later Nancy appeared at our door, bristling with indignation.

'Whit huv ye been tellin' oor Gracie?'

I was bamboozled. 'Whit dae ye mean?' I had forgotten my teasing.

'She's only ben the hoose, greetin'*, 'cos she cannie git up oan the roof tae learn tae flee.'

I laughed and said, 'Oh dear, ah wiz only pullin' her leg.'

Nancy railed at me, 'Ye should ken better, ye ken fine she believes aw' thing ye tell her.'

Gracie came knocking on our door that weekend to inform me that she knew I was telling fibs, folks cannie fly, an' wiz ah cummin' oot?

I told her with spiteful glee that folks could fly in aeroplanes, as anyb'dy wha wisnie daft knew. She blushed beautifully and I felt quite ashamed of myself.

I was having my own little squabbles at school, I was being left out of playground games. I was determined to find out why and after individually cornering and threatening to kill several class-mates, I found out who the culprit was – London Tony. He had told most of the class not to play with me or let me join in anything. On the threat of being duffed up, they complied.

I thought 'I'll give him duff up' and went to find him. I was really cross for he was always after me for his rotten rounders and five-a-side kick about, so what was he up to?

I found him with some of his, and once my, cronies. Pushing them aside, I grabbed him, 'Right you!' I bellowed. 'Whit's your game?'

He stared and I yelled at him, 'What's all this I hear about you not letting people play with me?'

I had forgotten the Glasgow 'twang' in my rage.

His London-cum-Glasgow was as bad as my twang. 'Ah'm no' tellin' ya.'

A crowd gathered as I grabbed him again, yelling, 'You'll tell, orrul knock yer heid aff!'

I let go of him as someone yelled, 'Belt him Bobbie!'

Something in his face alarmed me, and for one awful moment, I thought he was going to cry.

I turned and walked away from him, I wanted to be alone.

---

* crying

It had been raining and we were not allowed in the field, but I needed privacy so I went through the gate, closing it after me. I was perplexed for I could have sworn he looked hurt. Why should *he* be hurt? I was the one being picked on.

I heard the metal gate clang and thought it was the janitor coming to shoo me out, but it was London Tony coming towards me. As he drew level he said, 'Ah'm sorry.'

'It's OK, but what was it all in aid of?' I replied.

His face went very red as he blurted out, 'Because I like you.'

'Good grief!' I exclaimed. 'Do you always ostracise (new word we had learned to spell) the people you like?'

For a reply he asked, 'Why do you sometimes speak so funny?'

I sighed heavily and told him, 'Because I sometimes forget that I am in a foreign land.'

We both laughed and he told me, 'You can be my girlfriend, you're good at rounders.'

I did not know whether to thank him or punch him on the nose.

The entire school somehow heard about it and that our feud, if that is what it was, was over. All over the playground walls, the lavatory walls (at least the girls' as I cannot vouch for the boys') and on the pavements outside the school were drawings looking suspiciously similar in white chalk.

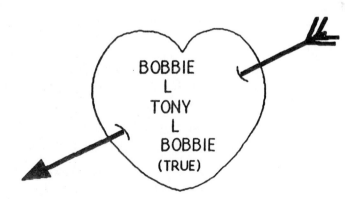

It was days before it rained again to wash it away, I could

have died of embarrassment. I was glad that John had gone up to secondary school in New Stevenston and was miles away. I had mostly played with boys for as long as I could remember, but I came to the conclusion that they were most definitely unpredictable. I could not rest until I found out why London Tony tried to warn off most of my pals.

He told me that he wanted to make sure that I had nobody to play with, so when he came along all gallant, I would be only too pleased to play with only him.

I wondered if they got any better as they grew up and would I ever understand them? I doubted it on both counts.

Our teacher informed us one morning that those girls in the class who could not knit were to be taught how to. That meant most of us. We were to make a knitted kettle holder and the boys were to make calendars from coloured cardboard, painting or drawing their own design. They were to pay two shillings to the school for materials and the girls would pay the same for wool and needles. We could choose from royal blue, red or green double knitting wool that came in skeins which had to be wound into a ball. One child would hold the skein across outstretched arms, whilst another wound up a ball of wool. We were continually told 'not too tight'.

I was eager to learn how to knit, for I was still smarting at the memory of having to wear one of Mum's disasters made the previous winter. It was a royal blue sweater, I think, for it did not resemble anything. She had not used a pattern, so I will leave the finished result to your imagination. Fit it did not, but I am sure some small furry thing would have just loved it in its bed.

I was obliged to wear it and endure the sneers of my classmates. I made no attempt to retaliate for I heartily agreed with their comments. The favourite taunt was usually aimed at class clipes*, but it served just as well, it went:

> Tell tale tit, yer mammy cannie knit,
> Yer faither cannie go tae bed, with oot a dummy tit.

I needed to learn to knit and the sooner the better. I could not suffer another of Mum's woolly wonders. She could not

---

* tell-tales

really see properly to knit and dropped stitches became ladders down the knitting.

I dreaded going home to ask for the necessary two shillings. The teacher had informed us that we could pay threepence or sixpence a week and we could keep the needles and the finished article. I worried that it was a long way from a kettle holder to a jumper, but it was a start.

It took me four days to pluck up enough courage to ask for the two shillings. I offered to use my pocket money to pay for it and was asked irritably, 'What pocket money?'

I explained about the threepence or sixpence per week, but she seemed to be only half listening. She railed at me, 'Sixpence! Sixpence! It's always sixpence!'

After a pause she demanded, 'What for, this time?'

I sighed and explained once more, getting one of her 'hoomphs' for a reply. She needled, 'If that school wants all these fancy goings on, they should pay for them. Tch, making things, going out, whatever next?'

I had a mental image of all her unsold 'Holy Joe' magazines that could be found in almost every drawer and cupboard in the sitting-room and I wondered how many sixpences they represented. I had told her once in a rage that they were the right size to fit the cat-litter tray and that was about all they were any use for, apart from perhaps kindling a fire.

She had raided my bedroom and burned all my newspaper cuttings, old magazines I had raided from dustbins and a comic on loan from John.

'There,' she said triumphantly, 'that'll teach you.'

'That's all right, Mum,' I crooned sweetly, 'I'd read them anyway.'

I got my hard fought-for money for the wool, but paid for it at least twice, or Mum did. The local tuck shop was too much of a temptation. Threepence went for the wool and the same went into the tuck shop. I hoped Mum would not realise how often she gave me sixpence.

I chose red wool, somehow I could not face royal blue! To start the work with casting on the stitches was, for me, like doing it wearing boxing gloves. I was dismayed to find how awkward I was and even more so when it seemed so easy to the other girls in my group. They were having no trouble at all, me, I was sweating blood!

I almost gave up in despair, until I had another try, this time casting on thumb method on to a left-hand needle. We were doing just plain knitting, so I was soon well away, row after row, leaving the others behind. Carol laughed at my 'cack-handed' approach, but she had only managed about three rows as she was pulling the stitches too taut.

Lizzie kept sliding hers off the needle and dropping stitches as they were too loose. Isobel threw hers, needles wool and shrieks of rage, across the room and was sent to retrieve it from a group of grinning boys.

I was just beginning to feel smugly superior as the teacher came round to see how we were doing. As she reached the desk where I was seated, she exclaimed, 'No, no, Bobbie, we do *not* knit backwards.'

She made me unravel the whole lot and begin again. I was like a fish out of water and so clumsy.

Margaret, the new girl, chipped in. 'She's cack-handed, like ma mither, she knits left-handed.'

She was told, 'Well, *we* do it properly,' and to me she remarked, 'You will thank me one day.'

Right then, I wanted to stick the needles up her nostrils. There were three of us having tantrums over that wretched knitting, so our teacher told us, 'Ask your mothers if ye can stay after school on Wednesdays for half an hour and we'll get yeez sorted out.'

I doubted that I would ever be able to knit, but Mum said it would be all right.

Wednesday after school was my time to sneak into the Catholic church for a few minutes to see Father Murphy or Sister Iggy, as I called her. Mum was always out on Wednesdays and I had to sit on the outer steps waiting for John to get home with the key to let us both in, so I was not missed.

Sister Iggy was usually around and had told me I would always find her in the little room by the vestries, that way there was less risk of being seen by someone who knew me, who might tittle-tattle to my mother.

When we met, she always threw her arms around me with a big hug, I found that a bit disconcerting at first, but soon realised that she greeted all the children that way. I could not determine how old she was and did not dare to ask.

I marvelled at the fact that although we discussed all

236

manner of things, she never tried to convert me. Father Murphy, however, never missed a cue or an opportunity to redeem my soul from Satan, but not so Sister Iggy.

She warned me never to call her that in front of 'himsel''.

'Sure an' he's an old stick in the mud, so he is,' she laughed, enveloping me in one of her hugs.

She showed me her rosary, which was made from jet. It belonged to her mother and her father had kept it with him in the trenches during the first world war. He returned home safe from France. It was wonderful to have her as a friend and I often wished I did not have to keep our friendship secret. It is odd that I never converted to the Catholic faith in later years, for they had given me so much. They gave me confidence in myself and in my future, peace and harmony when I was troubled, and showed me love. I learned to believe and trust in God, as they taught me the power of faith. It was done in a subtle way, not aggressive or bombastic. Father Murphy once told me I had the gift of laughter, a powerful ally in troubled times.

It was also odd that both John and I were destined to marry Catholics.

The knitting sessions were tiresome and produced many tears and tantrums, but my teacher won through eventually and years later I appreciated her patience and perseverance. It had been worth it, to be able to knit from any pattern without getting sloping stitched knitting.

I managed to finish the kettle holder to take home to Mum. She enthused over it at length, saying how useful it would be. She had not realised that she was still paying for it!

32

Indian Summer Uncle

The autumn days were creeping in with cooler evenings, but the days were sunny and bright. Mum told me it was known as an Indian summer and we enjoyed that lingering summer all through September.

Mum visited Dad in the hospital on her own and I wondered if something was wrong, why had she not taken us? John had not wanted to go anyway and I was just curious, so we left it at that.

When she returned in the evening, she seemed very nervous and edgy, but insisted that all was well. John asked what I was thinking.

'He's not coming back, is he?'

She gave us a nervous laugh, replying, 'I don't think so,' then a shrug, 'I don't know.'

I came home from school one afternoon towards the end of the following week to find Mum sitting in a chair, crying like her heart would break. I dismissed angrily her 'nothing' reply to my query as to what was wrong, and demanded to know what upset her. I did not need to ask 'who', I knew only too well.

She had been obliged by Dad to hand over the money order she had received from his employer at the end of August. I told her she was a fool to have taken it in the first place and how on earth did he expect us to live?

She began to sob again, telling me she did not know how we could go on, she only had her family allowance book and he had tried to get that as well.

I was furious and raged at her, 'He does not need money in hospital, he has an allowance. What does he want the money for?'

'I don't know,' she wailed.

I asked her why she did not remind him that he was responsible for three other persons. She told me between sobs, that she had tried to plead our cause, begging him to help us, only to be pompously told that he and only he would give her, what *he* thought fit. He had asked her irritably if she had a return warrant and she told him 'yes'.

'You don't need anything, then,' he niggled, and gave her nothing.

When it was time for her to leave, he had told her he would cash the money order and send her a 'little something'.

She argued, 'What about the rent, food, dinner mon...'

He cut her short by snapping at her, 'Ah'll see to all that, leave it to me, it's not a woman's place to 'ave money or deal with things.'

I stared at her in disbelief, gasping. 'For pity's sake Mum, why did ye no' punch his lights oot?'

She gazed at me watery-eyed through her thick lenses and sighed heavily.

I raged almost to myself, 'Ah'd keep that bugger in the hospital, ah'd put him in traction.'

She sighed, but almost smiled as she just whispered, 'Oh Bobbie, what *are* we to do?'

Of course, no 'little something' was received and we were back to bread and margarine. John and I had school dinners and I got milk at school, but there was very little of anything for Mum.

Fluffy seemed to know it was 'back to the usual', for he stopped pestering for food. I will never forget the look he gave me when I offered him bread and milk sops again. If he could have talked, I am sure he would have groaned, 'Oh no, not that again!'

Providence smiled on us, however, thanks to Mum's door knockings. She had returned to the Motherwell meeting house and had offered lodgings to the Browns, the couple who had visited us with the old man, when Mum was in hospital.

It meant some money coming in and also some company. They were a nice, friendly couple and we were very happy whilst they were with us. Mum had bought two old armchairs from a neighbour and put them in the Brown's room, so they could have somewhere private to sit and listen to their radio. I think the only time there was ever a fire in the grate of that room was while they were using it. Mum had moved on to the put-u-up settee in the sitting room.

One afternoon during her door knockings she met a Mrs Anderson, whose family were all grown up. She had two sons and a married daughter still at home living with her. The daughter had left her home, brought her baby with her to live with her mother and while she went out to work, mother looked after the baby. There was too much to do on her own, so she asked Mum for help for which she would pay her. I think Mum went twice weekly and as well as payment, Mrs Anderson gave Mum a meal.

Things were looking up for us and we got on with the process of living. At the half-term holiday I had to tag along with Mum, but John was allowed to look after himself. Mum had left us once, but we nearly burned down the kitchen trying to make chips. The kitchen curtains were a write-off, but it could have been much worse.

Mum did not know that John was using her precious gas trying to be the local conker champion. He would soak some conkers in vinegar then bake them slowly in the oven. First time out, his 'beezer' was left in bits dangling on its string, dashing his hopes of being Scotland's greatest conker champ.

After the chip episode I went where Mum went, so I found myself at Mrs Anderson's amusing baby Grace and trying to keep out of trouble. The younger of the two sons, whose name I cannot recall, worked in the local abbatoir and delighted in upsetting Mum by telling her what he had spent all day killing. I did not like him at all!

The older one, who I guessed to be in his twenties, was much quieter and I liked him on sight. Charlie was easy to like, he always had a smile on his face and was quietly spoken with a cheerful word for all he met. The red hair was the only hint of a well-hidden temper.

I found myself wishing that I had known Charlie when he was a small boy. Look closely at the small boy and you will see the man he will one day become, faults and all. Forget the catapults, pet crawlies and general scruffiness, just look at their nature. I was sure Charlie must have been a nice little boy.

We met many nice people in and around Motherwell and I think it was in Motherwell that we met Mr Ventura. We were going for our bus home to Newarthill when we made to call in at an ice-cream parlour that doubled as a fish and chip shop. There were quite a few around in those days and many of them were owned or run by Italians.

Italians are inclined to be vivacious, friendly people and Mr Ventura was no exception. He had come to the shop door to close up for lunch as we approached. We turned to walk away as he opened the door and called to us, 'Come een, come een!'

He made us feel like we had made his day by just calling in. Mum flustered, saying that we did not wish to intrude, we only stopped to have a cup of tea and an ice-cream and we had not realised he closed for lunch.

He pooh-poohed the very idea and called out to his wife 'come see', as a smiling motherly looking woman came into the shop carrying a tiny baby in her arms.

I moved in for a closer look, I had never seen one so 'new' and was told that there were 'many babies'.

We were practically kidnapped into their living quarters to meet the family. The place seemed to be full of curly-haired, dark-eyed children. I was introduced to a girl who was about John's age and thought how lovely she was. Her name was Vivienne, a pretty name for a pretty girl, but I soon found out that her nature did not match her looks.

By way of conversation, I told her she was lucky to have so many in her family, but it was obvious that she did not share my sentiments.

'Huh,' she replied grumpily, 'there's always another one, then another one.'

We were perched on top of a brick wall in their back yard, swinging our legs, when she announced regally, '*I* am going to be on television and in films when *I* grow up.'

I laughed out loud and nearly got pushed off the wall for my troubles. I did not think it funny or unlikely, but she was so intense. It was as if she would just die if she did not do either or both. I often thought about her in later years and hoped that she got her wish, and if she did, was she happy? I hope so.

I returned from school one afternoon to find a strange man sitting by our fireside. It gave me quite a shock to see him sitting there and for an instant I thought it was the grandfather we had once seen years previously in Corsham. I realised that this man was much younger, but was of the same ilk, and as I was trying to guess who he might be, Mum said to him, 'This is Bobbie,' and to me, 'Meet Uncle Cyrus.'

So, that was it, there was a connection, he was Dad's very much older brother. He looked like the grandfather, so I supposed Dad took after his mother for looks and build. I was instantly wary, I had not liked grandfather one little bit, was this just a younger version? He talked to me for several minutes before I felt at ease with him. John seemed content in his company, so I guessed he must be all right. I watched him closely, with John and I vying for his attention. I could not wait to get to school to brag about my real live uncle. He seemed to weary of all the attention we lavished upon him and Mum told us to leave as they had things to discuss.

I suspected that she wanted to tell him that all was well and we wanted for nothing.

I will never know what was discussed or what the purpose of the visit was, but we never saw him again.

Some months later there was a letter to inform the parents that the grandfather was dead, and had been for months. There was a snapshot of his coffin, I was curious as to how a man of grandfather's bulk could fit into what seemed to be a normal size coffin.

Mum was very vexed by it all and went on at length about not being told – had that been the purpose of Cyrus's visit? If there was a will we were kept in the dark about it. Mum felt that someone had gone to a great deal of trouble to ensure that we did not know anything about the demise of an oversized bully.

I could not understand why Mum was so vexed. I reminded her that Dad had often told us he was the black sheep of the family and wanted nothing to do with his relatives. I always had the sneaking suspicion that he had more to do with one of his relatives than we ever knew about.

Mum took the letter and snapshot with her when she next visited Dad. On her return she told us that he had cried. The father that he had feared and hated all his life was dead and nobody had bothered to tell him.

Mum told us we had a cousin who was older than John and showed us a photograph of her. I wondered if she knew about John and I and why were we kept away from our relatives. We saw nothing of Mum's family either and only heard vague mentions in hushed tones. When we first lived in Newarthill, we had met one cousin of Mum's, a Jack Gilfillan. She had seemed pleased to see him and I wondered why we were kept away from everyone. Was it perhaps because John and I were a problem? They were for ever telling us that we were millstones around their necks, and oh, what they could have been – or done – if only . . .

I told Mum once in a fit of pique, that I did not ask to be born and I wished she had not bothered, they both gave me nothing but misery. I was informed for the umpteenth time that I was a wicked, thankless child.

We were outcasts from our families. All attempts by me to wring some answers were floored with, 'It is not open to discussion.'

If there were skeletons in our cupboard, I was all for rattling a few bones – angry bones!

Mum got a travel warrant to visit Dad. He had sent no money at all and we were back on hard times once again. The weekend before her proposed visit had been particularly bad. Mum had collected her family allowance money at the beginning of the week, but as Mrs Anderson did not need her that week, there was no other money, which meant that by the weekend we were in dire straits. Mum had her railway warrant but no bus fare for the in-between journeys. She managed to sell enough magazines around the doors to get the fares but had no other money at all.

I watched her as she turned out her pockets in the hope of finding a stray coin. There had been no pennies for the gas and she had not had a cup of tea at home for about two days. She fumbled in the shopper she used for her magazines and in a side pocket found a penny. The look of joy and relief on her face made me want to weep, but I felt a boiling rage swell up at my father's total indifference to our plight. The fact that we were destitute was simply not his concern.

Mum went off to catch her bus and I wandered off to play outside. I noticed a crowd gathering at the top of the road and went to investigate. Kirsty and Gordon were there so I asked them what was going on.

'A weddin',' said Kirsty.

I asked what everybody was waiting for and was told by Gordon, 'Tae see the bride o' course.'

243

The crowd was waiting by the gate of Sofia's grandmother's house and I thought 'of course'. Sofia had gone on practically non-stop about being a bridesmaid for weeks.

Robbie MacDowell turned up and I wondered what that scallywag wanted to watch a wedding for. I nudged Kirsty saying, 'Whit's he wantin' at a wedding?'

Gordon chipped in, 'He's come fer the scramble.'

'The wha-at?' I asked.

'Tch,' sneered Kirsty, 'Dae ye no ken whit a scramble is?'

Gordon explained in exasperation, 'The bride's faither chucks oot pennies as the car drives aff wi' the bride, an' ye've tae scramble fer them.'

'It's lucky,' added the all-knowing Kirsty.

'Lucky if ye don't break a leg,' I thought. No wonder Robbie was there.

'Thurr here!' someone shrieked as a long limousine turned into the road purring to a halt by the gate, where the crowd of children and neighbours had gathered.

'Aw Geez,' moaned Robbie, ' 'tis only the frickin' bridesmaids.'

An elderly woman turned on him with, 'You mind yer mooth lawdy, orrul skite yer lug.'

'Sorry Missus,' said the contrite Robbie.

Two adults attired in sky blue taffeta emerged from the limousine – but where was Sofia?

'Aw, the nice,' smarmed one observer as Sofia daintily emerged, looking as pretty as a picture, also in sky blue. I spitefully thought 'she looks like a walking lampshade', but it was pure envy, especially as she was wearing *my* favourite colour.

She went through the gate, picking her way like she was treading on rice paper, then stopped a short way up the path. Turning to face the onlookers she gave a dainty curtsy, lifting out the folds of her skirt and releasing cascades of coloured confetti. Everyone clapped and cheered, she blushed beautifully as she waved and then went into the house. I, of course, was convinced that the wave was just for me!

After a wait of about twenty minutes, all three re-emerged to leave for the church in the dark limousine. Ten minutes later it was back to collect the bride and her father, or so I was told. I had never seen or been to a wedding and wished that I could be a bridesmaid.

'Fat chance,' I thought, my mother refused to set foot inside a church. I once got a clip round my ear for telling her that only witches were afraid to enter a church, in case the devil saw them.

The children were clamouring around the car as it prepared to set off. I thought that if pennies were to be thrown from a moving car, it would be wiser to stand back a pace. I saw the man in the back seat lean forward to pick up a paper bag, then saw the rear window slide down, this was it! Robbie MacDowell had seen it all before and gave me a sharp dig in the ribs with an elbow as he pushed forward towards the flying coins. I floored him with a rugby tackle an 'all black' could have been proud of, then sat on him whilst I scrabbled for as many pennies as I could snatch. By the time Robbie managed to heave me off, it was all over. It was pandemonium but very satisfying, especially when I counted six pennies to Robbie's two. Gordon was in tears, he had not managed to get any, so I gave him one of mine as Robbie was shouting how unfair it all was. The watching adults were unanimous in their verdict that my assault on Robbie was quite justified. He stormed off, well huffed, when the woman who had told him earlier to 'watch his mooth' sneered, 'Fancy lettin' a wee lassie git the better o' ye, tee-hee.'

The crowd disappeared and I wandered home. Mum had gone to visit Dad and I had no key to get into the flat. After thinking 'what now?' I decided to go off to the shops on the main street, to spend my snatched pennies. I spent tuppence on halfpenny chews and kept three pennies for Mum, so she could get gas to make herself a cup of tea, she did like her cup of tea.

I got home about four o'clock to find John was back. We supposed that Mum would return at about six o'clock and I hoped that she had managed to get some money from Dad.

There was only the usual in the cupboard, part of a cut loaf, some margarine, half a packet of tea, some sugar in a bowl and some in a bag, and an assortment of almost empty jam jars. It occurred to me that even if she succeeded in prising some cash out of Dad, the shops would be closed by the time she reached Newarthill. The chip shop by the bus stop would be open and doing a roaring trade as it was a Saturday. I began to fantasize about plates of steaming hot fish and chips when I heard her key in the door.

I looked at John and he looked how I felt – dejected. She came down the passageway and into the room where we were sitting by the fireplace, she was not carrying any shopping.

John went into the kitchen to put the kettle on for her cup of tea and she sat down heavily on the chair he had vacated. Her face told me all I needed to know, but I asked, 'Well, what happened?'

She shrugged her shoulders mumbling, 'Same as usual.'

I left it at that for she was plainly at the end of her endurance, but on the Sunday I asked her what had happened.

She had tried to plead our cause to no avail. She argued that we must have something, to which he replied, 'Tch, always complainin'.'

He had fumbled in his tray purse, taking out a ten shilling note which he tossed in her direction with, 'There, now let that be an end to it.'

I said nothing, but mentally I resolved to tell Father Murphy, someone had to make that man face up to his domestic responsibilities.

The Browns had left us after only a few weeks and Mum was back in her bedroom across the passageway from mine, even from there I could hear her sobbing in the night. I had made myself a promise that I had to be strong and I was going to do something about it, despite Mum's protestations of 'I have my pride' when I told her we must seek help.

I had forgotten the pennies from the scramble which I hid in the doll's cottage when I got home. I got them out and took them to Mum after breakfast on Sunday, telling her I got them from a wedding scramble together with a poke in the ribs for my trouble. She gave an odd little laugh, then took them saying, 'Thank you dear, we can have some toast today.'

I suddenly felt very guilty about the tuppence I had spent on sweets, that would keep her in gas for tea for two days.

I went out in the afternoon to play with Gracie and we played in her kitchen as it was cold outside. In the cupboard under the sink, her mother had a basket with vegetables and cooking apples. I could not remember when I last had an apple so I asked Gracie if I could have one.

'Thurr cookin' aiples,' she told me.

'I dinnie mind.'

246

She looked at me then asked, 'Huv ye no' hud nae denner?'
I shook my head and wished I had not seen those apples.
'Goan, ye kin hae yin,' she said adding, 'but dinnie tell ma mither.'
I was tucking into the green sour apple when Nancy caught us. Before she could say anything, Gracie told her, 'She's no' hud ony denner.'
All Nancy said to me was, 'That'll gie ye a belly-ache.'
It did!

33

Happy Birthday

At long last it was the day we were to visit the Empire Theatre in Glasgow to see *Peter Pan*. I was beside myself with excitement. It was early October and the Indian summer seemed reluctant to leave. The nights were drawing in with a hint of chill, but the days were still pleasant and bright. The light crust of white frost in the early mornings made everything look like it had been dusted with icing sugar and the changing colours of the trees shrouded in fine mist looked ethereal.

An early lunch had been planned for our class as the coach taking us to Glasgow would leave before the normal lunch-break time. At mid-morning break, a helper from one of the infant classes came looking for me in the playground, to tell me that Miss Hill wanted to see me urgently in the class-room. She was Gracie's teacher and I wondered what she wanted me for. I found Miss Hill unsuccessfully trying to pacify a sobbing Gracie. When Gracie saw me she howled even louder and Miss Hill said to me, 'I don't know whit on earth is upsettin' her so, she jist keeps sayin' your name.'

After a pause she added, 'Huv ye ony idea whit ails her? Tch, the wee sowel's bin fair upset all mornin'.'

I saw red! That little brat was hell-bent on stopping me from going on that outing – all week she had whined at me, 'Dinnie go, dinnie go, ah dinnie want ye tae go.'

I told Miss Hill that Gracie was vexed because I was going to see *Peter Pan* and she wasn't.

'Don't be silly,' she started, but I told her about the whinings and the fact that Gracie had people who could take her and I had not. I also explained that it had been a struggle for my mother to find the money to pay for the trip. I did not tell her how hard I had fought for it! I concluded the case for

248

my defence by stating that Gracie could go on a trip when she got up to my class.

'I see,' said Miss Hill and then turned to Gracie who wailed at gale force again.

Miss Hill sighed heavily, it was all too much.

'Could ye no' jist forgo it this time?' she pleaded, adding, 'Ye kin see hoo upset she is.' (More wails from Gracie.)

I had a strong desire to slap both of them, but instead I let fly at Miss Hill, 'I will not, she is a spoilt brat who needs a hard smack.'

As I fought to control my rage, I continued, 'It took my mother weeks to get me the money, that girl (pointing at Gracie) spends more in the tuck shop each week.'

Gracie wailed again and Miss Hill snapped at her, 'Oh do be quiet, fer goodness sake!'

To me she said, 'You had best go, leave her tae me, I'll sort her out.'

I left and as the break was over I went into the dining-room where our lunch was to be served. The helper who had come looking for me obviously knew what it was all about, for she asked, 'Well, *are* you going?'

When I replied in the affirmative, she whined, 'Is that no' a bit selfish?'

I glared at her and replied, 'Is it not selfish to try to prevent me?' and before she could comment further, I added, 'Especially by someone who always seems to get exactly what *she* wants.'

'Eat your lunch,' she snapped at me, and I did.

I was smarting at the unfairness of it all, why should I let her ruin my day out, even though she had almost succeeded in doing that anyway.

Carol chatted excitedly by my side, then asked me what all the fuss with Miss Hill was about. I told her I would explain later, I was too rattled to let on about it.

The helper was still glaring daggers at me, presumably for being so selfish, and suddenly let fly at me with a hefty slap on the back of my head. My head went forward onto the table edge stopping as my lip made contact with a thud. I thought she had knocked my front teeth out, but could feel nothing. There seemed to be an odd momentary hush before Carol leapt up yelling at her, 'Whit did ye dae that fer?'

249

'She wiz talking,' whined the helper.

'So wiz aw'b'dy else, why pick on Bobbie?'

One of the dinner ladies came marching over to demand, 'Whit the Sam Hill dae ye think yer daein'?'

'She gits oan ma nerves,' whined the helper.

'Yer no' fit tae be near bairns,' she was told by the dinner lady who then added, 'Ah'm goany report yous tae the heid.'

Another dinner lady gave me an ice cube to put on my lip which was swelling at an alarming rate.

'Ah'll see tha-at yin oot o'a joab or ma name's no' Bessie Wilsun,' she raged.

The first dinner lady put her arms around my shoulders and after 'therr, therr-ing' at me, declared, 'Ah'd like tae sink a fist in that yins' smairmy fizzog.'

I mumbled between sobs that she would have to answer to my mother and she would know about that.

'Ah'm still gaun tae the heid,' she grumbled.

For all my mother's irritating ways, she would not tolerate anyone who shoved me or John around and I felt sure that there would be trouble for that helper. Mum had always told John and I to stand up for what we felt was right, but at that particular moment it did nothing to make me feel any better. Turning the other cheek was not part of the Bible she paid any heed to and neither did I.

I felt sick on the coach, but managed not to disgrace myself. We arrived in good time and were shown to our seats. There were some parents with us as helpers and there seemed to be an adult for every group of eight children. We had a part-time teacher in charge of our group of eight and at the interval she sent Robert, one of the twins, to buy choc-ices from an usherette. The ices were sixpence each, twice the price of shop ones, but I had no money anyway. She bought a choc-ice for all her charges except two, London Tony and myself.

Carol asked over-loudly, 'Whaur's yours?'

I did not reply, neither did London Tony, but there was no stopping Carol and she turned to the helper, 'Bobbie an' Tony huvnie got an ice-cream.'

Our helper looked down her nose at London Tony, glared at me and then told Carol, '*I'm* not buying ice creams for aw'bdy, let them buy their ain.'

I tried not to let it bother me, but it seemed however hard I tried I was not allowed to enjoy anything. I did not mind too much about the ice-cream as I had not expected one anyway, but the last straw was when Billy Smith sneered in a sing-song taunt, 'Yous didnie git yin.'

Tony, being the nearest, did the foul deed and sneering William ended up with most of his ice-cream up his nose.

By the time we had returned to Newarthill it was dark and a crowd of mothers were waiting by the school gate. It goes without saying that my mother was not amongst them and I was worried about getting home alone in the dark. I was about to sneak off hoping that no one had noticed, when the new girl's mother asked, 'Is yer mither no' cummin' fer ye?'

I told her 'no' and she told me to walk with them as they went almost half-way to my home and the streets were lit up on the estate.

I knocked on our door and John let me in saying, 'You're in for it.'

'Whit dae ye mean?' I asked.

'She fergot ye were aff tae Glasgow the day,' he replied.

As soon as I walked into the sitting-room I was greeted by Mum yelling at me, 'Where *have* you been?'

I replied, 'Ye ken fine whaur ah've been, ye made enough fuss ower it.'

Before she could say anything further, I stormed, 'Aw'b'dy's mithers were there at skale tae see them hame, but no ma mither, ah'd tae git hame masel in the dark.'

She screamed at me, 'You *know* there is a meeting tonight and we're already late!'

I screamed back, 'You *knew* we were off to Glasgow today, how else could I return but on the school coach!'

She was marching up and down the floor, bristling with her comical 'righteous indignation', and suddenly she yelled, 'You'd no business to go, you *knew* it was the meeting night and *still* you went off to your dratted theatre!'

John was smirking and I wanted to slap his face, I had had more than enough for one day.

Mum nagged on in a whiney voice, 'You promised, you promised faithfully to attend *all* meetings and keep up with your studies, and you have deliberately defied me.'

I yelled back at her, 'I did not! I told you I wanted no part of your idiotic religion, so stop telling lies!'

251

She screamed at me, 'I'd never have given you that money had I known it would come to this – you're a backslider!'

She then screamed at me again, 'Backslider!'

I thought 'Christ, she's as daft as a brush', but could not trust myself to answer her, for I could not do so without using a string of expletives or obscenities. When I ignored her, she demanded, 'Well, what *have* you to say for yourself?'

'Whit's fer tea?' I asked.

John guffawed and Mum just gaped, then laughed and said, 'Oh get yersel some bread an' jam.'

As I sat down at the table to eat my tea, she peered at me closely, saying, 'Hey, huv you been fighting?'

I sighed and related the story of the day's events. As to Gracie's part in them, Mum told me, 'You keep away frae her, she's jist a spoilt little brat.'

I was right about the helper, Mum was coming to school with me in the morning with a promise of, 'Ah'll fix her.'

She was too late, the dinner ladies got there first and the helper had been dismissed. Seems several complaints reached the headmaster and the helper was told that her sort of help was not required.

Neither Mum nor John were the least interested in my day out to the theatre, so I decided to say nothing. I was still angry at Gracie's carry-on and so I called at her back door the following evening to let her know that I had enjoyed it enormously, despite her amateur dramatics.

Mrs Mac opened the door to inform me irritably, 'Gracie's no' cummin' oot.'

'Oh aye,' I replied. 'Kin she no' face me efter makin' such a fool of hersel' yesterday?'

'Ah heard aw' aboot tha-at,' Mrs Mac niggled, adding, 'Disgraceful, disgraceful,' and shaking her head.

I wondered if she meant that I was disgraceful and told her pointedly that I did not see why I should have given up the trip, I got very little as it was. Before I could add to that, Mrs Mac said, 'Ah should think no' tae, that yin got laldy* frae her faither an' she's no' gettin' tae see Peter Pan.'

Mum had received the money order from Dad's work for the end of September and had cashed it. She bought some pro-

* a thrashing

visions and some coal. She also bought some things for us, shiny black Wellington boots for me and some school gear for John. The new gaberdine school raincoat did not appear, instead Mum produced a raincoat that someone had given her for me when she went door knocking. It was made from a sort of oil cloth, which was dark blue, and it had a hood. It was a bit big and Mum enthused that it would do for two winters. I gazed at it dejectedly, it was nice, but when I mentioned that it would not keep out the cold, I got, 'Oh do stop complainin', you're never satisfied.'

I ventured, 'Can I have some long woolly stockings?'

'No you cannot,' she niggled, 'I've spent enough on you as it is.'

I was going to remind her that the coat was given and only the boots cost her money, but I thought better of it.

She said, to no one in particular, 'I don't know what yer father is going to say.'

So, that was it, she was worried about cashing that money order and what he might do about it.

I gazed at her pale, pinched little face, peering myopically at me, and told her, 'Well, ye kin be sure *he* will no' be cold or hungry, so we must do what we must.'

'Oh Bobbie,' she sighed, 'ye huv such an old head on yer young shoulders.'

'Aye,' I replied, 'an' we ken wha' pit it therr, don't we?'

She looked so forlorn, that I wanted to just hug her and tell her to 'never mind', but my mother was not one to be comforted. It came as rather a shock to me to realise that she enjoyed playing the martyr; if she enjoyed herself it would probably prove fatal.

I did however share her fear and trepidation over Dad's next course of action regarding the money order. He was a voluntary patient at Fountainbridge, and unless he did something criminal, no one could compel him to remain there. Mum was worried, there had been no travel warrant sent to visit Dad in early October, and I did not like the implications of that at all. I did not fear that something was wrong, it was more likely to be that we would not need it.

Mum had been very odd and quiet for days, it was like resting on a bomb, hearing it ticking away never knowing when it would explode. One morning she told me she would

253

meet me after school, by the gates.

'Whit's up?' I asked, wondering if it meant a visit to the dentist or suchlike.

'You'll see,' was all I could get out of her. Sure enough after school, there she was, waiting by the entry gate. She told me we would walk home via the shops, instead of cutting through the back of the estate. We went first to the newsagents where she bought some sweets. There was a display of children's annuals at the back of the counter, and Mum asked, 'Which one would you choose?' pointing to them.

I looked them over, then pointed to *Girl's Own Annual* 1952.

Mum nodded to the shop assistant and she took it down off the shelf. I wondered if Mum had had a knock on the head or something, she was behaving so out of character, but I said nothing. Further up the road, we went into the baker's shop, where Mum bought a loaf of bread, then whispered, conspiratorially to the assistant, 'Put three cookies in a bag.'

'Three,' I thought, 'must be for us.' When we arrived home, she told me we would have a cup of tea when John got in from school. She put the kettle on the stove when she heard his key in the door a few minutes later, then laid the things she had bought on the table.

When the tea was poured out, she said, 'Well, come on then,' opening the bag of cream cookies, and offering them to us.

We sat down bemused and she said to me a bit irritably, 'Well, go on, open your present.'

'A present?' I asked, gaping at her, 'What, for me?'

It was the annual she had bought. I gaped at it, then again at her.

'Oh for goodness sakes,' she niggled, 'don't you know what day it is?'

'It's the twelfth of October,' I told her, then realization dawned, it was my birthday!

I was nine years old, at least I would be at 6:55pm. Was there something wrong? For years our birthdays had been ignored, not even a mention. The one time I had asked why, I had been told in no uncertain fashion that such worldly things were of the devil's doing and not for the likes of us. They were forbidden, a taboo subject, like Christmas, along with presents, signs of affection and worldly pleasures – whatever they were!

I noticed that Mum did not wish me 'happy birthday', I suppose you can take a thing too far. Neither did John, he was too intent upon ogling my sweets.

'Well madam?' niggled Mum, 'Are you not pleased?'

'Thank you,' I replied, then added, 'a card would have been nice, like a proper birthday.'

When she made no comment, I asked, 'Will John get things on his birthday too?'

His birthday was in November.

'Oh for goodness sake,' she exclaimed.

I shared out the sweets with John, then went off to my bedroom taking my share and the new book.

Some time later Mum called that tea was ready, and there was no more talk of birthdays. I was lost in my own thoughts, wondering what the next nine years of my life might bring, when Mum brought me back to earth with a jolt, saying, 'Your Dad's coming home on Saturday.'

He arrived back on Friday night, neither John nor I had discussed his impending return, but I am certain John dreaded it as much as I did. We had had a fleeting glimpse of life without him, and it had been too good to be true. The memories of life with him would go with us to our graves.

Fluffy, being an uncannily clever cat, had made himself scarce.

It was touchingly sad to see how pleased he obviously was to be back home. He was full of how well and content he was, doctors were pleased with his progress etc. etc.

I thought 'huh, they don't have to live with him', it could not last, and judging by the expressions on Mum's and John's faces, they were thinking much the same. Mum was as near to tears as she could be.

He returned to work at the Carfin depot on the Monday, just to prove how fit he was.

After school that day, I met Mrs Mac coming down the path, and she quipped, 'Ah see it's back, then.'

'Aye, wurst luck,' I replied.

There was an ugly scene when Dad returned from work that evening. We were sent off to bed, but I for one was not deaf, and caught several snippets of their agitated discourse. Our parents never quarrelled, at least, not in front of us, mostly Dad dictated and Mum complied. She could cut him dead with a look, or destroy him with a comment, but they rarely yelled at each other.

He was demanding his money, and the few pounds she had hidden away for a 'rainy day'.

When she had told me about her 'rainy day' money, explaining what it meant, I told her, 'It disnie rain roond here, it pours.'

He raised his voice to tell her it was *his* money, she 'ad no rights at all, she was just a wife. I had to admire Mum's stoicism, I would have floored him with one swipe, but she kept calm. I would doubtless find her in tears again, once he left for work in the morning. She never gave an inch with the family allowance book, and he eventually tired of trying to get that off her as well.

It was not long before we were back on starvation rations and an atmosphere you could drown in at home. Mum threw herself into her religion with renewed vigour, John and Fluffy kept out of the flat as much as they could. Mac went where John went, except to school, and I went back to raid the allotments.

There was not much to raid, a few carrots, there seemed to be mostly potato drills, and row upon row of chrysanthemums. I wondered if they were edible.

Dad made an effort to be nice to us, there was no pinching, poking or punching, he even once gave us a half-crown each, telling us not to spend it all at once. 'He should talk,' I thought, for money burned a hole in his pockets. We were informed one Saturday that the parents were going to Glasgow for the day, and NO, we could not go, they had important business to attend to.

'Oh lah-de-dah,' I thought, but wondered what they were really up to, you never knew with those two.

They returned late afternoon with Mum looking like a cat that had just pinched the cream, sporting a new fur coat. We were told it was Beaver Lamb, and I was rude enough to ask how they could afford that, when there was never enough food in the house.

'Now, now,' I got from Dad, and a killer glare from Mum.

'Oooh,' said Mum, 'I can't wait fer it tae git really cold.'

I got the knife in again, by whining, 'It will surely be warmer than my oilskin mac, tha-at's no' even a proper winter coat.'

Another killer glare, but the coat was hung up in a cupboard, out of sight.

'Don't want the cat attacking it,' needled John.

Mum could hardly wait to show off her coat at the next meeting of her Holy Joes, and we all had to parade off as well. She refused to take it off during the entire session, and seemed oblivious to the smirks and sniggers around her. It had been really hilarious when we left the flat, for we left as Mrs Mac and Mrs McKissock, were having a blether* over the fence. Mrs Mac had ventured into part of my 'jungle' to do so, and I thought that was very brave of her. I could have died of shame, for I knew that both of them knew the way we lived, indeed, it was Mrs McKissock who fed the scraps to our cat. For all her yelling 'git that moggie aff ma gairden', I had seen her on several occasions giving him a plate of meat scraps. There were times when that cat fared better than John and I did.

They both gaped as we walked down the path to the gate, I waved to the pair of them, as Mum said snootily (I thought), 'Come along Bobbie.'

Mrs McKissock (bless her), guffawed, and exclaimed, 'Oh crivvens, wid ye gerraloady tha-at. Het's aw furr coat, an' nae knickers.'

Mrs Mac failed to see the humour as she shouted, ' 'Tud be mair the thing, if it pit some grub intae thae bairns.'

Mrs McKissock hooted with laughter and yelled, 'Geez, ah'v no' seen thurr cat fer days!'

The sound of her guffaws followed us out of earshot. Mum's face was beetroot red, it was really comical to see Dad propel her through the gate, almost frog-marching her up the road with her nose in the air.

Oh how I loved the Clydeside humour, there was no place for pretentiousness, it was enough to make the cat laugh. Mrs McKissock was ever curious as to why my mother never hung out any washing. It was always put on the kitchen pulley, to drip dry. She would snicker and say, 'She disnie want onb'dy tae see her knickers, tee hee, maybe she disnie wear ony.'

She made just such a remark to me once, as I sat on the fence watching her peg out a line of clothes.

---

* natter

I replied, 'Well, Mrs McKissock, awb'dy kin see your big bloomers, geez, ye could go campin' in thae passion killers.'

She flicked a wet tea-towel in my direction, laughing, 'Awa', ye cheeky wee scamp, an' git aff tha-at fence.'

The fur coat did not stay long, the payments were not kept up, and a man came to reclaim it. For the money paid, Mum was given a fur shoulder-cape made of long brown soft fur. John said it was skunk, and I thought it was the most revolting thing I had ever seen. I told Mum that I could not understand how people could walk about draped in dead animals.

34

A Day at the Seaside

School was out for the Michaelmas half-term, and autumn was slipping away, with nights drawing in bringing winter chills. Dad had a Saturday morning off work and we were told to go early to bed on the Friday, for we were to have a day in Ayr. In reply to our blank stares, Dad informed us that we were going to the seaside.

'The seaside!' I exclaimed.

'Yes,' he giggled, 'we are going to Ayr to see the sea.'

I thought it was a pity we could not have gone during summer, but did not say so.

I went off to bed, full of anticipation of our day out, hardly able to sleep at all. I drifted off into a dream of walking barefoot on the sand, filling one of those small buckets that children love, with all sorts of flotsam. I found shells one would normally only find on a South Seas island, as I paddled in clear blue water, scuttling crabs hurrying away from my tread. I built the biggest and best sand castle in the whole world, and watched as the waves crept up to wash it away. I ran towards those milky white waves to flee in delight before they could reach me. It was a beautiful dream, but a million light years away from reality.

We caught a train for Ayr and on arrival walked along to the sea front. We were on the side of the road farthest away from the wall along the sea front, and Dad pointed to it saying it was called a promenade. The wall blocked the view of the sands and the sea was far out, I could hardly wait, I knew the tide would turn, bringing it closer.

'Can I have a bucket please?' I asked Mum.

She glared at me, snapping, 'What on earth for?'

'For shells,' I replied lamely.

259

She ignored me, and I began to sense an awful feeling of foreboding, something was amiss.

Dad had been the one who had enthused about the trip to the sea, so I turned to him to ask, 'Can I go down to the sand Dad? I'll take ma sandals an' socks aff.'

'You shut up, an' stay 'ere.'

'But Dad,' I started, 'you said we could see the sea.'

'Well,' he niggled, 'you 'ave seen it, it's over there.'

He pointed in the direction of the wall, and laughed. I wanted to cry, but I was nine and constantly being reminded of the fact. From Mum I got, 'Now you are nine, drone drone,' and from Dad, 'You'll soon be into double figures.'

I did not know why being nine had to be so serious, or were they just amazed that I had lasted that long? I went to great lengths to ensure that no one saw me cry, and mostly succeeded in keeping it private, so it would just have to keep.

John interrupted my thoughts by asking petulantly, 'Well, where *are* we going?'

As we walked along the footpath, Mum pointed to a large building bedecked in banners and said imperiously, '*That* is where *we* are going, c'mon, hurry up.'

My heart sank, along with the expression on John's face. I noticed the banners bore religious slogans, and quite forgot myself as I exclaimed, 'Oh no, not another bloody convention.'

Dad roared with laughter, John smirked and Mum glared poison. I promised myself to be as big a nuisance as I could get away with. I often got the feeling that Dad secretly delighted in my giving Mum a hard time over her religious beliefs, it was more than he dared do.

We entered a large hall where seats had been set out in rows, and found four together in the centre of a row. We had to excuse ourselves past about eight pairs of feet, and I took care to tread on as many as possible, to a chorus of 'ohh, ouch, hey watchit.' My mood was murderous, but being pushed into a chair that squeaked brightened my ill-humour. I fidgeted and squeaked in that seat until Mum nudged me and glared. That was my cue to kick rhythmically at the legs of the seat in front, until I got a nudge and a 'stoppit'.

I sighed several times – loudly – and was told, 'Wheesht!'

'Ah'm bored,' I yelled out, to a chorus reply of 'tut tuts'

260

from around.

Being a brat can be fun, especially when Dad heartily approves, so I pulled a face at anyone I could catch the eye of. Dad was grinning from ear to ear, and John was pretending he had no idea who I was.

I got a nod and a wink from Dad, time for the master-stroke.

'Ah'm burstin'', I informed anyone who was interested.

Mum's face coloured up and she snarled in a whisper, 'Fer goodness sake, go off an' find something to do.'

I was off, as I passed Dad he whispered, 'Don't leave the building.'

There were eight pairs of feet hurriedly tucked well under chairs, as I made my exit along the row we were in. Oh, the relief of escaping the droning of the oaf up on the platform, talk about liking the sound of your own voice! I wondered if a person could die of boredom, as I went out into the main corridor of the building. I really did need a toilet and set out to find one, it was not difficult, the signs on the doors were large enough, I pushed through one marked 'LADIES'.

When I entered, I saw a crowd of girls playing with water in the wash-basins, and they were still there when I left the cubicle. One girl from the group asked me who I was, and where I had come from. When I told her, in my best 'pan loaf', she informed me that she and most of the others 'came frae Edinburry'.

'We're aw'frae Edinburry,' chipped in another girl, who went on to inform me that her Dad and Uncle were in charge of the catering, and would I like to help?

I just gaped at her, I had never given thought as to what went on behind the scenes at a convention. I knew lunches and snacks were provided for a fee, not that we ever had them, Mum always took sandwiches, but I never wondered where they came from. I would gaze in envy at the platefuls of hot food, and all the cakes and buns, and just wish we could have some.

'Oh yes please,' I eventually blustered. Anything to avoid having to return to Mum, never-endingly nudging me and chiding 'wheesht' or 'pay attention'.

I followed the group of girls down another passage, into a large room that was a veritable hive of activity. Some boys were washing up in a row of deep sinks, and judging by the noise, they were enjoying themselves.

Everything was in a rush preparing for the imminent lunch break, and I could not see how I could help, except by staying out of the way. There was a man in white overalls working at a large wooden table, icing and cutting what looked like huge square sponge cakes. He grinned at me and asked my name. When I told him he replied, 'Well, Bobbie Eriksson, wid ye like tae help me?'

Would I? Not half! But I smiled back and said, 'Yes please.'

'Right then,' he said. 'Ah'll git the sponges oot o' the tins, an' ye kin jam them up – OK?'

I nodded, and watched as he laid out four huge square sponges, each about one and a half inches thick.

I looked at the huge tin of jam and realised I would not be able to lift it, so I went over to where the boys were washing up to get a clean soup bowl and a large spoon. When I began to spoon jam into the bowl, he asked what I was doing.

'Ah cannie lift that,' I said, pointing to the jam tin.

'Oh right,' he said nodding, as he watched me spread jam over the sponges with a spatula, then added, 'That's it, when ye've done that, ah'll pit their lids oan.'

I watched in amazement as he turned out more large sponges, he made it look so easy, and I almost giggled when I thought of Mum's attempts at sponge cakes. She did not bake very often, but when she did she turned out some really nice cakes; but alas, the art of sponge cakes eluded her, they came out of the tins in bits. This man had it off to a fine art, and huge square ones at that. He tapped the sides of the tins, easing out the centre with a long-bladed spatula, and the complete sponge slid obligingly on to the table. I was impressed, and wished that Mum could see that.

'These are fer puddin's,' he informed me, as he put on their 'lids'. 'They've tae be cut intae sixteen pieces, kin ye dae that?'

'Of course,' I replied, 'four times four, nice square bits.'

'Yer a bright wee thing,' he commented.

I felt slightly irritated, and realised that he must have thought I was younger than I was, so I told him, 'Well, at nine, ye should be able to cut up a sponge cake.'

'Oh aye, right enough,' he replied with a smirk.

He plonked a chef's hat on to his head, and I giggled as he

announced, 'Right, that's the puddin's, now fer the wee ains.'

He laid out two rows of small round sponge tins, then lifted up a large metal vat of mixture.

He winked, saying, 'Watch this.'

He had tucked the vat under his left arm, and with his right hand got handfuls of the mixture and slung them, one after the other, into the lined up tins.

I laughed and laughed as he solemnly told me, 'Ye cannie footer* aboot wi' cakes. Mix 'em up, sling 'em in.'

John arrived to inform me that he had been sent to look for me.

'Well, ye've found me, so ye can just buzz off,' I told him.

Mum appeared about five minutes later to say, 'So, this is where ye are.'

The man looked at her, then at me and told her, 'She's bin here aw' the time, helpin' me.'

'Hoomph,' said Mum, sniffing, then niggled, 'She should be in the hall, listening to the talk, she's always backsliding.'

The man looked askance at her.

'Aw, come aff it sister, ye cannie expect a bairn tae sit through that.' He added with a sniff, 'Ah wouldnae.'

They tended to call each other brother and sister in that movement, a pretention I felt was rather silly. Mum looked down her nose at him and I almost laughed, him standing at six foot plus, and her at five foot two, then she whined nasally at him, 'She has to learn to buckle to.' (whatever that meant!)

He gaped at her in disbelief, and I had an aching urge to kick her shins. If she had half of the sense she was born with, she would have realised that her attitude was driving me away from any form of religion; it was only thanks to Father Murphy that I was not a total atheist.

The man was not to be swayed, 'I need her help here, she's doin' jist fine, all the bairns are given a job.'

Mum pressed her lips together hard, and I thought how much she looked like a mean, wicked little witch when she did that, and I almost sniggered.

'Very well,' she shrieked in temper, 'be it on your own head,' and stomped off.

She always said that when she could not get her own way,

---

* fiddle

especially where her religious idiosyncrasies were concerned. The man whistled through his teeth, then gasped, 'Is she aye like that?'

'Oh no,' I crooned, 'she's usually much wurse.'

He shook his head, saying, 'Folk like her git oor people a bad name.'

I spent the entire day having fun in that kitchen, and I was sorry when it was time to go home. I got a free dinner and anything I wanted to eat. John came to fetch me when it was time to leave, I expect he was told to 'go an' git that girl.' No doubt Mum realised it was prudent not to show her face again. Dad sat opposite me on the train going home, and wanted to know all about my day, Mum's face was as black as thunder. John hardly said a word, as I enthused about the art of catering. For Mum's benefit I ended my narrative of the day's events, by declaring that I had had a wonderful day, despite not being allowed near the beach. It was doubly satisfying to see Dad look shamefaced, but he made no comment.

From Mum we got the usual 'hoomph'.

My visit to 'see the sea' had been very strange indeed, but my dogged belief that 'something will turn up' had not failed me.

Father Murphy had once told me that we should always say a prayer to thank God for each day. I had never been taught any form of praying, except for the Lord's prayer, I learned at Sunday school in Corsham parish church when I was small. My prayers took the form of a formal letter:

'Dear God, thank you for (whatever). I'm Bobbie and I love you, Amen.'

I often wanted to ask for things, but somehow that did not seem right. It was all right to ask on behalf of someone else, and I just hoped God knew what I needed without having to be asked.

I found often that even in the face of some of the worst opposition, things somehow came right in the end.

35

No' Awa', Tae Bide Awa'

Dad came home one evening all excited and full of news, there was a transfer on offer and he had put in for it. Years later we found out that he put in for any transfers that were on offer, in the hope of getting promotion. He would tell Mum that he was to get a new suit, 'up for promotion' he would swank, but it never materialised. I think he got his transfers so his colleagues could be rid of him.

'It's off to White'all for me,' he said grinning, as Mum dropped her bombshell.

'I hope you enjoy it,' she snapped, 'we are not going, and certainly not to London.'

Before he could reply she went on, 'You go where you must, but we are staying put.'

'But—' he started, as she raged at him, 'I expect to be consulted on such matters, not told. You drag us about like suitcases, and for what? Nothing ever gets any better. No, we are not going.'

'Now Nance,' he chided, but she screamed at him, 'We are staying put, do you hear?'

I had never heard her yell at him like that and I wanted to applaud. She looked really angry as he gaped at her, ashen faced and open-mouthed. John and I slunk off to our rooms, leaving them to it, the coup was long overdue and the dictator was being ousted.

I left the flat to sit on my step and think, 'Oh no, not another move, another school, will it never end?' Had the move been back to Corsham, I am sure we would have been on the first available train, but London? Our last proposed move to London had left us homeless.

I wandered round to Gracie's, I had to tell someone, Mrs

Mac would understand. She opened the door to my call of 'Haw Gracie' and said, 'Come awa in hen, whit's up?'

Before I could reply, she grimaced saying, 'Het's him, is is no'? Aye, we ken fine it's back right enough.'

She had obviously heard the rumpus from upstairs.

'Whit's it done this time pet?' she soothed.

I do not know what happened, but the flood-gates just opened and I sobbed hysterically. Mrs Mac sat me down by the kitchen table crooning 'therr, therr'.

Gracie and Nancy looked in to see what all the commotion was and Mrs Mac shooed them out of the room. She sat down opposite me and waited for the deluge to subside.

'Right noo, ur ye goanie tell whit this is aw' aboot?'

Between sobs and hiccups I related what had happened, ending by telling her tearfully that I did not want to go to London, or anywhere else with him.

'Therr therr,' she soothed again, 'mibby it'll jist go himsel', an' lave yeez here.'

There were no holds barred, I told her falteringly that we would be abandoned, there would be no money sent and what was my Mum to do?

She took my face in her hands, lifting it up so that I had to look at her, then said, 'You lave that tae me, ah'm goanie settle that yin's hash, once and fer aw. We ken fine whit he's like ye ken, an' he's no'gittin' awa' wi' it, ye'll see.'

As she rose to her feet, she told me, 'You gaun hame the noo, an' dinnie let on onythin' tae thame.' She thumbed towards the ceiling. 'Say nothin', right?'

I nodded and as I left she whispered to me, 'Dinnie fash yersel', ah'll sort it.'

I went back to sit on my step and after a short time John came to the door, saying when he saw me, 'Oh there ye are, yer tae come in noo.'

As I got up he asked, 'Whit ur ye dae'in' oot there in the dark?'

As I pushed past him he exclaimed, 'Hey, huv ye been greetin'?' Before I could tell him to drop dead he soothed, 'Ach dinnie greet, he's goin'.'

'Good,' was all I said.

I went straight into my bedroom and after a few minutes Mum came in. She stood looking around the room, all that was

266

in there was the bed in one corner and two old suitcases in another, I could not imagine what she was thinking. She sighed and told me that Dad was leaving on the Saturday.

'And us?' I asked, hardly daring to breathe.

'We are staying put.'

There was a bus outing from her meeting-house on the Saturday, to a convention in Paisley. On the return journey Dad would be dropped off at the bus station in Glasgow with his suitcase and we would return to Motherwell. Dad left the coach with Mum for a brief farewell, but he just ignored John and me. I cannot recall much about that day, but on the journey back to Motherwell I was being fussed over by a lady who told Mum, 'Whit a shame, she's that upset.'

He had not even bothered to bid us farewell, but I could hardly tell the woman that I hoped he would never return. Mum seemed much happier in the weeks that followed and we saw much more of the cat and John. The latter came home one afternoon from being out with a friend, clutching a jute sack and looking very sheepish.

'Ah'v found something Mum,' he ventured.

I noticed that the 'something' in the sack was moving and thought 'What now?'

He gently placed the sack on the floor and out of it crawled two of the most adorable kittens I had ever seen. Mum and I practically fell on them with oohs and aahs as the tiny balls of black fur squirmed in our hold. Mum looked at John and asked, 'Where have these come from? They can't be very old.'

He shuffled his feet awkwardly and stuffing his hands into his pockets, told her that he and his pal had found them on the towpath by the canal, they were tied up in the sack.

'Just two kittens?' asked Mum.

'Er, no, there wiz five, but ma pal took three o' them.'

'Oh goodness,' exclaimed Mum, 'whit ur we tae dae wi' three cats?' She thought for a few seconds then added, 'Whit's Fluffy goanie think aboot these?'

John shuffled again to say, 'We'll huv tae feed them wi' a dropper, thurr no' weaned yet.'

'Poor wee things,' said Mum, totally taken over, then sighed, 'Oh dear.'

I chipped in with, 'We'll need tae git them started on to solids, then mibby a neighbour can gie them a hame.'

Both John and I knew that by then there would be no way we could part with them; that left just one problem: Fluffy.

It said a lot for John's perseverance that both kittens survived. He used a mustard spoon to slip food into the tiny mouths, giving them first milk and arrowroot pudding, then mashed up bits of fish and cat food.

As for Fluffy, he was as besotted with the fur balls as we were. He had come in, via the kitchen window as usual, from off the roof of a neighbour's shed, sauntering in like he owned the place, when he stopped in his tracks to stare. I had made up the doll's bed with an old jumper and the new arrivals were curled up together fast asleep. Fluffy began to creep up on the sleeping kittens as we watched, ready to grab him if he made to attack them. We need not have worried. As he reached the bed by the hearth, he sniffed first one then the other, as they stirred and just looked at him. Neither could purr nor meow yet and we were ready to act if need be. Fluffy leaned forward, first to lick one then the other as we said 'ah' in unison. He was not that old himself and perhaps he remembered what it was like to miss mother's attention.

Mum said, 'Would you believe that? Who could want to drown them?'

John said that whoever it was obviously could not go through with it, for the sack was left on the towpath. It was wonderful to watch that tom-cat mother those kittens, lick-washing their tiny faces with a look of smug satisfaction on his face. We had to keep the kitchen window closed, in case the kittens tried to follow Fluffy out, so we gave them a litter tray. To see him show the kittens that tray was just hilarious. Mum would let Fluffy out of the main door, but he was reluctant to remain outside for very long, he took his nursery duties very seriously. If the kittens got overly boisterous, he would cuff them around the head with a paw. Poor old tortoise Mac came in for a lot of teasing from the little rascals, but got his own back on them by walking into them whilst they tried to snooze on the hearth rug. We had not named them at first for fear they might not survive, but once they were on to solids and we knew that they were male, we had to choose names. They were almost identical, so after much deliberation, it was agreed they would be named Bootsie and Snudge, after two characters on the radio.

We had hours of fun with those cats, but it was becoming more and more difficult to keep them indoors. We had a P.D.S.A. van that came around the estate about once every two weeks and I asked the man in charge, when did I need to take the kittens to be neutered, or whatever it was they did to tom-cats? He told me they would need to be about six months old, and yes it was all right to let them out, but advised me to keep them in at night if possible. That way they would not stray or get into fights. We mostly managed to get them in by feeding them at night.

They had outgrown the doll bed and moved in with Fluffy on to mine, I could not move for something furry poking me.

All went well at home until Mum got a letter from Dad's work, sending her a money order. She could not understand why one had been sent for November when Dad had been out of hospital since early October, they must know they had transferred him! She was relieved to get it but puzzled, and fretted over what Dad might do about it. The amount was less than when he had been in hospital, but what was it all about?

I had forgotten about Mrs Mac's threat to 'settle his hash' and Gracie had told me her Mum went to the Carfin depot, as she put it, 'tae sort yer faither oot'.

'Oh heavens,' I thought, 'it's all going to come out, with me right in the middle of it all.'

I dared not tell Mum, anyway 'he' was away in London, too far away to bother us.

'Needs must when the devil drives,' I thought, but how wrong can one be!

He turned up like the proverbial bad penny the following weekend, armed with a travel warrant and a suitcase full of dirty washing.

'I need that for Sunday,' Mum was told, no 'please' or 'would you mind'.

He was full of himself, how wonderful his new post at White'all was, how important 'e was, blah blah blah. We were getting the full throttle on his Mr Nice Guy routine, it was almost nauseating. I felt really angry, just what was he trying to pull off? We listened in silence as he enthused about life in London, oh yes, 'things were much better there, never should'uv come 'ere'.

He got up, put his small attache case on the table and began to rifle through it, then closed the lid and locked the case.

'What's in there Dad?' I asked, 'State secrets?'

'You shut up,' I was told.

He had a brown paper carrier-bag with him also and from it he produced a small carton, which he opened, telling John and me to 'come see'. It was full of half-pound bars of milk chocolate. We gaped at them and John said 'Wow!', and I asked, 'Who is that for?'

He sniffed then replied belligerently, 'None o' your business, it's not fer you two.' He started to close the carton.

'What, none of it?' exclaimed John.

'Nope,' he said with a sniff, as he lifted the carton off the table and went out to the cupboard in the passageway. It was an airing cupboard, but there were not very many things in it, so he placed the carton on the topmost shelf, with the warning, 'Don't yous touch.'

We had followed him into the passageway and Mum came to see what was going on. She had filled the sink to make a start on Dad's laundry and was drying her hands on her apron. She had bought a new electric smoothing iron and I wondered if Dad had found out yet. John and I looked at each other as Mum demanded, 'What's going on here?'

I told her, 'He has got a whole box of chocolate bars, an' he says we're not to have any.'

She turned to Dad to niggle, 'Fer goodness sake, can ye no' give them some? They get little enough as it is.'

'They'll git nuthin' frae me,' he announced, sniffing noisily.

'Chocolate makes me feel sick,' I said. 'Ah'v only tried it yince an' it was awful.'

I was sowing the seeds of a plan that was forming in my mind. Oh the fun of it, but I would have to be careful, every detail had to be perfect. We were dismissed with the usual 'Git tae yer beds.'

I knew there was trouble brewing and was pleased to escape, I had some thinking to do. No one, but no one, would know what I intended to do, but like Mrs Mac, I intended to settle his hash.

I fell asleep with no particular plan worked out and on the Saturday, after John returned from his paper round, Mum told me that she and Dad were going out. I was to remain indoors, but when John got leave to go out, I said that I did not want to

270

be left alone and could I go to Gracie's?

I was told, 'All right, if you must.' Then, 'Be here when John returns.'

'So far so good,' I thought, it was all falling into place without too much planning. I just had to ensure that at no time during the day would John or I be alone in the flat. John went off with the assurance that I would be at Gracie's when he returned late afternoon and the parents were expected back at the same time. I could hardly keep a straight face, it was all too easy. All I had to do was make sure that I left the flat last, leave the lock on the latch position and make a big fuss of closing the door. The door was a bit weather warped, so it could appear to shut fast when a push would open it.

As we left, Dad followed me down the inner stairs and I panicked, I had to be last out.

'Must get a hanky,' I gasped, rushing back up the stairs past Dad.

'Hurry up,' niggled Mum, 'we'll miss our bus.'

'You go on,' I called back, 'I'll pull the door to.'

They were hovering by the foot of the outer staircase, but I got the latch up as I left the doorway. I thought it clicked as loud as a pistol crack, but they seemed not to notice as I pulled the door hard to closed.

I blew my nose noisily, as Mum accusingly asked, 'You got a cold?'

'Nope, jist snotters,' I replied.

'Bobbie – really!' she raged. 'You get off tae yer pal's, an' keep a look out fer John coming back.'

I went round to the back of the building and waited a few minutes, checked that the parents were out of sight, then let myself back into the flat.

I got a dining chair from the sitting-room to reach up and lift down the carton. There was one bar missing, so I supposed that Dad had eaten it the previous evening. My original plan had been to remove some of the bars, but somehow the thought of Dad's attitude made me take the lot. They were stashed away under the loose floor-boards that only I knew about and could remain there for as long as I wanted them to. I had to drag the bed away from the wall and move a piece of torn linoleum. My bed had been placed in the corner to hide the floor-boards where a piece of linoleum was missing and it was quite difficult

271

to move it all back again. I left the bed unmade and the room seemed exactly as it had been before. I replaced the now empty carton, then the chair, leaving the door partially open as I had found it. One final look round, then I left the flat, this time dropping the latch. I went to Gracie's to be sure that that was where John would find me and just waited for his return. My plan went like clockwork, the parents returned first, followed by John a few minutes later, then he was sent to fetch me from Mrs Mac's. I was itching to tell John of my trick on Dad, but I knew that I dare not. When it came to the showdown, he would not be able to brazen it out.

The parents did not tell us where they had been, but both were in a foul humour. John and I were not allowed out again as it was dusk, or gloaming as it was called locally. That twilight time between day and night, when the light sky slowly fades into darkness.

Mum was complaining that she would have to iron dry Dad's laundry, as he was leaving on Sunday morning. I quipped, 'It's a long way tae come tae git yer washin' din,' and was told by Dad to shut up.

I thought the evening would never end, we had our usual bread and jam tea and at eight o'clock Dad told me, 'Git tae yer bed you.'

'Whit aboot John?'

''E's older than you, now git,' he snarled.

I saw the smug expression on John's face and almost laughed. Oh boy! Were those two in for a shock! It was like sitting on the edge of a volcano, waiting for it to erupt.

I got washed and ready for bed and as I left the bathroom, Dad appeared to open the airing cupboard door. I had my clothes bundled under my arm and had to wait, almost behind the open cupboard door, as he fetched down the carton. 'This is it,' I thought, as I saw the look on his face as he lifted down the now empty carton. He shook it in comical disbelief and I was fighting not to laugh out loud.

'Oh goody – chocolate,' I squealed.

'It's no' fer you,' he snarled.

'Is that why ye scoff it when we're no' aboot?' I asked.

At that instant I knew that he knew, but the expression of open puzzlement on his face was almost too much for me. His face also told me that he knew there was no way he could ever find out what had happened to the contents of that carton.

He was clearly puzzled. How had I managed to do it? I could almost hear him thinking. I watched his face as he tried to think, then he suddenly bellowed, 'W'at 'ave you done with it?'

I ignored him, just watching his facial contortions.

Mum came from the kitchen as John came to see what all the commotion was about and why Dad was shouting.

'She,' he shrieked, pointing a finger at me, ' 'as taken it!'

He was agitated, shaking his fist at me, as I backed out of his reach almost into the bathroom doorway.

Mum and John had no idea what he was on about, until he held the carton upside down.

'It's empty – empty!'

He grabbed me by the arm, digging his fingers into the flesh as he shouted, 'W'ere is it, w'ere?'

He pushed my head against the door frame with a bang as Mum yelled at him, 'That is enough! What on earth do you think you are doing?'

He let go of me to yell back at her, 'She took it, her, she took it!'

'Enough,' yelled Mum. 'Control yourself for goodness sake! Really, what a palaver! You've only yourself to blame – and you know it!'

He looked really peeved, but calmed down, to sulk like a small boy. John was watching me closely and I tried to make my face as expressionless as my aching arm and throbbing head would allow. It only strengthened my resolve to make sure that he never saw that chocolate ever again, I would give it to Old Nick before he would have it back. Something in my nature that I am not at all proud of would not allow me to back down, come hell or high water.

Mum was rattled and turned on me, demanding, 'Well, *did* you take his dratted chocolate?'

'No I did not!' I exclaimed, thinking, I stole it, purloined it, redistributed it, removed it, hid it, borrowed it, but no, I did not take it. I put it somewhere else.

Dad tried his Mr Nice Guy approach, to wheedle, 'Now dear, if ye've taken it fer a joke, that's OK, jist 'and it over.'

I glared at him and Mum snapped, 'Go to bed Bobbie, this has gone quite far enough.'

To Dad she snarled, 'You jist leave her alone.'

'Ah, ah!' cried Dad in triumph, as he barged into my bedroom, switiching on the light.

I usually came and went in the dark and did not need a light on. He went over to my unmade bed turning everything upside down, including the mattress, then dumped it all on the floor. He opened the two old suitcases which contained some clothes and odds and ends, dumping them on the floor also.

'Are you satisfied?' asked Mum, and when he made no reply she added, 'Now leave her alone, damn you and your stupid chocolate.'

I was shocked, I had never heard Mum swear – ever! Drat and darned were her strongest words. I had a varied and colourful collection of expletives, used mainly to annoy her, but I had picked them up elsewhere.

Dad glared at me, then left my room muttering, 'Ah'll find it, ah'll find it.'

Mum helped me to get the mattress back on to the bed, leaving me to make it up and pick up the things from the floor. I rolled up the sleeve of my nightdress to reveal a huge purple bruise on the top of my arm. There was a small lump on the side of my head which hurt to touch, but I almost giggled when I thought, 'I'll live to fight another day but he will never see that chocolate again.'

Dad left for London the following morning, but only Mum went to the door to see him off, John and I did not even bid him farewell. Oddly enough, neither Mum nor John mentioned the missing chocolate, so about one week later I removed it from its hiding place, taking care to cover up the loose floor-boards. I placed it on the table in front of Mum and John, relishing their looks of amazement. They both stared at it for some seconds before Mum said, 'So, you did take it after all.'

I laughed and told her, 'No, I removed it.'

To my surprise she laughed and laughed, gasping 'Well, I never!'

She looked at the pile of bars and said, 'You haven't eaten any of it.'

I answered, 'No, I don't like it much, it really does make me feel sick.'

'Then why?' she asked in exasperation.

274

I explained that something about his attitude, and him saying that John and I were not to have any, got right up my nose.

'Well I never,' she said again and after a pause, asked, 'Weren't you afraid he would get it out of you?'

I replied, 'No, and he did not, did he?' As she gaped at me, I added, 'He cannie bully *me*.'

She sniffed and replied, 'Apparently not.' She pulled a face then asked, 'What will ye do with it?'

I told her that I did not care two hoots what happened to it, then asked her if she wanted some.

'Certainly not! !' she exclaimed angrily.

John was flabbergasted, 'Whaur did ye hide it?'

But my secret stayed with me, I never knew when I might need it again.

Oddly enough he did not want it either, although he could not resist just one bar, the rest went to local children, a gift from our Dad!

Mum sometimes bought sweets from Mrs Anderson's daughter who had a job in a sweet factory. Mum would give her a half-crown, for a bag of broken toffee or misshapen sweets, but we kept those for ourselves.

The next thing we heard from Dad was when a parcel of dirty laundry arrived, with a note advising Mum that it was required A.S.A.P. We had heard nothing for almost three weeks and he had obviously relieved Mum of the worry of housekeeping yet again. I found her in tears one afternoon when I arrived home from school, she had left the door on the latch for me to let myself in and I found her in a state of upset, trying to read his scribbled note.

Life in London, it read, was busy and expensive, so he could not manage to send her anything. Would she please return his laundry A.S.A.P.

'The nerve of it,' I thought, but of her I asked, 'How come he's sendin' or no' sendin' you money?'

She looked at me but made no reply, so I went on, 'I thought the money came to you, it has all been sorted.'

'What do you mean?' she snapped, adding with a sniff, 'What would *you* know about it?'

I thought 'uh – oh, careful,' then drawled, 'Well, you got one money order, so I guessed as he is in London his employer was sending you part of his wages.'

When she made no comment, I added, 'They must know about him.'

'What about him?' she sneered.

I lost my temper to rage at her, 'Oh Mum, for goodness sake, come off it! Awb'dy kens *him*, the whole street kens he hus left us destitute.'

'Oh do they indeed?' she sneered, then bristled with irritation to add angrily, 'I won't have our business discussed by all and sundry.'

She fidgeted in her seat, fiddling with the hem of her skirt, then whined, 'I have my pride.'

I sneered, 'You and your stupid pride, we starve and live like animals, but never mind, *you* have your pride.'

She burst into tears and I felt really awful, but asked her, 'Why don't you stick up for yourself? Why don't you ever learn?'

'You don't know him, you don't know what he can do.'

'Has he hit you?' I demanded.

'No – no,' she wailed, and I thought, 'no, he doesn't have to, he could teach tricks to the Gestapo.'

I made to leave the room, asking her as I left, 'For Christ's sake Mum, why did you marry that shite?'

I could hear her wails as I went down the stairs to leave the flat.

John was just coming indoors and he asked me, 'Whit's up wi' your fizzog?'

'Oh shut up,' I told him and slammed the door.

I went to sit on my step to think and wondered if things would ever be any different. How could I do anything about our problem when Mum would not back me up?

The following Monday morning at school, I joined the queue for dinner tickets, but when I reached the head of the queue I was told to wait until the end. My teacher informed me, with a deal of embarrassment, that my tickets had not been paid for in weeks. I could feel the heat rising on my face as I told her that my Dad was supposed to pay for them, but he had gone.

'GONE!' she exclaimed, then in hushed tones asked, 'What do you mean – gone?'

I was sure that the entire class was staring at us and I just

276

wanted to disappear through the floor. I blurted out, 'He's gone tae work in London an' he doesnie send ma Mum ony money.'

It was her turn to blush as she mumbled, 'Oh dear, well.'

She did not seem to know what to say, but dismissed me with, 'All right, just go and join the other queue.'

I had a mental vision of Mum wringing her hands, saying, 'I have my pride.' I thought, 'she's goanie do her nut.' I stood behind a girl called Christine, who had watched as I made my way from one queue to the other, and she turned to ask, 'Whit ur ye dae'in in this line? Your faither's no' oot o' werk.'

I replied, 'Ma faither's gone.'

She gaped at me in wide-eyed astonishment.

'Geez, ye lucky bugger.'

She stared again before adding, 'Wisht ma bloody faither wid go, aw he's ony yiss fer is gettin' plootered* every nicht.'

I giggled and she asked angrily, 'Whit ur ye laughin' at, het's no bloody funny.'

'No,' I agreed, 'it's no', he'll maist likely come back.'

'Aw jings,' she moaned, 'so he's no' awa' tae bide awa'.'

We both laughed, God knows why!

A boy prefect from the top class was issuing the welfare tickets, checking his list and ticking off the names. I was last in the queue and he asked my name. Before I could tell him, he informed me that there were no more names on his list. He hollered across the room to the teacher, 'Haw Miss, she's no' oan ma list.'

Miss hollered back, 'Then pit her oan yer list.'

'Ah'v nae mair tickets.'

She came across the room to where we were standing to tell him irritably. 'Fer goodness sake! Gie her Robert Brown's tickets, he's aff seek, ah'll sort it wi' the office.'

I told Mum all about it when I got home and I was right about the wringing of the hands and her 'doing her nut'.

'Oh dear, oh dear, what *am* I to do?'

I think if she had mentioned her 'pride' I would have slapped her. I told her she would have to do something, she could not got on pretending that nothing was wrong. She was not really listening, she prattled on about how she had got our

---

* drunk

old wireless set to work by removing the valves then replacing them.

'Must've been dirt,' she mused.

She gave an odd little snigger then told me, 'Winnie the windbag is Prime Minister again.'

'Oh,' I replied, 'ah thocht he wis deid.'

She sniggered again, saying, 'He is dear, but he just won't lie down.'

The King was very ill, she told me he had cancer. I thought that that was a sign of the Zodiac, but said nothing, not wishing to display my ignorance, and it did sound really serious.

I knew that Dad's star sign was Cancer – the crab! ! !

36

Goodbye Good Friend

The next letter from London contained travel warrants and instructions for the three of us to go to London for a few days. Mum was in a state of panic, what trick was Dad trying to pull this time? John pointed out that the warrant included returns and we got the 'will we won't we' debate, with John telling her that he could not prevent us from returning. I told her to keep the return warrant well-hidden, I did not trust that so-and-so!

Mum announced that we would not take much with us and I reminded her that we did not have much anyway – getting a scowl for a reply. Arrangements were made for the furries and Mac. 'No,' Mum told John, 'you cannot take Mac.'

With very little ceremony and even less cash, we set off for Glasgow to get on the train for London. The warrant did not make allowance for a sleeping compartment, so we would just try to get a compartment to ourselves, with Mum's assurance that mid-week travel would not be busy. She was wrong!

We spread ourselves and our belongings around the compartment, to make it look fully occupied, and almost succeeded in keeping it to ourselves. The idea was that John and I could stretch out and sleep during the long journey. Just as the train let off steam to jolt into movement, a last minute passenger almost hurled himself in with us. It was a corridor train and we were in a compartment next to the entry door. He flung open the compartment door and fell into the seat next to Mum, gasping and wheezing from the effort of his last minute dash.

He was a strange little person, rather shabbily dressed and carried only a small attache case for luggage. He removed his well-worn overcoat, huffing and puffing as he took off his steamed up, wire-framed spectacles, to wipe them on a not very white handkerchief. All this I watched whilst fighting an urge to giggle. John nudged me and whispered, 'Crippen,' and I lost the battle to stifle the giggles.

As Mum glared at us both we giggled even more. As for the little man, he behaved as though we were not even there, after he had had a good look at all of us.

I lost interest in him and settled down to listen to the train 'talk' as it rumbled over sleepers and points, gathering speed. It was a game we played on trains, with everyone having different opinions as to what was being said, it usually ended in an argument or with us laughing. To me it sounded urgent, in a hurry: here we go – here we go – mustn't be late – mustn't be late.

Our travel companion was absorbed in his own thoughts and everyone soon settled down to the inevitable boredom of travel. It was dark outside so there was not much to look out at. Mum was watching the man, I guessed that she was not happy about him being there, and would doubtless try to remain awake. We had not been travelling long when he put his attache case on his lap, opened the lid to fumble about inside, crouching over it in a furtive manner, as if he did not wish us to catch a glimpse of its contents. He placed something metallic on the seat beside him whilst he closed up the case, then put it back on the seat also. I recognised it as a 'cut throat' type razor at about the same instant as Mum did. I saw her blanch then look above the door to where the communication cord was. John was staring at the man as I watched Mum mentally judging the distance between her and the emergency pull, she would only just be able to reach it. I would have to stand on my seat to reach the one above the window, but one false move from that man, I am sure, would have sent all three of us leaping for that cord. He was oblivious of the silent drama going on around him, quite unconcernedly removing his left shoe, then the sock. He wiggled his toes a bit, then opening the razor, proceeded to pare his corns with it.

John stifled a snigger, I gaped, Mum giggled, then we all burst out into gales of laughter. The man stopped paring, to look from one to the other of us in utter amazement, then asked peevishly, 'What's so funny then?'

When Mum had managed to compose herself, she told him, 'You should do that in private,' then giggled again.

'Eh – what?' he flustered, then grumbled, 'Oh I see.'

280

It was clear he could not see what was so funny, but he closed and pocketed the razor, then replaced his sock and shoe, looking most put out.

It was some minutes before John and I could stop the smothered sniggers, but I must have eventually dropped off, for when I next looked, the strange little person had gone. Mum said he left the train at Crewe and the rest of the journey is a blank.

Dad met us at the station and we had a short bus ride to where his lodgings were. He had the use of one room, sharing a kitchen and bathroom facilities, in what looked like an apartment block, I think in Paddington. The place thoroughly depressed me and I was feeling unwell after the journey. I worried that the whole exercise was a ploy of Dad's, to force us into a move that fitted in with his plans. The food I was given made me feel ill, with dizzy headaches and vomiting. We were on bread and jam rations as usual, the bread was crusty with tiny black pips all over it – poppy seeds Mum told me, adding that it was probably them that made me feel sick. She removed the crusts, tut-tutting about the waste and told me to stop being a pest.

We saw no one else at the flat during our brief stay, only a policeman by the entrance, who wore a funny helmet, not a hat like the police in Newarthill wore. We were not allowed out at all, not even to play in the vestibule of the building. The policeman was there because that week an elderly woman had been found murdered in her room. The police believed that her killer had not found what he was looking for in her room and just might return.

It was early November and the weather was really gloomy. On the Saturday we were to visit a colleague of Dad's, who would tell us how wonderful life in London was. The look on Mum's face made me want to laugh, who was he trying to fool? But she made no comment. It was only a short walk away and we did not stay very long, but when we made to leave and return to the lodgings, we got quite a shock.

Outside was blanketed in fog, thick enough to collect in a bucket, a dark, wet, clinging filth. Dad exclaimed, 'Oh no! Quick, back inside, it's smog.'

He rummaged in his pockets for a few seconds, producing two crumpled handkerchiefs, while Mum found two smaller ones in her bag. We were told to cover our noses and mouths and breathe only through the cloth. The cloying filth seemed to stick to us as we made our way slowly back to our lodgings. Mum niggled at Dad, 'Ah hope you know where you're going.'

He replied, 'Yes, yes, stop witterin'.'

It was almost eerie, late afternoon on a Saturday, with hardly any people about and very little traffic. I never could have believed that I would be pleased to be back in our dismal lodgings. We removed our makeshift masks, which were covered with what looked like wet soot, and Dad told us solemnly that all that muck would have got in our lungs without a mask.

As if to add weight to her argument, Mum niggled at Dad as she removed her coat, 'You kin keep yer bloomin' London, we're goin' back to Scotland.' And we did!

I only vaguely recall our arrival back in Newarthill, I had asked Mum if were were going to move to London and was told, 'No, not to London, not London.'

She had a far-away expression on her face and I did not like the implications of her vague response, it hinted at a move of some sort. She could not be pressed further and I was told that it had nothing whatsoever to do with me.

In the afternoons after school, in that mysterious gloaming period before it got dark, I would venture into my 'jungle', to look for 'critters'. Not that I found anything much in November, unlike summer when it would abound with wonderful crawly things. One such afternoon, I decided to keep out of the long grass as it was all frosted and very cold. As I made my way back towards the path I heard a low yowling noise. 'Tiger,' I thought and giggled, moving slowly towards where the sound came from, as another yowl warned me to be careful. It sounded like an animal in distress, so I cautiously edged forward, gently parting the long grass, to find a very large tabby cat. It spat and snarled in fury at me, and in the fading light I could not tell if it was grey or brown. I thought that I knew all the neighbourhood moggies but it was huge and seemed quite wild, I had never seen anything like it before.

I reached down to gently stroke the enormous head as it uttered another warning yowl. Talking softly to it, all sorts of gibberish, I began to stroke the forehead with the back of my hand. I noticed that the ears were tufted and decided that the animal must be injured, for it made no attempt to flee. It was clearly distressed and as I stroked the head, I gingerly felt around the limbs for any obvious injury. It remained in a crouching position, emitting low growling sounds as I eased my hand along the length of the huge back. 'This,' I thought, 'is no household pet.'

My hand touched something damp as the cat snarled its fury at me, I had found the injury. I needed to fetch help, the cat was too big for me to handle, Mr Mac or Mr Powell would be home.

I slowly backed away from the now snarling cat, talking soothingly to it, but I noticed the angrily swishing tail and realised that the cat was poised to spring at me. My reflex actions were swift, I was used to dodging swipes, but as that angry frightened animal sprang at me, I only just managed to leap out of its reach. It landed by my feet, spitting and snarling as I tried to back away. I dared not turn my back on it to flee, for it was poised once more to spring. I dodged aside again as it leapt at me once more, but screamed in pain and fright as razor-sharp claws tore into my legs. I went on screaming as the cat yowled and spat its hatred. I heard Mr McKissock shout and I screamed again.

It was almost dark as he called out, 'Whaur ur ye?'

'Over here, over here,' I shrieked, not daring to take my eyes off the cat. It had backed up ready to spring again, that brute was measuring the distance and I had to be ready to take evasive action.

Mrs McKissock let fly with a sweeping broom and it howled at her, then fled. She must have ducked through the fence to reach me so swiftly, following the sounds of my screams and the cat yowls.

Mr McKissock took the broom and followed the direction the cat had taken, but it was long gone. My legs felt like they were on fire and I thought I was going to faint as Mrs McKissock lifted me up like a rag doll. I was amazed at her strength, but shook convulsively as she carried me up the path, then up the steps to the door of our flat. Mum and John were just coming out to see what all the commotion was about, saying that they had heard a cat fight and they thought it was Fluffy. I told them through chattering teeth that he was asleep

283

on my bed with the kittens.

'Naw, het's this yin that's hid a fecht wi' a cat,' they were told, as Mrs McKissock pushed past them to carry me up to the flat. She was taking charge, despite Mum's protestations.

'I'll see to her now, thank-you – I'll take over, no need for you to come—' she trailed off. It all fell on deaf ears, so she followed us into the sitting-room. John was told to fetch a towel and put it on the chair. All this time Mrs McKissock rocked me in her arms, cooing 'Therr, therrr.' Could this be the same old bat, I wondered, who was forever yelling at me to 'Git aff tha-at fence you'?

She placed me on the towel covering the chair, to assess the damage. The cat's claws had torn the edge of my skirt and I worried what Mum would do about that, but she said nothing. Both legs from the knees to the ankles were raked with claw marks that oozed blood. Mum fetched a bowl of warm water, along with a small bottle of disinfectant and Mrs McKissock cleaned up the wounds.

There was a pile of newly laundered things on the table, that Mum was waiting to post back to Dad. She had told me earlier that she would send them on when he sent her some money – she was learning!

A handkerchief taken from the pile was used to bathe the scratches and John was sent off to Mrs McKissock's house to fetch a bottle of iodine. Mum glowered at her when she was told to get a hot sweet drink for me. I was helped out of my clothes and into a nightdress that had been amongst the newly laundered things. The drink, warm milk with sugar in it, was handed to me, but I could not hold it as I was shaking all over, my teeth chattered on the edge of the cup as it was held for me to drink from.

John arrived with the iodine and two rolls of bandage, wrapped in dark blue paper. Mr McKissock had asked if a doctor was needed, John said he had asked something about tetan— before he could finish Mum snapped, 'That won't be necessary.'

I could not help thinking that if she had been the cat's victim it would be an ambulance she would want, never mind a doctor!

I gasped as the iodine stung like fire, but the wounds were not as bad as they might have been.

'Therr,' announced Mrs McKissock to me as she bound up the last piece of bandage, 'Ye'll live tae fecht anither day, but nae cats mind.'

She turned to Mum, whose facial expression would turn milk, to tell her, 'Aye, ah heerd tell o' a muckle great cat here aboots, that wifie Simpson's dug chased it oot o' thur gairden jist the ither day.'

'Hoomph,' was all Mum could say.

As Mrs McKissock closed up the iodine bottle she said, 'Aye, noo, that'll stope ony infection.' She shook her head and added, 'Ye nivver ken whaur that brute's bin.'

All the time she dressed my wounds she gazed around the room, taking it all in. Mum always kept everything clean and tidy, which seemed to surprise Mrs McKissock.

Mum remarked that the cat sounded like a Scottish wild cat and what was a thing like that doing around a built up area? Through chattering teeth I told them both that it should go up to the farm where they were plagued with rats, then realised too late that I was talking to the celebrated street gossip.

Mum niggled, 'You stay away frae that farm – you hear? An' that waste ground.'

She turned to Mrs McKissock to grumble, 'She's always in there, fooling around.'

Mrs McKissock laughed heartily and replied, 'Aye, so ah've heard.'

I never knew what Mum had against the farm and its occupants, Rita and her family were always kind to me, making me feel welcome whenever I went there. For my part, I was told 'not to bring that girl here'. When I asked Mum why I could not bring friends home, I was told that she did not want people interfering in her business; at least she had given up the 'those sorts and disassociation' speeches. Rita's dad was usually around when we played at the farm, so we were in no danger, the only time we were at risk was the day the nasty old boar got loose in the yard and we showed Rita's dad that when it came to making ourselves scarce, we could move like greased lightning.

We landed ourselves in trouble one afternoon, when we decided to find Rita's dad for a ride on the tractor. We spotted him about two fields away and set off to reach where he was working. When he saw us he yelled at us, waving his arms about and telling us to go back. We could not see what all the fuss was about and carried on regardless, but when we reached him and clambered over the fence, he told us off good and proper.

Seems we had just trudged across a bog, but as it had not rained for some days, it was only spongy. He angrily told us that he would skelp* the pair of us if we did not stay in the farmyard. The fenced off fields were all bog, although he could sometimes put sheep into them.

When Mrs McKissock left she told Mum to keep me at home the following day, as she would be round to change the dressings. Mum niggled after she had gone, 'Aye, an' she'll huv anither guid gawp roond.'

I told Mum that that cat was dangerous, especially now it was injured, what if a toddler came up against it? She said she would visit the police station after Mrs McKissock's visit in the morning and make sure that something was done about it. I was annoyed with Mum for she had not thanked our neighbour for her help, and I knew that had it not been for her, I would have been in a sorry state. Next day she stayed for the tea and fairy cakes that were offered, after the dressings were changed. We had some petroleum jelly and I was told to use it on the scratches. Mum's offer to pay for the bandages was waived aside.

Mrs McKissock declared that the wounds were clean and would soon heal, there might be scars but they would fade with time.

The police, she advised Mum, had been told about the cat and had several complaints. 'Mary Buchanan's man's efter it wi' his air rifle.'

'Poor thing,' I thought.

We tried to keep Fluffy in until the cat was caught, but it was not easy. He got out of the bathroom window down on to a neighbour's shed roof and no amount of coaxing could get him back in, two days after my confrontation with the cat. I told Mum that I could not go to bed until I knew he was safely back indoors. John kept going to the door to call for him but there was no sign of him. At about nine o'clock we heard a cat fight and John and I rushed downstairs to go out to where the

---

* smack

286

sounds were coming from, they were somewhere in my jungle. Mum quickly followed, she had stopped by the coal cupboard to get the hand shovel, the one I had once used as a weapon whilst playing in the snow years before in Corsham.

I was going into that jungle to get those cats. Mum said, 'Oh do be careful, for goodness sake,' as she handed me the shovel.

I told her if it was that brute, I had a score to settle with it. I never made it into the long grass, something fast, furious and furry brushed past my legs, followed by a large dark shape. It was too dark to see which was which, but instinct made me strike out at the larger shape. I hit something really hard, but no sound came. John went indoors to fetch a small torch he had and we spent several minutes searching the area that Dad had cleared some months before, to find what I had hit. The grass there was now quite long, but we found Fluffy by following his pitiful mewing. John lifted him up, he thought that I had hit him with the shovel, but I told him I was feet away when I hit something much larger than Fluffy.

We got him indoors and laid him on the side of the kitchen sink. He was covered in blood and lay very still, breathing in shallow little gasps. Mum and John sponged him down with warm water and disinfectant, cleaning all his fur. He made no sound as they poked and prodded around him looking for injuries, and it was soon apparent that they were cleaning off the other animal's blood. He had lost a few patches of fur, his ears were torn and he was totally exhausted, he had put up a tremendous fight.

Mum warmed up some milk, added a little sugar and John painstakingly held the cat's head whilst he spooned the milk into its mouth. He rallied a little and Mum rubbed a smudge of nasal decongestant under his chin to ease his wheezing. I wrapped him up in a clean towel, as Mum put the soiled one in to soak, then took him off to my room to sleep on the end of my bed. I was told to get off to bed as I was returning to school the next day. Mum came into my bedroom to see us settled in and took the kittens off to their box in the sitting-room. She told me the P.D.S.A. van would be on the estate on the Wednesday and I was to take Fluffy for a check-up. She asked if I had hit the other cat and I told her I had hit something, very hard.

At school next day, at morning break, a boy was telling a crowd of children about a huge cat his dad had found in their garden, a real wild cat. I dared ask if it was all right.

'Oh no,' he replied, 'it wis deid, someb'dy hud bashed its heid in.'

I could not help feeling relieved, but also a bit sorry. It was a beautiful wild thing and had probably come looking for food, only to be hounded to death.

The boy eyed my bandages and asked, 'Wis it you it scratched? We heard aboot it.'

I thought, 'Yes, and I know who from,' but just nodded my reply.

The P.D.S.A. vet listened to my sorry tale, as he examined Fluffy, then told me that he had treated some local cats for some really horrendous injuries, having to destroy two of them.

'Wha ivver bashed yon brute's heid in, did us aw a favour.'

I said nothing.

Fluffy had never really recovered, he was totally lethargic and the vet pointed to the reason. We had looked all over him for bite marks, but just by his anus was a large lump, oozing pus. A tom-cat's bite, he told me, can be poisonous, it was the cause of most fight injuries, adding that Fluffy's had gone too far. He explained gently that it would be kinder to put him to sleep – no antibiotics in those days!

He offered to take him there and then, putting him into a cardboard carrying box, which he placed under the bench he worked on. I made him lift it up again, so I could give Fluffy a goodbye pat, then I had to sign a form. I handed over the five shillings fee that Mum had given me and left with my heart breaking.

The van had parked a few doors away from our gate and as I returned home I met Gracie. She asked where Fluffy was and between sobs I told her what had happened. She had heard about my trouble with the 'muckle great cat' but did not know about Fluffy. She soothed and commiserated, saying we still had Bootsie and Snudge, whilst she had nothing. I asked her what she meant, and she tearfully told me that they had to have their old black labrador Lass put to sleep. In my own miseries I had not noticed that she was not around. That old dog used to follow us everywhere, she took her guard duties very seriously, wherever we went Lass was never far behind.

I went indoors to tell Mum all the sad news, then escaped to the privacy of my bedroom, to cry for the pet that had meant so much. There would be no ceremony in a garden for Fluffy. For weeks afterwards, I kept imagining that I could see him sitting on my bed, preening his fur, lying by the hearth and once, sitting on the draining board by the sink waiting to be let out of the window. It was difficult to accept that he was gone forever and I would never see him again. There would be no soft purring head by my pillow, no paw poking me in the face, no comforter when I felt lonely. The kittens came round for fusses, but Fluffy had been special, we had been through a lot together.

37

The Last Rose of Summer

The impending Christmas holiday was all my class-mates could talk about, for my part I was dreading it. I listened to their excited chatter about what they wanted from Santa Claus and got more and more depressed. Everywhere was a buzz of activity with preparations. Fir trees festooned in multi-coloured fairy lights lit up many windows. Shops were decorated with paper chains, colourful lanterns, shiny stars and all manner of baubles. It was impossible not to be caught up in the excitement. I loved to hear the band of the local Salvation Army on a street corner playing carols, and groups of local children, muffled up against the cold, going from door to door rattling their collection tins as they sang out, 'Ding dong merrily on high.' Oh how I longed to go carolling, but Mum said 'Don't answer' when they knocked on our door.

One night, coming home from one of her meetings, I remarked how nice it was to see all the pretty trees at the windows.

'Tch,' she complained, 'ye jist cannie git away frae it, silly pagan customs.'

'Tut tut,' I mocked, 'silly me, we cannie hae folk enjoying owt, kin we?'

I asked her if she had Christmas presents when she was a child and when she did not reply, I persisted, 'Well, did you?'

She sniffed then replied, 'That was different.'

'Oh,' I sneered, 'all right fer you, but no' fer me an' John.'

She sniffed again, a habit of hers that really annoyed me, then told me, 'We know better now, now that we are in the truth.'

I sneered at her, 'Huh, you widnie ken truth if ye fell over it.'

290

Had she told me there was no money for Christmas, that was simple enough to accept, but professing to be a Christian (and better than most according to her) and shunning the very festival that started it, was just beyond my comprehension. I could rearrange the facts to suit my own purpose, but she had it off to a fine art. She was simply not prepared to see anyone else's point of view, she and only she was right. I annoyed her further by asking if we could have a traditional dinner, to make a change from soup and toast.

'We'll see,' she replied, translated it meant 'forget it'.

We made our paper chains at school, along with paper lanterns that were used to decorate the assembly hall. There was to be a party on the last day of term, I was afraid that I would be obliged to miss it, until our teacher told us that no one was to leave until school finished at three-thirty. I went home to tell Mum, expecting the worst. She whined, 'Kin ye no' jist leave after lunch?'

'No,' I replied, 'we have been warned that no one is excused before three-thirty.'

'Hoomph,' was her only reply to that.

I added wickedly, 'I expect the teachers did that on purpose, so's naeb'dy wid miss oot on the end o' term fun.' She glared at me without making a comment, so I added, exaggerating the accent, 'Nivver mind Mum, ah'm sure no' tae enjoy masel, efter aw, awb'dy'll be in party claes, an' yours truly will be her usual raggedy sel'.'

She coughed, went very red in the face, then yelled at me, 'Go to your wretched party if you must, but don't you join in on anything – you hear? I *won't* have you consorting with worldly things.'

'That's aw richt Mum,' I cooed, 'dinnie worry, it wouldnie be Christmas withoot Scrooge.'

She gave me an odd look then demanded, 'Have you been reading books again?'

Books were not allowed, we had a set of children's encyclo-paedia that Dad had bought when we lived in Corsham, and he had shown them to John, telling me that they were not for me, I was not to touch them. I was left on my own enough to read them several times over. I would read anything I could get my hands on, often salvaging books from rubbish bins. I had been given a volume of Greek mythology a neighbour was about to throw away, and loved reading tales about half men, half beast, and that wonderful Medusa, who could turn to stone all who gazed upon her. She reminded me of my mother who could practically kill with a look.

I returned from school one afternoon to find Mum hovering over that book, like the black death.

'Where did you get this?' she screamed at me, waving the book in the air.

'Enjoyed reading it, did you Mum?' I replied.

'You will tell me this instant where you got it from,' she shrieked.

'Oot o' a rubbish bucket, whaur aw ma reading material comes frae,' I told her.

I thought she was going to explode as she shrieked, 'You, you rummage in bins?'

'Aye, ah wis lookin' fer grub, but aw a foond wis a mouldy auld book.'

I was laying it on as thick as treacle.

'Oh my God,' was her only reply. She sat down, visibly shaken, then proceeded to give me a lecture about reading 'worldly' literature, telling me that I could read her magazines or the Bible if I must read at all.

I almost caused her to have an apoplexy when I replied rudely, 'Ah dinnie read trash.'

She went very quiet and I left her to go into my bedroom. She had turned everything upside down, things all over the floor, so I set about putting them back. There was not much in the room, so it did not take very long, but I resolved to make more use of my hiding place under the floor-boards, even though it was difficult for me to shift the bed. Meanwhile, my book had gone on the fire.

The day before the school party I had arrived home from school, to be told to go and look in my room. There, draped across the bed, was a buttercup yellow satin frock. It had satin rosebuds on the waist, with bands to tie at the back, and two small pockets that also had satin rosebuds on. It had seen better days, but at least it was a party frock, with a full skirt that really needed a buckrum petticoat under it, but it would have to do. I thanked Mum for it, not daring to ask where it had come from, as she hovered close by, telling me to try it on.

It was intended for a much taller, heavier person than me

and buttercup yellow was certainly not my colour.

'Oh dear,' complained Mum, 'you look like the last rose of summer.'

She pointed to a paper bag, saying, 'Thurr's shoes in that.'

I opened up the bag to find a pair of buckskin shoes that had also seen better days, but oh how I had craved a pair of those soft white shoes! They were too big, but Mum stuffed paper in the toes and as they had a strap fastening, I managed to keep them on.

John had arrived home during the dressing up and he informed me that I looked like Minnie Mouse.

At bedtime, I had to endure having my hair done up in rags to make ringlets.

Next day we were to have an early lunch, then those who lived near the school could go home to change, the others could bring their clothes to change into after lunch break, the party was to start at one o'clock. A huge Christmas tree was put up in the hall, decorated with all the things that the children had made. I thought it all looked so wonderful and could hardly wait for the lunch break to come when I could rush home to change into my party clothes. Mum tidied up my hair after I donned the frock, which hung around my skinny legs like a damp dish-cloth. She had whitened up the shoes with tennis shoe whitener and bought me a pair of white socks. I was told to wear the shoes as it was not raining, but the frock hung down about four inches below my oilskin mac and I hoped that nobody would notice amidst all the excitement.

Some girls were in the cloakroom when I arrived back at school, chattering excitedly and comparing attire. I slunk in to hang up my mac and navy woolly cardigan, hoping that nobody would notice me. I made to put my handkerchief into a pocket of the frock and noticed with dismay that there was a small tear in it; perhaps it would not be seen, I hoped.

I looked longingly at the collection of taffeta and tulle, satin and velvet, then saw Carol. She had seen me and my frock and I felt really dejected. She came over to where I stood, eyeing the frock, but she made no comment, just took my hand saying, 'Come oan Bobbie, let's gaun intae the hall.'

I had not seen myself in the yellow frock as we did not have a full-length mirror, but I imagined that I looked just awful. Carol's frock was a frothy layer upon layer of blue Shantung, ballerina length with puffed sleeves. With her dark hair and high colouring she looked really lovely and I told her so.

'Thank you,' was all she said, eyeing my frock.

She was friend enough to make no comment, but Sophia, of whom I expected better things, almost fell over herself to tell me how awful I looked.

'Where *did* you get that dress?' she sneered.

'Het's a hand-me-down,' the delightful Isobel informed her.

Sophia blushed, adding lamely, 'It's not your colour.' Then she turned and walked away.

'You look like a rag doll,' accused a girl from a higher class, who was floating in white organdie, tied with a dark green cumberbund.

'You're lik' the fairy aff the tree,' I snapped back.

I had promised myself to try and curb my temper and not let fly verbally, or with feet and fists. I was to cease being a hooligan, but oh dear, how I was being tempted, it was almost too much!

We were told to make up groups of eight for a reel, so I went to join a group of class-mates, but was elbowed out by Isobel who told me, 'We've got eight, clear off.'

A tall girl with vibrant red hair took my hand, saying, 'C'mon, we need anither yin,' and the man with the piano accordion began to play. I liked Scottish country dancing, at least I liked to watch it, I was not too keen on doing it, all that birling* made me feel giddy. The first boy I had to dance past looked me up and down, and on the second circuit informed me that my dress was ghastly. On the third circuit I informed him that his manners were appalling and we left it at that. I felt smugly pleased with myself, for it was not that long since I would have floored him for his rude remark.

I wanted to go and sit the dances out, but the girl with the red curls would have none of it.

'Dinnie mind him, he's jist iggerant.'

It was a relief when the dances ended, I never could do them right. I loved the music but all that leaping about was just exhausting, all I wanted to do was collapse into a chair.

'Over here,' called Carol, so I joined a group of my class-mates. London Tony was sitting with Joyce, he had completely

* spinning

ignored me since his arrival, I consoled myself with the belief that it was the frock that was to blame. I looked at the dresses my companions wore, the beautiful styles and colours, and sighed, thinking dejectedly, 'a weed amongst the flowers.' For some peculiar reason I remembered something Dad had said to me years before, when we lived in Corsham. I had been watching him dead-head some chrysanthemums and pull up the weeds around them. When he saw me watching him, he had smiled and told me, 'The flowers fade and die, but you can never get rid of the weeds.'

That memory cheered me up enormously and I told myself, 'You are what you are, not what you wear.'

A teacher who had been playing the piano, announced that it was party piece time.

'What on earth is that?' I asked Carol.

'She wants folk tae sing or play the piano or whitever.'

A boy played the piano and everyone clapped, then another boy sang *Silent Night*. I almost sniggered, there was nothing silent about the way he belted it out! The girl with the red hair recited Edward Lear's *The Owl and the Pussy Cat*.

Carol nudged me to whisper, 'You kin sing – go on.'

'No fear!' I told her, but before I realised what Carol was doing, she was standing up calling out, 'Bobbie kin sing Miss – she'll sing.'

'Well, come on then,' called out the teacher.

'Oh heavens, what can I sing?' I thought, as I made my way up to the front of the hall.

I had to walk almost the entire length of the hall to stand by the teacher at the piano, my face scarlet as she asked me what I would sing.

'*O, Holy Night*,' I told her, adding, 'it's an Italian Christmas carol.'

'I *know* what it is,' she said irritably, then asked, 'What key?'

'I dunno,' I mumbled, wishing I was thousands of miles away.

I was told to sing the first word, then on the count of three.

I faced the audience of grinning, leering faces, my stomach doing somersaults, but tried to mentally blank them out. I remembered what Dad had told me, 'Sing out, let the sound come from deep within, let it flow then gently fade away.' I finished with 'O night, o night de-ee-vine,' and when I looked, everything was still, silent; nobody moved.

'Oh dear,' I thought, 'they didnie like it,' so I bowed and made to leave. Suddenly everyone seemed to be clapping, even the teachers, and I thought, 'It couldnie huv been that bad after all.'

The pianist caught my arm as I made to return to my seat and asked, 'Who taught you to sing like that?'

'My Dad,' I told her.

My class teacher came up and said to the pianist, 'Ye could do with Bobbie in your choir fer the festival.'

The pianist sniffed, replying, 'Ah already have all I need, thank you,' and turned her back on both of us.

I returned to my seat to find Carol in tears.

'Whit's up wi' you?' I asked.

Margaret, who was trying to pacify her, said, 'It wiz your song, it wiz that sad.'

'Oh dear, ah'm sorry,' I replied, puzzled.

School was out, we all had a sugar mouse from the headmaster, dressed up in a Santa Claus outfit. We said our goodbyes and 'happy Christmas' and went home.

38

Oh Little Town of Newarthill

I had dreaded the holidays, they meant very little hot food, no milk and very little of anything. Mum received nothing from Dad, but he came home for the Christmas break bearing nothing but a bag of laundry. There was very little cheer and certainly no spirit of goodwill. Christmas was a taboo subject in our house and we were supposed to be oblivious to what went on around us.

A package had arrived from Canada with a card, a box of chocolates for John and a box of toffees for me. The toffees, Mum told me, were called candy kisses and had come from Grandma. She was Mum's dad's second wife, an American lady he met in Toronto after Mum had returned to Scotland. He had died some months before and I had had to read out Grandma's letter to Mum telling her about his funeral. The Canadian branch of the British Legion had arranged his funeral, with his coffin being carried on a horse-drawn gun carriage 'Hm, very grand,' I thought. Mum had declared that it meant nothing to her, she felt nothing for a man she had not seen for years. I told her we should write to Grandma, to thank her for the presents and let her know that we were thinking of her. I was told in no uncertain fashion that we would do nothing of the sort. Mum snorted angrily, 'She's nothing to us, she's not your grandmother.'

She bristled with irritation, adding, 'She's no right to send you things.'

The card was thrown on the fire, never to be mentioned again.

Poor Grandma, no card, no letter and her just widowed for the second time. I looked at my parents, so wrapped up in their own importance, so detached from anything normal and felt almost sorry for them, but I was determined that neither of them would be offered any of my sweets.

Dad had not mentioned his missing chocolate, but he pointedly ignored me, which suited me just fine. We had a picture of him on the wall, put there by him. It was one of him in Navy uniform, a very nice one, but I had annoyed Mum once by commenting, 'Looking at that, ye wid never ken it wiz sic' a pig.' The picture frame had been made and given to him by some shipmates. The frame was a replica of a lifebuoy, about the size of a dinner plate, painted white with gold coloured braid around the outer rim. On the top of the buoy, in gilt lettering, was H.M.S. SEABORNE. The photograph was glass-fronted and the backing was a piece of plywood, cut from a packing case. The piece of ply had been cut around a trade mark on the case, a black inked chain, bearing the word DUREX. John had tried to explain what that was, adding that Dad must have been a right Jack the lad in the Navy, with a girlfriend in every port. He would not explain further, and neither would Mum when I asked her, she just had a queer expression on her face!

I took delight in turning that photograph with the face to the wall. When Dad had arrived home he asked what his picture was doing with its face to the wall. It was hung up by the braid, on one of Dad's infamous nails, above the fireplace, way out of my reach! I had to stand on a fender stool and reach across to turn it over.

I announced that it was always like that, however many times we turned it back it would always end up with the face to the wall. I added almost casually, that it must be another poltergeist. The look on the parents' faces almost made me laugh. I was up at the crack of dawn each day that Dad was home, to turn the picture to face the wall, it had a wonderfully unnerving effect on both of them. Eventually the picture was put away in the sideboard cupboard.

Christmas Eve was the same as any other day, we had some coal in the cupboard and a big hearty fire had been in the grate since Dad's arrival, and was to remain until he left. He did not buy any more coal. He just used up most of our supply, what we might do when he left did not seem to concern him.

At around eight o'clock we were told by Dad, 'Git tae yer beds.'

John complained that it was too early and was told he
needed his sleep. I quipped to John, 'We mustn't be awake
when Santa comes,' but nobody thought it was funny.

It was freezing cold in my room as I had left the window
open, I closed it up then noticed that the kittens were already
snuggled down in my bed. I wondered if Mum would let me
borrow the hot water-bottle until she went to bed, so I went
back to the sitting-room to ask her.

'You git tae yer bed,' Dad yelled at me, but I totally ignored
him and went to the kitchen to find Mum. She was just coming
through the doorway carrying a large potato in each hand. I
was amazed to see her place them in the ash can under the fire
and wondered what she was doing.

'What is it?' she niggled at me.

It seemed to me that she could never talk to me without
sounding thoroughly irritated.

'Could ah borrow the hottie bottle until yous gaun tae bed,'
I asked, but before she could reply, I added, 'Whit are ye
dae'in burnin' thae tatties in the fire?'

Dad sniggered, Mum sighed heavily and replied, 'Fer
goodness sake, git tae yer bed.'

I left and returned to my room, I heard the sitting-room
door being firmly shut, I suppose so I could not eavesdrop on
them. I switched off the light, climbed into bed, heaving the
furries over to one side as they snuggled down, purring noisily.
I wondered what Mum was thinking about, why waste food
when there was so little of it?

'Of course, silly me,' I thought, 'she was baking those
potatoes, not burning them, no wonder Dad sniggered.' They
were up to their old tricks again, sending us to bed so they
could have their supper.

I fumbled in the darkness to find my socks to put them back
on, and wondered if I should put on my cardigan also. The
door opened and Mum brought in the hot water-bottle. She
had not put the light on and I covered up the kittens in case she
tried to take them away. She pushed the warm rubber bag
under the bedclothes and told me she would collect it later.

'You come mind,' I warned, 'ah'm not wantin' him ony-
where near me.'

She did not reply, she left without even a 'good night' and
certainly not a 'Merry Christmas'.

In the dark, I could not tell which kitten was which, but one was washing everything it could reach, whilst the other purred contentedly. I lay on my back trying to remember the words of the carol *Oh Little Town of Bethlehem* and somewhere between 'while mortals sleep' and 'angels keep' I drifted into oblivion.

A noise outside woke me and I sat up to listen. The water bag had gone and so had the kittens. Mac the tortoise had gone for his winter sleep in the airing cupboard, with strict instructions from John not to disturb. I listened to the sound of voices, recognising Mrs Mac's and Nancy's, but could not make out what was said. I decided that they must be going to the midnight mass, Gracie had complained that she was not allowed to go until she was older. She had asked me what I was having for Christmas and I told her, 'Same as usual,' and changed the subject.

Christmas morning I awoke to find Dad hovering over me, holding a plate of toast and a mug of tea.

'Wakey wakey, rise an' shine,' he sing-songed.

I sat up staring at him, standing there grinning like a benevolent sprite as I took the proffered plate and mug. I thanked him and when he left, I found myself thinking about a Christmas morning that seemed so long ago, something about a red racing car and big dark blue balloons. What had gone wrong in our lives? Why did everything have to be so glum? Was there a reason why we were starved and neglected? Dad was never out of work, out of sight mostly but not out of work. Why was there no love? Were we really the millstone around their necks that they kept reminding us of?

Dad had told me often enough how evil and worthless I was, what a burden and disappointment. Mum went on at length to both of us, about what she could have done, been, if only ... Oh dear, it did seem that we were the bane of their lives. Mum would whine on about how she could have been this or that, oh yes, she was cut out for better things.

I once commented that, for a miner's daughter who left school at fourteen to work on a farm in the Canadian outback, she had some big ideas about herself. She had sniffed and informed me that I was just a nobody.

During Dad's week at home, John fell ill with influenza. He had been out in all weathers, delivering his newspapers. There had been severe frosts and biting winds, and neither of us had adequate warm clothing. He was feverish and could not keep down the soup he was given. Dad moved John's bed into the sitting-room where it was warm, but no doctor was sent for. Dad told John he would have to sweat it out of him and kept tucking the blankets around him, piling our rapidly diminishing coal supply on the fire, the room was like a furnace. He refused to give him a drink until the fever was out of him. I was frantic, I had not forgotten about that sneaky 'Angel of Death' and John looked so ill.

I was told gruffly by Dad, 'Clear off you, we don't want another one ill.'

I crept into the room during the night, I was paranoid about that 'angel', it would not dare come whilst I kept watch. By the time Dad returned to London, the invalid was sitting up taking notice, with no real enthusiasm.

Whatever John had had, I got with knobs on!

We had been to one of Mum's meetings, despite the bitterly cold weather and had been waiting around for the bus home. My feet were warm enough due to the fact that I was wearing a pair of Dad's warm woolly socks, stolen from his suitcase before he left, but the rest of me was numb with cold. I had a throbbing headache and felt really feeble. I had told Mum earlier in the day that I did not feel well and she had told me that I needn't think that I could get out of going to the meeting. I complained that my head felt full of cotton wool and I felt queasy, she replied, 'Oh do stop complaining, you're not going to be ill are you?'

I was. Somehow I got home, we had boarded a bus in Motherwell, seating ourselves on the side seats by the platform. After a few stops a man got on, carrying a baby. He settled himself down with the infant on his lap, then took stock of his surroundings. When his gaze fell upon me, he looked really alarmed, and lifting up the baby he got off at the next stop. I obviously looked as ill as I felt. As we got off the bus at our stop, a woman who had been seated opposite me and next to the man with the baby, said to Mum, 'That bairn,' pointing at me, 'should be at hame in hur bed.'

Mum totally ignored her, but bed was where I remained for the following three weeks, lost in shadows of delirium. I missed the entry of 1952 and the first flurries of soft white snow. I could only recall vague sounds of voices, needle pricks and some person pummelling my back. I was sometimes aware of being in my own bed which had been moved into the sitting-room, and I would stare at the white painted doors of the cupboard on the opposite wall. I would see vivid pictures on those doors and could hear my own voice calling out.

I heard Mum ask over and over again, 'What about the King, dear?'

I kept replying, 'He's going away.'

I had really weird dreams, one in particular that kept recurring, so much so that I began to know what would happen next. It always followed the same sequence, like a film replay over and over.

I would be floating in a black void, lost and crying, when a voice that seemed to come from far away would tell me, 'Go to the light Bobbie ... go to the light.'

I would twist and turn as if weightless, floating until I saw a tiny flicker of light, like a candle flame. Somehow I seemed to be able to propel myself towards the light, which would get bigger and brighter as I approached it. I would find myself standing in a doorway looking out over a vast amazing garden, full of flowers and plants that glowed and sparkled. The colours were very strange and I found that once I was awake I would be unable to recall the colours at all, even the sky was a strange colour, almost iridescent. I would hear the sound of voices and laughter and try to reach the source of the sound. I would cross the strange garden as if floating, to enter a huge valley filled with people wearing long white robes. The people all smiled and moved aside as I floated past, but none spoke. I saw a group of laughing children, also dressed in white robes, playing around a tall figure, whose face I could not see. Everyone seemed so happy, but try as I might I could not reach the figure. I felt that it was watching me, although I could not see the face, then I would hear a voice that seemed to come from everywhere, echoing, 'Not yet Bobbie, it is too soon ... too soon ... too soon.' I would feel a sensation of being dragged backwards, away from the laughing children, back through the strange garden, to be hurled into a purple vortex, a deep purple abyss, spinning as the colour darkened to black. The last time I had the dream, I heard voices through the blackness calling my name.

An urgent sounding voice was saying, 'She's out of the wood

now, she's coming back.'

I heard my own voice call out, 'Not a wood, a garden ... a garden.'

I saw Mum's face through a blur of dizziness and heard her ask, 'What garden?'

'I want to go back to the garden,' I sobbed, 'I don't want to come back.'

I felt a needle prick in my thigh, then oblivion.

I can never see the colour purple without thinking about that garden, but I can never remember the amazing colours of it.

Some hours later I was awake and clamouring for food.

'Ah could scoff a scabbie donkey,' I told Mum, but settled for some broth and bread.

Mum laughed and told John 'By hokey, we ken she's back right enough.'

'Back?' I asked. 'Back, well whaur huv ah been?'

She thought for a few seconds, then replied, 'God only knows.'

39

In the Bleak Mid-Winter

I had a visitor, the doctor was just leaving as he arrived, so Mum had to ask him in, appearances and all that. I heard her voice as she came back up the stairs and along the passageway, saying, 'Oh, an' jist how do *you* know my daughter?'

I heard a man's voice reply, strangely familiar, but I was very befuddled. As Mum entered the sitting-room, she announced in her 'hoity toity' voice, 'But we are not Catholic,' making it sound like an infectious disease, then I saw him. It was Father Murphy, oh how glad I was to see him, but I had to be careful.

Mum would persist, bristling with indignation, 'I want to know, how you know *my* daughter?'

'Ah tae be sure now, an' don't ah know ahl t' bairns here aboots,' he replied, throwing up his arms in a gesture of exasperation, to add, ' 'Tis a penance ah'll be doing, visitin' all the sick o' me parish.'

He was poking fun at her! Oh the joy of it! He was like a ray of sunshine on a gloomy day.

'Well then,' Mum started, but he cut her off with, 'Ah'll be havin' a sit down wi' the bairn, yersel' kin go brew a pot o' somethin'.'

He was laying on the accent as thick as treacle and it was all I could do not to laugh out loud, he was just the tonic I needed.

'You're not to talk to her,' threatened Mum, as he fetched a chair to sit by my bedside.

'Ah'll jist be sayin' a wee prayer, nae herm in that, sharely,' he crooned, as she peered down her nose at him. She left reluctantly with a muted 'hoomph' to go into the kitchen, but left the door wide open.

Father Murphy winked at me, but obeyed the edict not to

talk, he took hold of my hands to bow his head in prayer. I wondered if he had come to check up on me, as I had not seen him for some time. He raised his head, put an index finger on my forehead, patted my shoulder then made to leave.

Mum was back, hovering to ask him, 'Will ye take some tea?'

He declined, thanked her kindly, saying, 'Thurr's mony sick, I must away, God bless yeez all,' and with that he left.

Mum saw him safely off the premises, but was soon back. I had no idea she could backtrack up those stairs so quickly. She was demanding to know how I knew 'that man'.

'Awb'dy kens him,' I told her disinterestedly, adding, 'Ye must've seen him roond the hooses, he's only dae'in whit you dae.'

'Oh, an' whit's that pray?' she sneered.

'Shovin' his religion doon folk's throats,' I sneered back.

I thought she was going to hit me, but instead she snarled, 'You jist keep awa' frae him – ye hear?'

I was not listening.

I was back at school by the end of January, we had had very little snow, but it was bitterly cold, with dark heavy clouds that threatened much more. I was spared most of the post-Christmas tittle tattle, but a girl from Gracie's class came up to me in the playground one afternoon, to tell me that I was a liar.

I gaped at her, then she said, 'Awb'dy git somethin' fer Christmas.'

So, that was it, Gracie had been gossiping, I should have known. I told the girl to go home and ask her mother to tell her the truth, before calling other people liars.

Carol pushed her, yelling at her to leave me alone, then quietly asked, 'Did ye really no' git onythin'?'

I told her we never did and she soothed, 'Is that no' awfie?'

Isobel, who as usual had been ear-flapping our conversation, gave us the benefit of her wisdom by informing us, 'Only good children git pressies, the bad yins git nuthin.'

Carol rounded on her, shrieking, 'You! You jist shut yer fat gob, orrul pit ma fist intae yer kisser.'

'Oh dear,' I thought, 'I expect she gets that frae me.'

Gracie could not be convinced, Nancy was sent round to rout out the truth and cornered me by our outside staircase, some days later.

'Is that right?' she wheedled. 'Yeez didnie git onythin' fer Christmas?'

I had had enough and yelled at her, 'NO, ah didnie, neither did John – no' this year, no' last year an' no' since ah wis fower.'

I stopped to draw breath as she gaped at me, I then added, 'Satisfied?'

I glared at her and went on, 'D'ye no' think it's bad enough, withoot folk aye goin' on aboot it, ah dinnie need or want remindin'.'

She turned and fled without a word.

I was cold, hungry and ill-humoured. Since my illness, I had found it difficult to shake off the feeling of lethargy and depression. John felt like a stranger to me and told me accusingly that I never seemed to laugh any more. He must have been right, for my school friends had remarked much the same.

I seemed to feel sick and light-headed all the time, with a perpetual headache. When I got really hungry, my whole body would shake and shiver. I found that if I ate sugar it helped, but it left me feeling really ill and feeble. I told Mum about it, but all she said was, 'Oh fer goodness sake, whatever next?' and threw up her arms in a gesture of despair. That was something she did when either John or myself went to her with a problem, seems she could not cope with our problems on top of her own.

'Ye'll jist huv tae git on wi' it,' she whined, 'whit dae ye expect me tae dae aboot it?'

I was the last straw, she had all the aggravation she could handle.

After a pause, she niggled, 'Whit *is* the matter with you, anyway?'

I told her that it happened when I was hungry and I seemed to be hungry all the time.

'Don't you think I am hungry too?' she asked angrily, then accused, 'You get school dinners, so stop complaining.'

One Saturday in early February, when a fresh covering of snow had fallen, making everything look dusted with icing sugar, I wandered up to the farm to call on Rita. It was early afternoon, very bleak, with dark clouds threatening more snow, you could almost smell the snow. Mum had told me that it was ozone and you could smell it by the seaside also. There was nobody at home at the farm, so I went into the field where the sheep were. How I envied them their thick woolly coats, but they were huddling into the hedgerow, as if they too could sense the impending blizzard. I was feeling sick and giddy again, but was puzzled, I had had a bowl of soup for lunch, nice it was too. It came from a tiny box of powder that had to be mixed with water then boiled up. Oxtail, Mum said it was, and I thought it was a strange thing to make soup from, no stranger than bird's nest.

On the ground around me I noticed some small round objects that appeared to have been cut up for the sheep to eat. I kicked the ice off a piece and picked it up. It was odd, I had not seen anything like it before, similar to a turnip, but a different colour. If sheep could eat it – well why not?

I bit off the dirty tough skin from the piece I had picked up and spat it out, pocketing the remainder, then looked around for some large pieces.

There was an old hut in the field that Rita and I had played in during the previous summer, which may have been used as a store at some time. I pushed open the door and went in, followed by a nosy old sheep bleating at me, probably because I was trespassing and I had pinched some of her food.

She was coming in too and no amount of shooing would dissuade her, so I pulled the door closed and looked for somewhere to sit. A pile of sacks that Rita and I had used in the summer were still there in the corner of the hut, so I sat down on them after poking about to make sure that they were not occupied. I remembered the rats in the barn and shuddered.

I bit the skins off the pieces of vegetable I had picked up, then crunched into the flesh – not bad at all. By the time I had finished them, I had decided that they must be swedes. I wondered if I could collect enough pieces to take back to Mum for her to boil, but what would she think about me stealing from a sheep?

The sheep that had followed me into the hut, insisted on staying really close to me and had plonked her head on my lap. I told her she was a sheep, not a lap dog, but she just bleated dolefully at me, rolling her eyes. I wondered if her thick woolly coat had ticks in it, but fell asleep without really caring.

A thud on my rump awoke me, I had slipped over on to the

307

floor and that funny old sheep was butting me with her head. When I sat up she baa-ed at me and I thought that was really funny, it was almost as if she was scolding me, bidding me to go home.

I left the hut, my limbs stiff and aching, with woolly-back trailing after me bleating her head off. The more I shushed her, the more noise she made. It had gone very dark and I had no idea what the time was. I could see no stars at all, which meant that the chill wind had not blown the snow clouds away. I hurried up the field, hoping that the sheep's bleating would not attract attention, and climbed over the fence near the road. Woolly-back saw me off before she gave up her bleating. As I crossed the field, I had tried to find some more pieces of swede, but it was too dark. After picking up several clods of snow I gave up, how could I explain where they had come from anyway? I wondered if I would ever be able to look a sheep in the face again. Although the wind had freshened it did not seem so cold, but as I reached home the flurries of snow came thick and fast.

When I got in Mum wanted to know where I had been, did I not know what time it was? Did I realise how worried she had been? I niggled unkindly at her, that she had not been worried enough to bother to come looking for me. It was late afternoon and we were in for a blizzard.

We had taken to going to bed early, in an attempt to save our rapidly diminishing coal supply, so after some soup and toast I told Mum I was going to bed, I did not feel very well. I asked if I could keep my socks and cardigan on as my room was cold and she told me to fetch my pillow and blankets, to move in with her, we would keep warm together. I gave a blanket to John and transferred my few belongings, thinking it was a good idea, especially as Mum had the hot water-bottle. There was a fireplace in that room, but the only time it had been used was when the Brown's had lodged with us. The kittens were quick to transfer also, but they curled up in the old armchair. I wanted John with us also, but Mum would have none of it.

One snowy afternoon, on my return from school, I found Mum using a dinner knife to cut up my little doll's house. She had wrenched one side off it and was trying to cut it up like kindling. I was shocked, she knew what that little house meant to me; apart from the doll bed, it was the only toy I had, a reminder of happier times. She destroyed any book she found and was now intent on an act of spiteful vandalism, destroying the one thing I treasured, my dear little cottage.

All I said was, 'Why?'

She sniffed in her annoying fashion to reply, 'We need fuel.'

I told her she would get precious little warmth from that tiny piece of wood, lovingly fashioned into a little house for me.

She sniffed again to whine, 'We all have to make sacrifices.'

I would not give her the satisfaction of a temper tantrum, I just went off to my room and sat on the floor. I touched my mattress which felt damp, looked around the room at the two suitcases that I played on and thought, 'Well, there is not much more to take.' I saw the doll bed that the two kittens had vacated, the companion piece to the now destroyed cottage and thought 'right', and returned to face Mum. I found her in the kitchen – the cottage had gone up in a no doubt brief flame – and snarled at her, 'You touch my doll bed and I will destroy every one of your Holy Joe books and trash that I can lay hands on.'

She looked at me aghast as I left the room screaming, ' *That*, lady, is a promise!'

I was too angry even to use an exaggerated accent on her like I usually did, but she made no comment and the doll bed was never touched.

One Friday evening we were sitting around the table when we heard a key open the main door of the flat. That was followed by the plod-plod of heavy footsteps up the stairs then along the passage. None of us moved as Dad came into the room, all smiles and suitcase, cheerily saying, ' 'Ello, it's me.'

I looked at the suitcase thinking 'laundry'. What now?

Mum gaped at him, and John, ever so quiet who never said owt, snarled at him, 'What are you wantin'?'

Everyone stared at him as he scowled at Dad. We never knew what John was thinking, he was so quiet. Nobody was left in any doubt as to what I was usually thinking, for I was outspoken to a fault and was not the one to spare feelings.

Mum flustered, 'You never said you were coming.'

Before he could reply, she went on, wringing her hands to tell him, 'We've no coal an' hardly anything to eat.'

'It's his darned neck she should be wringing,' I thought angrily, as I watched them both.

He dismissed it all with a wave of his arm.

'Oh, ah'll sort all that, ah'm 'ome now.'

John stood up from his place at the table and made to leave the room. As he left he glared at Dad, saying, 'Why don't you stay in London?'

To say I was flabbergasted would be an understatement, but I was worried, just what was Dad up to?

It occurred to me that I would have to move back to my own room, so I retrieved my blankets and got a sheet from the airing cupboard to remake my bed. I usually used one double sheet, folded over, and was pleased to get a flannel one. I asked Mum if I could borrow the hot water-bottle to air my bed as it felt a bit damp.

'Oh go on, if you must,' she snapped.

As I waited for the kettle to boil, she came into the kitchen with the bottle to empty it out. I whispered to her, 'It's no' ma fault he's hame.'

'Wheesht!' she replied. 'He'll hear ye.'

He was home, it seemed, to try to persuade Mum to move to London, chance of promotion for him, blah blah. Mum would have none of it, she had heard it all before, no amount of wheedling or threatening would change her mind.

John and I did our 'merge with the furniture' routine, making ourselves scarce, but I heard Mum yell at Dad, 'An' ye neednie think ye kin force us oot by yer starvation an' neglect, either.'

Was she learning? Could it be, at long last, she was fighting back?

Neither John nor I were about when he left for London on the Sunday and neither could have cared less. He had given Mum a ten shilling note to buy a couple of bags of coal, telling her for the umpteenth time that living in London was expensive.

'Well,' she had told him, 'come back to Scotland.'

Our radio was broken again, the valves had, as Mum put it, 'given up the ghost.' We did not have a daily newspaper, so we were a bit out of touch with national news. I arrived at school one morning to find that all classes were to gather in the assembly hall. A large box, a coffin I soon realised, had been placed at the front of the hall. The table it rested on had been covered with a black cloth and the coffin was draped with a

Union flag. We were informed that King George VI had died in his sleep. For one awful moment, I thought he was in that box on the table, then realised that it was a quite uncalled for piece of cheap theatrics. I wondered if our headmaster thought we did not know what 'dead' meant. We went through a repeat performance on the fifteenth of February, when the King was buried at Windsor Castle. We had a two minute silence after prayers, and I wondered why it was that half the school chose those two minutes to cough or clear their throats. It irked me that they could not maintain silence for even two minutes.

As we filed out of assembly to return to lessons, Billy Smith niggled, 'We-ell, tha-at's wan parasite less,' and our teacher smacked his ear.

Mum told me we had a second Queen Elizabeth and she hoped this one would not be a tyrannical despot like the last one.

'Remember her, do you?' I asked, giggling.

As she glared at me I told her, 'Not our Princess Elizabeth, never.'

'Hoomph,' she replied, to add nasally, 'there will be no need of royalty when this system of things ends.'

'Silly bitch,' I thought, but told her, 'It's a guid job she's no' the first, ye'd be in the Tower of London fer treason, an' serve ye right tae.' I was treated to one of her killer glares for a reply.

40

Winds of Change

The snow continued, whipped into blizzard conditions by gusting wind. There were power cuts and coal shortages, the latter being something we were quite used to. There were no woodland areas nearby to collect firewood from, so we spent a lot of time huddled in bed. Meat was still rationed and food subsidies had been cut. Mum went door knocking in all weathers, with me on tow at weekends and half-term.

One afternoon we went by bus to Wishaw a few miles away, taking along another woman from Mum's sect. It was a wet blustery day, which got progressively worse. We were in a tenement close, when one woman told Mum off for pestering her. She had answered the knock on her door and as she opened it, a gust of wind blew out the light on her gas stove. She railed at us for pestering folk, and on such a day too. Mum and her friend apologised profusely, then moved on to pester next door.

The woman who answered the next knock behaved as if she had been waiting in all day for our arrival, saying cheerily, 'Come awa' in, yeez must be fair frozen.'

We were glad to, we were frozen. She bustled and fussed, sitting us down by a roaring fire in a highly polished grate.

'Ah'll awa' an' pit a kettle oan, yizzel be wantin' a brew.'

It was a statement rather than a question and nobody argued.

The tea arrived amazingly quickly and she explained almost apologetically, 'Aye, ah heerd yeez at auld torn-faced's nixt door, an' ah kent ye'd be here nixt, so a pit oan a kettle.'

She thumbed in the direction we had just come from, almost whispering, 'Yeez'll no' git onythin' ooty tha-at yin, tight as a duck's bahouk, so shizz.' She laughed to add, 'An tha-at's

312

watter tight.'

During the adults' small talk, the woman turned to me to ask, 'An' whit dae they cry you hen?'

I told her 'Bobbie' and she exclaimed, 'My, but that's rerr!'

So I explained grumpily that I was supposed to be a boy.

'Och no,' she crooned, 'ye're jist fine as ye ur, ye dinnie git a lawdy wi' sic' bonny hair.'

We finished our tea, thanked her and made to leave.

'Yizzel be headin' fer hame noo, I 'spect,' she said, then added, 'thurr's a souster* blawing up oot therr.'

We assured her that we were heading for home, then bid her farewell.

It was blowing a howling gale outside, with bits of chimney pots and roof slates crashing down on to the road. We had to get to the end of the street to find a bus for Motherwell, and Mum told me to walk close to the tenement wall, to avoid the flying debris. A violent gust of wind caught me, literally blowing me along the pavement, out on to the road that was strewn with broken roof slates. Every time I tried to get back on to the pavement, the wind blew me into the road. I did not know whether to laugh or cry, I was powerless to go in any direction other than the way the wind was blowing. Mum and her friend came running after me and managed to keep hold of me long enough to struggle back to the tenement walls. As we left the road, something large crashed into the road from aloft. Mum said something, but it was lost in the roar of the wind.

We got on a bus for Motherwell, with the conductress telling us that hers was the last bus to run until the storm abated. It seemed much calmer in Motherwell when we bade farewell to Mum's friend, but before we caught a bus to Newarthill, we called in at a small haberdashery shop. Mum bought me a pair of brown woolly stockings and something that looked like a vest, with rubber buttons down the front.

When we got home I tried the stockings on and they fitted, but I could not see how one got them to stay up. Mum cut two lengths from a card of elastic that she had also bought, tied a knot in each, saying with a flourish, 'There ... garters!'

I wondered if that was how she kept her stockings up; no one, but no one, ever knew the secrets of her underwear, they

---

* south westerly gale

313

were more mysterious than the whereabouts of the Holy Grail. I decided there simply *had* to be another way, I could not imagine ladies of the sort one saw in glossy magazines keeping up their silk hosiery with a length of laggie, tied in a knot!

The vest was something else! A torturous looking garment with body panels, fastened with a row of rubber buttons down the front. I had seen them on girls at school and on Gracie and I thought they were just awful.

'It's a liberty bodice,' announced Mum.

I could not imagine anyone having much liberty of movement in one of those ridiculous garments.

'How Victorian,' I sneered. 'Ah'm no' wearin' tha-at thing.'

'Ye should'uv had one long ago,' grumbled Mum.

I replied, 'There are a lot o' things ah should'uv had long ago, but that,' pointing to the vest, 'ah kin dae wi' oot.'

She sighed, pushing it back into the bag, saying, 'Ah suppose ah kin exchange it.'

I caught a cold and Mum made me stay indoors saying, 'We're no' wantin' you ill again.'

She had gone out one afternoon while John was at school, leaving me to amuse myself, so I did some of my school knitting. We had gone on to do bigger things and were knitting scarves. I had chosen red wool again, paying threepence a week for it. This time I did not take anything for the tuck shop, for I knew that Mum did not have very much money and we had our once a fortnight bag of sweets from Mrs Anderson's daughter, who worked at a sweet factory.

It was overcast outside and gloomy inside, so I decided to switch on Dad's wall-lights. We rarely used them as Mum did not trust his handiwork. As it happened, she was right not to trust it!

I was knitting away quite happily, kittens asleep in their box by the hearth. Mum had told me to keep an eye on the fire, not to let it go out, but go easy on the coal, as it had to last. I caught a whiff of burning rubber, looked up from where I was sitting, to see wisps of smoke coming out of the nearest wall-light. I have often pondered over it, but I will never know what made me stand up and poke it with a metal knitting-needle.

There was a loud bang and a bluish flash as both lights went out. There was a black smudge on the wall by the light that I

314

had poked and a nasty acrid smell in the air.

'Oh heck, I'm for it now,' I thought, wondering what to do next.

I tried the kitchen light-switch ... nothing, then the lobby one ... nothing. I would have to go to Mr Mac for help.

As I went down the stairs to the main door, somebody hammered hard on the door, making me jump with fright. I opened the door to a very angry looking Mr Mac and a flustered Mr Powell. My knees were practically knocking as Mr Mac demanded to know what was going on.

'Our lights went bang,' I told him, quaking.

'The whole bloody block's gone bang!' he exclaimed. 'Whit the blazes huv ye bin up tae?'

I told him, 'Come see.'

Mr Mac was first into the room and he whistled then gasped, 'In the name o' the wee man, wid ye gerraloady tha-at!'

Mr Powell shook his head saying, 'Thurr should be a law against the likes o' that.'

Mr Mac looked at me puzzled, then asked what had happened. I told him about the smoke wisps and me poking the fixture, which made him utter a string of expletives, ending with him saying, 'Ye could'uv bin kill't.'

Mr Powell soothed, 'Het's a blessin' in disguise, so 'tis.' He patted my shoulder and said, 'Dinnie fash yersel' hen, well sort it.'

'Aye,' agreed Mr Mac, adding vehemently, 'this lot's cummin oot ... noo.'

Mr Mac left to collect some tools and Mr Powell asked, 'Your faither dae this?' waving at the wall-lights.

I nodded and he added, 'Is thurr onythin' else ah should see?'

I ushered him into the bathroom to show him the wall-fire, the holes in the wall leading into the kitchen and the plug and socket he had made from a single to double socket.

He shook his head in disbelief and announced, 'This lot's cummin oot afore we hae a fire or it kills someb'dy.'

Mr Mac returned with the tools and some fuse wire and the pair set to work, muttering in undertones to each other. They had almost finished when John arrived back from school.

Mr Mac told him, 'You see yer faither disnie dae ony mair electrics.'

315

John just looked at him bemused, I could not bring myself to tell him about my part in the drama. Mum arrived as the two men were leaving and wanted to know what was going on. She was told and Mr Mac warned her no to let 'that man' do any more handiwork on electrics.

Mum sniffed to retort angrily, 'Huh, he won't pay any attention to me.'

Mr Mac's reply was to the effect that he would get the man from the council and she could explain to him how they had a power failure and almost a fire, to boot. I told her about the smoking light fixture, but left out all the little incidental details!

When Dad came home for a weekend, a couple of weeks later, Mum read him the riot act, so he poked fun at her attempts at D.I.Y. She had bought three tins of fabric dye, one each of red, green and yellow, mixed each in turn with water, then, using an old shaving brush of Dad's, she daubed the lobby walls with splashes of the colours. The walls had been painted an offish beige and it brightened them up no end. He was only jealous, for all he ever seemed to do was spoil things.

He was a bit quiet and subdued during that weekend and had been almost nice to us all. He laughingly told me that he knew about me pinching a pair of socks out of his case and was sorry I had been ill . . . was I better? I could not help being just a bit suspicious, especially when he left on the Sunday night, instead of in the morning as was usual. What was he up to now?

I had to wait until Monday after school to have my suspicions confirmed. My cold had dried up and I was anxious to return to school pals and hot dinners. Mum told me that she had something to tell us when John got back from school. My heartbeat was keeping double time and I was filled with a feeling of foreboding, I knew from experience that all was not well, something was about to happen. It was obvious from the expression on Mum's face that whatever it was, there would be no cause to jump for joy, it was like sitting on a bomb.

It was almost Easter 1952 and the world for me was a very insecure place. I wondered if things would ever be any different, what kind of person would I grow up to be? Would I ever find happiness? It was too depressing to think about. John eventually arrived home, to an atmosphere fraught with doom and gloom, then we were told the news. Dad had a transfer back to Scotland; not to Carfin, it was scheduled for closure, but to Almondbank.

John and I exchanged looks but made no comment, not even to ask where that was. I needed John so much, but we were drifting further and further apart. I knew that my future path would be taken alone, my prospects did not look very bright.

Mum looked from one to the other of us, shrugged her shoulders and said with a sigh, 'It's in Perth.'

41

I Belong to Glasgow

All I knew about Perth was that it was the place our school choir went to for the music festival. They had won a baton and for weeks afterwards, on each assembly, we had to listen to their winning songs. Once, twice was nice, but oh they did wear thin! There is only so much one can take and we got more than we needed of *Grandma had a goat* and as for the 'sweet white rose' – it withered! Eventually the music teacher got the message and we thankfully returned to singing hymns. One thing we all learned from the exercise was not to let success go to our heads, and we also became adept at stifling yawns.

After the revelation of our impending move, John retired to his room no doubt to sulk and I went off to my step to do likewise. Gracie came round to play, but I was in no mood for company. I told her about our move and where to, she recoiled in horror, exclaiming, 'Oh no – no' Perth, that's an awfie snobby place so'tis.'

I could not help but laugh, you would have thought we were off to the depths of Hades. I told her I would not be bothered by snobs, no point being snobby with me. I was however, disturbed. I did not relish the idea of yet another school, another sea of new faces, more questions, another gauntlet to run, of hostility from people who did not approve of my mother's religious persuasion. Good heavens, were they really that awful? I was getting very weary of constant changes, there just seemed to be no point in setting down any sort of roots, just to be moved on again. Saying goodbye all the time was just too painful. I thought of my friends at school, then of Father Murphy and Sister Iggy, would I ever see them again? Oh Lord, would it never end?

Mum seemed to be in a perpetually foul humour.

'You for one,' I was told, 'will have to mend your ways, watch your Ps and Qs. There will be none of this, that and the other in Pe-erth.'

'Bugger Perth,' I thought savagely, 'if they cannie accept me as I am, they can bloody well leave me alane.'

'Don't sniff Bobbie!' yelled Mum one afternoon after school, adding the now habitual, 'You can't do that in Pe-erth, there'll be no runnin' round in bare feet, gittin' colds in Pe-erth.'

It went on and on, I once asked her in my best 'pan loaf' if it would be all right if one pumphed in Pe-erth.

She threw a shoe at me and I sneered, 'Tch, tch, ye cannie go throwin' things in Perth.'

She laughed then wailed at me, 'I don't want to go to that place.'

'Huh, you an' me both,' I grumbled.

We were both being most unfair to the so-called fair city of Perth, neither of us had seen it, or knew much about it. I told myself firmly that I must keep an open mind, take as I find, after all, it would be a perfect opportunity to 'people watch', if nothing else. I would have to sink the 'Glesga' slang and opt for the 'pan loaf', but that could be a giggle ... about as funny as a fart in the dark!

Dad came home one weekend after Easter, to tell us all about his new posting. We were to have a flat in a block of four again, on a new estate being built on the outskirts of the city, called Letham. I asked if there was a school nearby and was told, 'We'll see.'

Well, that usually meant 'forget it' or 'no way', but this time I supposed it meant, 'shut up and mind your own business.'

'Damn it,' I thought, 'it *is* my business.'

'You must know where our schools are,' I persisted.

Dad glared at me, to reply almost pompously and he was very good at being pompous, 'You shut up, you 'ave no say on the matter, you do not count in this 'ouse.'

We were seated round the table during that discourse and Dad told John and I, in a threatening tone, 'You are not, I repeat not, to tell anyone about our move.'

John and I exchanged glances.

'Oh dear, oh dear,' I quipped, adding wickedly, 'Oor teacher kens, the neighbours aw ken, half o' Newarthill kens, ah've telt jist awb'dy.'

Dad blanched, John smirked and Mum stifled a giggle.

'Ur we goannie dae a moonlight then?' I asked, to Dad's obvious discomfort.

'Dinnie be daft,' exclaimed John, 'awb'dy wid see the van!'

The expression on Dad's face was just comical, if he had been planning to dodge off out of some debts, I had just snookered him, he would get his come-uppance, I hoped.

On Saturday afternoon, we were told to behave, remain indoors and not answer to any callers. The parents had to go into Motherwell on important business. They both looked smugly pleased with themselves and Dad was being smarmy.

Would we like anything brought back? Some sweets or a comic?

'A creme filled egg, please, they cost threepence.'

I had seen friends at school with them, but had never had one. All afternoon I waited in anticipation of that egg, covered in thick milk chocolate, its centre full of sticky white and yellow creme. The parents arrived back around early evening, looking well-pleased with themselves. We were told that they had bought some new furniture.

'Oh aye,' I drawled, 'on the never-never ah suppose.'

'Shut up,' snarled Dad.

There was no sign of the egg, no tell-tale paper bag, so after tea when I could contain myself no longer, I asked if they had remembered my egg.

'What egg?' snapped Mum.

'Dad did ask us if we wanted anything brought back,' I replied lamely, as she scowled at me.

'Hoomph,' she sneered, 'you should know better than to ask for things, those who ask, don't get.'

I looked from one parent to the other, Mum 'hoomphed' again and Dad went all pompous.

'*We* 'ad more important things to see to, you an' w'at you want, does not matter one bit, you 'ave no place 'ere, *you* are not important.'

I almost blew a raspberry at him, but instead I left the table, omitting the ridiculous, 'may I leave the table?' and as I left the room I asked them, 'Tell me, with all the people there are in the world, how come I got landed with a pair like yous fer parents?'

They both gaped foolishly at me, as I added, 'I must've done something really evil in a former life.'

As I closed the door I heard Mum say, 'By jingo, that yin's bin here afore an' no mistake!'

After the Easter break I returned to school to tell everyone about our move to Perth. We had not been told when, but as Mum was packing everything that was not nailed down, it had to be soon. She told John that he could not take the kittens as cats did not like to be moved, I suspected that Dad was behind that edict. Homes had been found for Bootsie and Snudge, it was all well-planned, but they would only be a few doors away from each other.

John asked, 'What about Mac?'

'Oh I suppose you can take him if you must,' she niggled.

She had been picking on him a lot and it really annoyed me, his life was bad enough without her starting on at him. A neighbour's boy had come to the door, telling tales about John, he was being cheeky, he said, telling lies and swearing. Mum asked me who it was who called, and what did they want. I told her it was just come kid trying to make trouble for John.

'I demand to know the truth,' she shrieked at me.

'Oh come off it Mum! That brat is a known trouble maker.'

'I will have the truth!' she shouted, storming out of the room.

She returned with a red fabric belt she had removed from a dress in her wardrobe.

'What are you doing?' I asked her.

'I will get the truth out of him,' she bristled in her own foolish indignation, red in the face with rage.

'Why don't you jist ask him? You can't hurt him with that idiotic belt, besides, you have no right to hit him at all.'

She glared murder at me as I yelled at her, 'Don't you think his life is bad enough without you starting on him, do you *have* to pick on him all the time? We both have enough to put up with from that pig you were stupid enough to marry.'

'Don't you start!' she shrieked.

'Huh,' I snarled nastily, 'ah finished wi' you an' that pig long since.'

She opened her mouth to snarl something nasty back, but John arrived, unaware of the tirade he was about to face. It was bad enough having to endure Dad's verbal abuse, but when it came to emotional battering, she could leave him standing. She succeeded in reducing John to tears and I left the flat in a cold rage.

I would not tolerate anyone doing anything to my brother and I set out to find the offending clipe*. I found him outside his house with a crowd of boys. He had his back to me as I approached, so I tapped him on the shoulder. He about turned and got my right fist full in his face as my left foot found his shins. As his lip swelled, oozing blood, his eyes filled with tears and he stuttered, 'Wh-whit ur ye, whit w-wis that fir?'

Before he could finish I yelled in his face, 'That's fer clipin' oan ma brither, ye wee shite poke.'

'Ah'm s-sorry,' he sobbed as I turned to storm home, still seething.

When I got back to the flat, Mum let me in demanding, 'Jist where do ye think you have been?'

I did not answer her, but went into the bathroom to run cold water over my aching hand. She followed me in to ask, 'Here, huv you bin fighting?'

'No Mum,' I told her, 'jist fixing a wee clipe, ah'm no' a hooligan.'

John told me off for fighting his battle for him, but I told him I was spoiling to thump that kid anyway.

Dad had a few days off for the removal, a van took away our belongings, along with the new furniture that had been delivered a few days before. We were left to spend the night on the floor of the now empty flat, with a couple of blankets and only the barest of necessities. A visit to the local chippy took care of tea, so all we had was the clothes we were wearing, a couple of blankets, some crockery, cutlery and the two old suitcases. Bootsie had gone to his new home a few doors away and Dad said Snudge could stay until the morning. Mac was safely settled into a shoe box, with some dandelion leaves to nibble on, with John checking up on him every five minutes, or so it seemed.

Nobody got much sleep on that last night at Gowkhall, but we had a lot of laughs with the antics of Snudge as he crept up on each of us in turn, to pounce playfully at anything that moved. He did not have Bootsie to play with, so he made the

---

* tell tale

322

most of the available humans.

I got very weepy the next morning, when the neighbour came to collect him, but consoled myself with the certain knowledge that he was going to a better home.

We had some tea and toast, gave Mac a drink and some left-over cat food, then John settled him into his box for the journey to Perth. The key to the flat was to be left on the kitchen drainer, the new tenant was given a spare and they were to move in the next day. They had a daughter Anne, who was in my class at school and I imagined that she would be having my bedroom. I hoped that she would be happier in it than I had been.

John took charge of Mac Sporran, Dad had the suitcases and Mum and I had a collection of paper carrier-bags. We left, saying goodbye to no one. I had asked the previous evening if I could go and bid farewell to some of the neighbours. We had not been allowed out at all the previous day, and I wanted to say 'cheerio' to Rita, the Mac's, Powell's and the McKissock's.

I was told curtly, 'You'll do no such thing, you're not going anywhere!'

I had not been told the day of our move, so I had not said goodbye to my school friends or Father Murphy and Sister Iggy. She had gone to Ireland on a visit, and oh how I needed to see her, it was all too much.

'I don't want to go,' I wailed.

'Oh do shut up girl,' snapped Dad.

'Leave her be,' Mum niggled at him.

John just looked at me like I had come from another planet, 'big bother' just could not understand 'tag along', and what all the fuss was about.

We struggled on to the bus for Motherwell with all our luggage, we must have looked like refugees. I was feeling very foolish, for I could not seem to stop crying, the mixture of emotions that overwhelmed me were beyond my control.

'You shurrup orrul give ye a fourpenny one,' threatened Dad.

'Fer goodness sake!' said Mum. 'That'll do a lot to stop her bawlin' an' ah don't think!'

Two days before our departure, Mum had told Dad, 'That girl cannie go tae Pe-erth looking like that.'

323

I needed some shoes, so the parents trailed me around numerous shops in Motherwell, with Dad announcing in each one, 'Ah want the cheapest shoes ye 'ave fer 'er,' pointing at me.

None it seemed were cheap enough and I just wanted to curl up and disappear, I felt so ashamed. Outside the fourth shop we had gone into, I asked, 'Kin ah no' jist hae some gutties, they're cheap?'

'Good grief no!' exclaimed Mum. 'Ye can't wear plimsolls, in Pe-erth.'

'Oh, silly me,' I sneered.

In the umpteenth shop, an assistant produced a pair of weird looking black shiny shoes, that had square, silver coloured buckles on the fronts. I thought she had to be joking as I tried them on.

'How much?' snapped Dad rudely. 'They'll do, let's 'ave done wiv it.'

The assistant looked at me and asked, 'Dae ye dae the Heilan' dancin'?'

Before I could reply, Mum said irritably, 'No, she does not.'

'Oh!' exclaimed the assistant. 'Whit wid ye be wantin' wi' these then?'

'Just wrap them up,' snapped Dad, adding in his 'pompous' voice, 'You 'ave too much to say fer a shop girl.'

The girl's face went scarlet, but she persisted, 'Ye cannie walk oot in thame, thurr only fer the dancin', they've only got compressed paper soles.'

'Oh fer goodness sake!' shouted Mum. 'We have wasted enough time on her already.'

'An' money,' needled Dad.

As we left the shop, my face feeling like it was on fire, Mum pushed me and threatened, 'You jist see they last.'

'An' whit if it rains?' I ventured.

'Oh shut up girl, do,' moaned Dad.

So there I was, waiting for a bus to Glasgow, feeling like a prize idiot, wearing what had to be the silliest shoes in Scotland. The shoes I could live with, but having to leave Lanarkshire was almost unbearable. Somehow we arrived at the railway station and found the correct platform. The train was in, so we boarded it and found an empty compartment. We did our usual trick of spreading things around to make it look full, in the hope of keeping it to ourselves, then settled down. The parents seemed happy, John's face was expressionless and my heart felt as heavy as lead. I was having difficulty breathing properly and was fighting to control a sensation of absolute panic. I did not realise it then, but that was the first of the anxiety attacks that were to affect me for years to come.

I wondered if John felt as unhappy as I did, or did he just not care? He kept the box containing Mac on his lap and would lift the lid every so often, to check on his pet crusty pie, with no hint of his feelings displayed on his face.

I gazed out of the compartment window at the hustle-bustle on the platform – people rushing to and fro, trolleys full of luggage being loaded on to the rear of the train – and wondered what was the point of it all.

One very scruffy, ill-kempt gentleman of the road was being forcibly ejected from the train by two burly policemen. He was extremely drunk and looked heavy as he was half dragged, half carried across the platform, giving vent to a lusty rendering of 'I belong tae Glesga'.

I thought, 'You an' me both,' and we were both being forcibly ejected.

There were doors slamming shut, people hurrying along the train's corridor, with all sorts of last minute panic that seems to precede most journeys. There were some people on the platform waving goodbye, but not to us, we were almost sneaking off.

A hiss of steam, a jolt and we were off. The pain in my chest was almost choking me, I could scarcely breathe as hot tears coursed down my face, blurring my view of the rapidly disappearing platform.

Would I ever see my beloved Glasgow again? It was as if unseen hands were tearing the very heart out of me. I told myself that I had to try to rise above it, as I listened for the train to 'talk'.

'Going away – going away – never come back – never come back,' it seemed to sneer.

'Whit's up wi' your fizzog?' asked Dad.

'Leave her alone,' chided Mum, 'can't you see she is upset?'

She leaned forward in her seat to chide at me, 'Bobbie, don't sniff.'

She settled back in her seat with a sigh, crossed her legs and said, almost to herself, 'Ye can't do that, in Pe-erth.'

To follow: